STRIKING STEEL
SOLIDARITY REMEMBERED

In the series
Critical Perspectives on the Past
edited by Susan Porter Benson, Stephen Brier, and Roy Rosenzweig

STRIKING STEEL

SOLIDARITY REMEMBERED

Jack Metzgar

Temple University Press
PHILADELPHIA

Temple University Press, Philadelphia 19122
Copyright © 2000 by Temple University
All rights reserved
Published 2000
Printed in the United States of America

Library of Congress Cataloging-in-Publication Data

Metzgar, Jack.
     Striking steel : solidarity remembered / Jack Metzgar.
        p.   cm. — (Critical perspectives on the past)
     Includes bibliographical references and index.
     ISBN 1-56639-738-3 (alk. paper)
     ISBN 1-56639-739-1 (pbk. : alk. paper)
        1. Metzgar, Jack.   2. Iron and steel workers—Pennsylvania—Johnstown Biography.
     3. Strikes and lockouts—Steel industry—Pennsylvania—Johnstown—History Sources.
     4. Solidarity.   I. Title.   II. Series.
     HD8039.I52 U574   2000
     331.892′869142′092—dc21
     [B]   99-36085

To Judie and Judd
for being such good friends,
among other things

Contents

STRIKING STEEL
SOLIDARITY REMEMBERED

Introduction

The last conversation I had with my father, we argued. That was not unusual, since we had argued for almost as long as I can remember. He liked to argue, and so did I. But since we now saw each other only once or twice a year, we had learned to argue with one another without getting angry.

I was thirty-seven then and he was sixty-eight. In my late teens and through most of my twenties, we couldn't argue without fighting, without getting bitterly angry at each other in ways that made it impossible to talk at all for a while. In fact, in order to get along during those years, we tried as much as possible to avoid "touchy" subjects, which at times seemed to include just about everything. But he had retired twelve years earlier, after nearly thirty-nine years as a steelworker. After he had retired, he was less tense and less subject to the bursts of temper I had grown up with. And, at some point, I no longer had to prove to myself that I had a mind of my own.

But in our last conversation, I got angry. And though I had said much more bitter and hateful things to him in earlier years, I was surprised to hear myself harangue him in such a bitter tone. We were arguing about President Reagan, for whom he had voted. He had been explaining how Social Security was in trouble because the government had allowed "the welfare cheaters" (who he portrayed as if they were an organized group) to dissipate the Social Security funds. It was not the first time we had discussed this subject, so we

1

both knew the limits to which we could go, and we observed those limits scrupulously. Still, I was frustrated with the conversation.

What I liked to talk with him about were his years in the mill, particularly the 1930s. He had been a shop-floor organizer as a young man, which means that he was one of the thousands who solicited his fellow workers to sign cards indicating their desire to be represented in a labor union by the Steel Workers Organizing Committee (SWOC). Then as now, you could be fired for such activity, and in a steel town then it was an act of bravery to "talk union," not only in the mill, but anywhere in town. One of my favorite stories was about my father signing up my Uncle Stan. Stan's signature had to be kept secret from my Aunt Ruth, who found out about it only after the first contract with U.S. Steel had been won. She then refused to talk to my dad, her younger brother, for some months. In Ruth's view, Dad and Stan had jeopardized her family's livelihood.

My father always argued from experience—his own and that of people he knew and trusted. He didn't believe anything in the newspaper or on television unless it fit with his experience. He had lived in one town—a western Pennsylvania company mill town—all his life, and since most of the news and public issues presented in the media were difficult to fit into his experience, most of his ideas about the world outside were pretty screwed up, in my view. But about the mill and the union, and about anything that was part of his direct experience, he was a shrewd and perceptive observer, and what he had to say was always worth hearing. He had been a griever for the union, an early opponent of Steelworker president David J. McDonald and later an opponent of I. W. Abel, after Abel unseated McDonald as president. He eventually quit being a griever because he felt the union "wouldn't let me represent the men." He could tell a good story, and I had heard most of the best ones more than once. The more I read of twentieth century labor history (something I had never been taught in school), the more I valued his stories and opinions. On labor issues we generally agreed, or at least didn't violently disagree, and that's what I preferred to talk about.

But he liked to talk with me about politics, which is what, in one way or another, we had always argued about. He had been a lifelong Republican, but that didn't say much (directly) about his politics. He had voted for Roosevelt three times (he had been too young to vote in 1932) and had been active in the grassroots labor campaign for Truman in 1948. After that, he always voted "for the man, not the party," as he said, and being a Republican was less a reflection of his political views than it was a way a Protestant German family differentiated itself from the Catholics and "foreigners" in the local Democratic machine. His father had been a Republican in the Progressive Era and had experienced what my grandfather saw as the "treachery of Woodrow Wilson" during and after the Great Steel Strike of 1919. Thus Dad and Ruth were Republicans. But religious and ethnic differences shaped his politics more than party labels. He voted against John Kennedy in 1960 because he genuinely feared that the "infallible pope" would be running the country. And in 1968 he was one of those who couldn't decide between Gene McCarthy and George Wallace, tending toward Wallace more because of his Protestantism than his racism. But for as long as I can remember, my father always supported strikers in any labor dispute—whether they were women school teachers, Chicano farmworkers, or black sanitation workers in Memphis.

He always argued from experience and acknowledged no other basis for knowledge or opinion. Thus, in our last conversation he was recounting various stories about "welfare cheaters" he had witnessed or been told about. It was when he added this one from his own observation that I blew up: "These [coal] miners, kids a lot of them, all spring [1981] on strike. They drive up in brand new pick-up trucks and pay for their groceries with food stamps. They're on strike and they get food stamps! Reagan changed that."

"Shame on you," I exploded, sounding like an angry father. "I don't know whether the miners have a legitimate beef or not, but *they* think they're fighting to preserve their union. Where would we be today without the Mine Workers? What would your life have been like without the miners' union? And now that you're well off, you want to see them starved off a strike! Shame on you."

After I'd had my say, I gulped. I didn't want a big fight. I didn't get to see him that often, and I didn't want to ruin our day together. But I had insulted him, and he was not one to overlook that. Ordinarily, he would have come back at me with some choice words about the deficiencies of the college-educated.

Instead, he looked away from me with a puzzled expression. He said nothing, and I started fumbling to take back the tone of what I'd said without giving up the substance. He seemed calm, not agitated, but more than a little sad and humiliated. Some seconds passed and he said, "Let's get some coffee," and he got up to go to the kitchen. He was confused, not angry—which surprised me. "You're right about the miners' union," he said, as I followed him to the kitchen. "We owe them, you and me." And then he returned to his argument about the role of the welfare cheaters in undermining our society.

"The miners' union." It's a phrase that goes way back in my memory. The debt my father and I acknowledged had to do with the formation of the CIO and with the United Mine Workers (UMW) having devoted money and staff to organizing the steelworkers in the 1930s. My father had witnessed it, had been a part of it, and in my early years he spoke of "the miners' union" with the same reverence and gratitude that he usually reserved for God. There was a story my father told that I can't remember any of the details of, but I remember the feeling and the lesson. Somehow, in one of the Steelworkers' fights, "we" looked up and there were the miners, "hundreds of them" marching arm-in-arm in support of the steelworkers—like the cavalry arriving. It's one of those things a father tells his son with such genuine emotion that, though the details of the story fade, the point of it remains: The miner's union begat the Steelworkers union, and the Steelworkers' union begat all that was good in our lives.

By 1981, when our last argument happened, my father himself had forgotten that sense of genealogy and obligation he had instilled in me. That, I concluded later, was what puzzled him. He was a stubborn, overly proud, "I-don't-take-shit-from-nobody" kind of man who rarely conceded an argument, especially with me. But when I reminded him of a truth that had been central to his life and outlook, he not only had to concede, but he was genuinely and sadly perplexed about how he had, temporarily, forgotten it. After my anger subsided, so was I.

By 1981 I had a ten-year-old son of my own. After a few years of consciously trying to raise him differently than I had been raised, I found myself reverting to my father's ways. At first when my wife would say "You're just like your father," or "That's just what your father would say [or do]," it hurt and humbled me, because we were agreed that he was a negative model for our lives. But as time passed, I came to see that he had had his virtues, and before he died I let him know that. I hadn't realized how hard it was to be a good man and a good father, and I came to conclude that, all things considered, he had been both.

He didn't drink, for example, so my sister and I didn't have to deal with all the problems that children of alcoholics have to confront, as my wife and so many of our friends have had to do. Though he was an authoritarian patriarch who eventually made my mother's life nearly intolerable, he never abused any of us, and as my mother, my sister and I gradually freed ourselves from his grip, he had enough grace to let us go without much rancor and animosity. He was not anything like a distant father, one of those who are never around enough or say enough to make much difference, except by their absence, in their children's lives. Rather, most of our problems with him had to do with his being too involved in our lives, his taking too much responsibility for us.

As a mid-level skilled steelworker in the glory days of the U.S. economy, he was a good breadwinner for our family, and he brought a self-discipline and dedication to that role that gave it dignity. He was a deeply religious man, a fundamentalist evangelical with a strong (and sometimes weird) sense of both social and spiritual obligation. Though he was an irritating, dominating, and ultimately unlikable man, he demanded, and usually got, genuine respect from those who knew him. Above all, he was somebody who thought things through, and though highly arrogant and irritating in communicating his views, he was sincere and capable of genuine communication. Though nobody was less like the carpenter from Nazareth in his daily manner and style, for example, you could always get him to rethink his view of things if you could aptly refer to the way Jesus would have seen or done something.

Johnny Metzgar was a formidable person—intelligent, shrewd, and indomitable. But he was not ambitious. In fact, he distrusted ambition even as he insisted that his children have it. Though he virtually herded my sister and me into the professional middle class, he had what I have come to view as a classic working-class philosophy of life and a considerable ability to communicate it, reason about it, and argue for it. This book is an attempt to articulate part of that philosophy, the conditions out of which it grew and the institutions—the family, the church, the federal government, and above all the union—that sustained it. It is not a philosophy for all time, nor is it one that I, as a middle-class professional, can fully endorse. But it is a way of looking at things and of living a life that has a depth, complexity, and integrity to it that is easy for the professional, middle-class observer to overlook or distort. It is also a philosophy of life that has a lot to offer the achievement-oriented middle class—as an antidote, if nothing else, to our own worst tendencies.

My father was not a typical worker or even a typical steelworker; there is no such thing. The American working class is and always has been considerably more diverse than the middle class—in fact, so bewilderingly diverse that middle-class professionals routinely resort to the crudest of stereotypes, including the myth of classlessness, to shield themselves from its complexity. But neither was he unique or extraordinary in any meaningful sense. He fits many of the stereotypes of the white male blue-collar worker of his time—a sort of Joe Six-Pack without the six-pack. He fits even more easily into a certain working-class social type, what Richard Feldman and Michael Betzold, in their excellent typology of 1980s autoworkers, call "union advocates"—except that he had no ambitions to advance in the union or to take on additional responsibilities beyond his own work area.[1] As a griever, he was a shop-floor leader responsible for knowing what was going on in the industry, the union, and national and Pennsylvania politics (up to a point, of course), but he occupied the lowest position in the union, above which you could no longer be a regular guy.

Johnny Metzgar was a regular guy. What's more, he believed heart and soul in being a regular guy, and he could explain it and argue for it better than anybody I've ever known. That's what I hope will make him a good point of entry into understanding working-class culture during a time when it was less limited, less inhibited, less hemmed in by other classes, than at any other time in our history.

How could such a regular-guy union advocate forget the debt we owed the miner's union? It's understandable that my sister and I would forget, or that the generation of steelworkers who followed my father into the mill would forget. It wasn't part of our direct experience. But my father entered the employ of the U.S. Steel Corporation fresh out of high school in 1930, and he worked, very irregularly, without a union for seven terrible years as a molder's helper. As a child he had seen his own family and many others decimated by industrial accidents—and still scores of others ground down over time into drunkenness and demoralization. After the union firmly established itself throughout the steel industry in 1941, he saw nothing but improvements—over time, dramatic improvements—in every aspect of his life. He retired at the age of fifty-six and lived comfortably on a Steelworker's pension, with Steelworkers' health insurance, even spending the winter months in Florida! No regular guy in the history of the world had seen the material conditions of his life improve more dramatically. And he *knew* that it had not just happened, as if by magic. He knew it had had to be fought for, that people had died for it and suffered for it, and, most of all, endured for it. How could *he* forget?

What we remember and what we forget is complexly determined not just by our own personal history, but by what our larger culture emphasizes, focuses on, and tells stories about. When I was a child, Johnny Metzgar was one of those who would not let anybody forget "what we all owe the union." But it gradually faded from his mind because nothing in the broader culture reinforced it, and much in the broader culture made it difficult to retain.

It's not just that the broader culture has become anti-union, though in many basic ways it has. It's more fundamentally that our national culture, and therefore our national memory, is shaped by the professional middle class. And the professional middle class is generally not interested in other classes, often not even aware that there are other classes, unless those classes become problems. When they're seen as problems, as the African-American "underclass" has been for the past three decades, then the middle class debates whether they are more sinned against or sinning. Liberals see them as victims and conservatives as perpetrators, but the debate is fundamentally shaped by a "social problem" paradigm.

The industrial working class was once one of these problems, and as long as workers could be easily viewed as victims in a social problem paradigm, they got the attention, and the support, of the liberal middle class. But once workers became empowered through their unions and were therefore no longer credible victims, the liberal middle class lost interest and left the conservative middle class free to portray them as perpetrators. Industrial workers like my father saw the larger (middle-class) culture shift from seeing them as victims to seeing them as one of us, and then to seeing them as the principal perpetrators of racism, sexism, and narrow-mindedness in American society. Who could remember that unions had once been more than a white male plot to keep blacks in their place? Who could remember that the labor movement, as a social movement that made a difference, laid some of the groundwork for the Civil Rights, community organizing, and women's movements? People must be either victims or perpetrators, and neither of these categories appealed to my father, nor to very many others in the working classes I have known, black or white, male or female. Though I never heard him use such a phrase, like many others of his kind he eventually took a "fuck 'em" attitude—none of this had anything to do with him, and he figured there was no use trying to explain who he was and what he was about to people who insisted on such a constricted set of categories and judgments.

Unfortunately for him, the time was passing when you could ignore the larger national culture and fully preserve and live within your own ethnic, religious, class, neighborhood, or even family subculture. Through the ubiquitous television and other forms of mass media and the explosion of educational opportunities, among other things, the period of my father's maturity was precisely the period when the professional middle class established its cultural hegemony. Postwar America was a middle-class society not because of anything having to do with income levels or home ownership, but because — though an oligarchy of wealth would continue to rule, and though for a time the working class would have real economic and political power — the professional middle class would determine what was right and what was wrong, what would be emphasized and what forgotten, whose stories would be told and whose ignored. By 1981 the national middle-class culture could reach right into your memory, even while you were trying to make sense of things on your own, and only a professional middle-class son could help you remember what had been basic to your way of looking at things.

THIS BOOK is about class in postwar America, part of an attempt to understand two broad class cultures as I have experienced them in the second half of the twentieth century. I'm one of those who "got out" of the working class during that time and became a full-fledged middle-class professional, a university professor. My wife of more than thirty years is another one; she's a highly paid accountant who grew up in what was for the most part a single-parent welfare family. After the last of seven children entered school, her mother was a department store clerk earning just above the minimum wage.

Neither of us has been able to enthusiastically embrace the professional middle-class way of life. We *have* embraced it, but it took us a long time, and we didn't get over our ambivalence and confusion until we had mistakenly passed it on to our son. Though we wanted the income and working conditions of the professional middle class, we didn't want to let go of the working-class way of looking at and being in the world. Because of our shared ambivalence, we were acutely conscious of the two class cultures — she because of her strong ties to her family of origin, and I because of my jobs and intellectual and political interests. For the past quarter century, I have taught working adults at an urban commuter university in downtown Chicago, spending some of those years as a labor educator. Though my father's generation was the last in my family to be steelworkers, my brothers-in-law and nephews from my wife's side are well represented in what's left of the mills. Most of our friends either come from similar backgrounds or—because of their jobs as teachers, labor professionals, or organizers of one sort or another—have lots of contact with and appreciation for working-class people and their ways. None of this was intentional, or at least not entirely. It just sort of happened that way. Middle-class professionals whose entire lives and experience have been within the professional middle class do not find us interesting, and we find them not quite "down to earth" enough for us.

There is an implicit theory of classes here, but it is a simple theory, with only a few classes, and it is based on the broad vernacular's way of understanding class in America. Sociologists concerned with status differentials and economists concerned with incomes and occupations find dozens of "classes" that are significant to understanding our society.[2] But politicians, journalists, and other middle-class professionals who are not engaged in sustained scholarly analysis generally think in terms of a three-class model: rich, poor, and middle class. In this schema, there are only a handful of rich people and a larger handful of poor ones, while the vast majority is called middle class. Though this schema would seem to be based simply on income, when we discuss the dividing lines it usually becomes clear that all kinds of moral and status judgments are involved as well. In general the middle class is good, if perhaps a little boring, and the rich and poor are suspect.

This broad, everyday theory of social class shapes the way we experience our society's problems and prospects, and the generally positive valuation of the so-called middle class is an important part of our democratic ethos. But it makes people like my father nearly invisible, and it makes my own and many others' life experiences incomprehensible. A four-class model, one that is sometimes found among sociologists and historians, accomodates these realities while retaining some of the basic simplicity of the rich-poor-middle-class schema. It simply divides the middle class into two parts—the working class and the professional middle class. The vernacular often recognizes this difference, and while the three-class model is overwhelmingly predominant, everyday conversation often slides back and forth between three and four-class models. Though most middle-class professionals are uncomfortable with the term working class, they'll use "blue collar" or "factory workers," "clerical workers," "working people," or even "ordinary people" (not to mention "rednecks" and "hardhats") in ways that only make sense within a four-class model.

None of this is very precise, but I think an objective basis exists for distinguishing between the professional middle class and the working class, one that is roughly captured in the basic labor-force composition categories of the Bureau of Labor Statistics. Like all other workers, "managerial and professional workers" (who now constitute about one-quarter of the workforce) work for a wage—and would be considered proletarians in Marx's basic class schema. But unlike the rest of the labor force, though we too have bosses, we have substantially more control over all aspects of our labor process—including exactly when we'll work and when we won't, in what order we'll do the tasks we've been assigned, and most importantly how we'll get the job done. As in all human realities, there are lots of exceptions across a continuum, but the basic expectation is that, as managerial and professional workers, we do not need day-to-day supervision, whereas the rest of the workforce does. We usually have college educations and are paid "salaries" rather than "wages," and our annual income is usually substantially higher. But the most important difference between us and the working class is the amount of discretion we have in what we do day in and day out—including all the skills, attitudes, qualities, and characteristics that go with exercising that discretion.

That's the basic theory of classes that informs this work, and there are elements of it that I'm not too happy with. Push it hard, try to make it precise and rigid so that it easily decides all difficult cases, and it will fall apart. But of a few things I'm certain: first, that you cannot *not* have some theory of classes that informs the way you think about the society in which you live; second, that the predominant three-class model hides and disguises a huge part of our social reality—nothing less than the American working class; and finally, that steelworkers and professors, department store clerks and accountants are not difficult cases. The two categories in the middle class are in fact different classes of people, with different ways of doing, seeing, valuing, and being. They know it. We know it. The mystery is how they can be so often absent from our conception of our society and its history.

THIS BOOK is an attempt to remember the golden age of the American working class and to account for why it has been virtually forgotten. My thesis is not that there has been some kind of professional middle-class plot. Rather, I want to explore how what we remember, and how we remember it, is shaped by our values and goals, our senses of who we are and where we're going—that is, by our interest in whatever future we're striving for.

My father's insistence in the 1950s on remembering what we all owed the union, for example, was related to his hopes for what the union had still to do and his fears of losing what had already been gained. In later years, as both his hopes and his fears diminished (largely because most of the hopes had been realized), so did his memory. Likewise, some of the memories recalled in this book were not available, or not valuable, to me until triggered by some event or activity that made them relevant to my goals and my sense of the future. In broad terms, until the 1980s I took unions and the larger New Deal framework in which they thrived for granted; as a New Left radical, I scorned "the liberal consensus" and its half-hearted ameliorations of the capitalist system. From the mid-1960s I was frustrated with my father's lack of class consciousness and the inherent limits of his vivid trade-union consciousness. Now, when so much of what I took for granted has been lost and more is endangered, I feel and remember differently.

The strategy of this book is to take one highly visible event of which my family was a part, the 1959 Steel Strike; to place it in its historical, institutional, and familial context; and then to do some speculating about the implications of remembering or forgetting this event. I have chosen to focus on the 1950s for a complex of personal and intellectually strategic reasons. The '50s was a time when the working-class sense of possibility was large, and there was a unity and coherence to working-class life then that there is not today. But the 1950s also has an important symbolic role in the middle-class imagination and national memory—as an era peculiarly middle class in its ethos, a time of affluence and repression, prosperity and intolerance, consumerism and family values. Important policy debates and battles in our current "culture wars" are cast in terms of their stance for or against the '50s. The 1950s that both sides remember in these contests is a time in which the 1959 Steel Strike could not have occurred. The 1950s, as remembered in the middle-class imagination today, does not include labor unions, which are what created the "golden age" I want remembered.

On a personal level, the 1950s were my formative years, and my memories of them are more vivid and less filtered through the various interpretive lenses adults develop; they were also the last time I was a part of the working class and knew only its world. My choice of the

1959 Steel Strike as a focal point is, therefore, not innocent. It was an absolutely crucial strike during a perilous time for unions, it was the largest strike in U.S. history (as measured in "man days idled"), and no published work has yet dealt with it in depth; but if I had grown up in an autoworker's or electrical worker's family in the 1950s, I would have chosen a different event.

Looking at postwar U.S. history from the vantage point of the 1959 Steel Strike, however, offers a lot of advantages. It establishes that there was a working class then, and that at least a part of it was politically and economically powerful. The strike, which was the last of six massive, nationwide steel strikes, was a showdown between labor and management in an industry central to both the American labor movement and the American economy at the time. It centered on an issue—union work rules—that is essential to American unionism, but particularly difficult for middle-class professionals to understand or sympathize with. And the attitudes and characteristics necessary to winning that strike reflect crucial aspects of American working-class culture, a culture that is by no means as dead in our current reality as it is in middle-class imaginations.

The design of this book, then, allows for a great deal of what is often called subjectivity, and I do not apologize for that. In fact, a rigorous and responsible cultural relativism demands that we abandon the notion that we can have the point of view of God—standing outside our society and observing it—and requires instead that we attempt to place ourselves within the society and history we seek to understand. The undisciplined arbitrariness that most people reject in denigrating "subjectivity" cannot be overcome simply by pretending that we are not a part of the picture. In fact, as I hope to show, such pretending leads to the disappearance of cultures unlike our own, distorts our self-understanding, and tends to make our professional, middle-class cultural hegemony either oppressive or irrelevant for most people in our society.

THE 1959 STEEL STRIKE
Prologue

have almost no memory of the 1959 Steel Strike, during which my father, as well as my Uncle Bill and Uncle Stan and about one of three households in my neighborhood, went without a paycheck for 116 days. I was fifteen when it started and was driving my father's car by the time it ended. It isn't that I don't have clear memories of those days. Like most people, I can remember the year I turned sixteen more vividly than almost any other. I just don't remember much about an event that should have been pretty memorable.

I remember my father cackling sometime before the strike began, "I'll be on strike then. Oh, it's going to be a long one." He was looking forward to it, and I remember him laughing in that too-loud, taunting, irritating way he had when he knew he was outside the bounds of common feeling. It was both phony-sounding and a bit menacing, like the voice of the villain in a cartoon. He hated the steel companies and, on more than one occasion, chanted something like, "We're going to teach them a lesson they'll never forget." He was also looking forward to having some time off and had planned an elaborate, back-country fishing trip to Canada for during the strike.

I think I remember this incident, unlike so many others, because it initiated in me a complex of responses to my father. On the one hand, that taunting laugh when other people were fearful embarrassed me, because he was both showing off and being mean. On the other hand, I liked his independent, contrarian spirit—it kept things lively at family gatherings—and I knew well that his hatred for the companies and his love of the union were anything but phony.

I remember my mother complaining during the strike about him being around the house so much and being in such a good mood all the time. Though gregarious in public settings, at home he was often sullen and stern and didn't want to be talked to. When working, he was in a bad mood a lot of the time, and he had a bad temper that could flash at you at any moment, no matter what mood he was in. My mother, my sister, and I had learned how to maneuver around those bad moods and temper flashes. His being in a good mood was both irritating and unnerving.

I remember too, when it must have been late into the strike, him preaching to me about this fellow who had not prepared properly for the strike and was now complaining about the union's not getting it over with. "I told him it would be a long one, that he shouldn't buy that car, that he should hunker down and get ready," I remember him telling me. "But some people can't see beyond the nose on their face." He liked to pop off at other people to me, and I liked to listen to him do it. He made it dramatic, and there was always a moral to it, something specifically for my benefit. "Remember that," he would say. "If you don't look ahead, if you don't plan, if you don't figure what *you're* going to do, then *they'll* live your life for you, and you won't even get a say in it."

This "they" didn't refer just to the steel companies and their treacherous foremen (of whom I heard plenty). It also went for used car salesmen, wives and families, the preacher at church, or anybody, including the union, who tried to control you by means other than rational persuasion. My father even railed against the president of the steelworkers' union, of which he was a member. "And who does he think 'the union' is anyway —David J. McDonald? Not in your life. McDonald would just as soon kiss their [management's] butts on a golf course somewhere. But we're the union, all of *us* are the union."

That's it. That's all I remember of the 1959 Steel Strike. Though that year, that time in my life, is full of vivid memories (instances when I can remember how hot or cold it was, what something or someone smelled like, where I was and how I felt, in a flash of precise detail) that is all I remember of what was a definitive event in the life of my family.

For, indeed, my father had been right. In 1959 the Steelworkers taught the companies a lesson they never forgot. And though the 1959 strike was not the most important turning point in our lives, it was the culminating event of two decades of labor struggles that established a freedom and dignity for me and my family that, if you think about it, is pretty awesome.

The problem is that almost nobody thinks about it. I'm not the only one who doesn't remember the 1959 Steel Strike very well. Almost every history of the 1950s gives considerable attention to the fact that Charles Van Doren cheated on a TV quiz show. Van Doren finally 'fessed up to his sins during the 1959 Steel Strike, and that jolt to American innocence is well remembered. Conversely, the steel strikes of 1949, 1952, 1955, 1956, and 1959 are of no significance in American history. Of eighteen histories of the 1950s, only seven even mention that they or any other strikes occurred.

Some people, especially those concerned with the labor movement and those with a special interest in the steel industry, remember these events. But the memories are not good ones. Tom Geoghegan, a labor lawyer and author of the best-selling *Which Side Are You On? Trying to Be for Labor When It's Flat on Its Back*, remembers: "It was a long, bitter strike . . . and at the end of it the men had gotten nothing. It was like a family scandal. Something the older men didn't talk about, as if they had once tried to strike and had flopped at it."[1] John Strohmeyer, a Pulitzer Prize–winning newspaper reporter and steel-town editor, on the other hand, remembers the 1959 Steel Strike as one of the causes of the decline of the West: "The union won all it had hoped for . . . [but] while the outcome of the strike was good for labor . . . it was devastating for the industry . . . [T]he forces set in motion by the 1959 strike were soon to overwhelm the steel industry."[2]

Memory is a strange and mysterious thing. As Alessandro Portelli has vividly shown, it is as revealing in what it forgets and distorts as in what it most accurately remembers. An oral historian of working-class life in Italy and America, Portelli has taken a special interest in mistaken memories: "'[W]rong' tales . . . allow us to recognize the interests of the tellers, and the dreams and desires beneath them. . . . The discrepancy between fact and memory . . . is not caused by faulty recollections . . . but [is] actively and creatively generated by memory and imagination in an effort to make sense of crucial events and of history in general."[3]

My interest is to tell the story of the days when unions were strong in American life, when workers in major industries banded together to get a say in their lives. My dreams and desires are centered around making it so again. Remembering one strike in its historical context may help others remember how powerful, how transcendent, unions used to be, and how carefully and responsibly the industrial working class used that power for a time. To remember may be to rekindle, for—to twist Santayana's famous maxim—those who cannot remember history will not be able to repeat it.

I am thankful to Geoghegan and Strohmeyer for at least remembering. But Geoghegan represents a leftish point of view common among labor and social historians that hesitates to see what unions accomplished *after* they became stable and bureaucratic institutions. There were no violent confrontations in 1959, few colorful rallies or pageants, and certainly no noble if hapless victims of capitalist society—just a very civilized, grind-'em-out, wait-'em-out strike by a very powerful group of men. Likewise, Strohmeyer represents a plague-on-both-your-houses "community" point of view: The greedy Steelworkers, aided by a weak-kneed and complacent management, did themselves, the industry, and their communities in. The unions became too powerful, and they killed the goose that laid our golden eggs.

Of these two remembrances, I prefer Strohmeyer's, not just because it is more accurate (the Steelworkers did not "flop" at striking in the 1950s), but because it recognizes the Steelworkers as a causal force in the history of the United States. I like that remembrance better because it allows that we were there and had an impact, even if I can't remember it, and even if Strohmeyer's assessment is terribly one-sided and wrong. What follows, then, is my story of the 1959 Steel Strike—and of my and other people's memory, and lack of memory, of it.

Five years after the strike, grown up and married, I remember leaving Johnstown, Pennsylvania, the grimy, semirural steel town in which I grew up, for New York City. I remember saying to people as I left, in a softer version of that smirking way my father had when he was outside the bounds of common feeling, that I wanted to go where history was happening. It was a genuine feeling, and I'm glad I got out of there when I did. But I regret that I didn't know then that history had happened in Johnstown and that my family and I had been a part of it.

1

Getting to 1959

> I joined the CIO because I wanted to feel like a man for once. . . . It was a matter of spirit. When I joined, nothing happened right away, but I felt different.
>
> —Joe Molony, running for USWA vice president in 1965

> What have I got to complain about? Since my senior year in high school in Aliquippa [1956], my life has been a miracle.
>
> —Mike Ditka in 1993, after being fired as head coach of the Chicago Bears

Though I have few distinct memories of the 1959 strike, I have many memories of my father calmly explaining the problems and issues of his workplace. He was such a volatile, edgy man, so easily excited and prone to not letting people finish their sentences, that when he spoke calmly to me, listening carefully to my questions, developing careful analogies in relation to my experience, often confiding the secrets of being a "good man" (which of course I assumed he knew), I listened intently.

He did this often, usually as a pause in the midst of doing something else. I particularly remember summer days when he was working the 3-to-11 shift, as he sat on a porch step to lace his steel-toed shoes. He was usually calm and thoughtful as he prepared for work—his innate cockiness expressed as a quiet determination rather than an in-your-face blustering. I'd ask him something, something serious, to get him going, and he would pause and answer carefully. Or I'd just

17

go sit by him, and he'd start to tell me whatever was on his mind. He was always instructing, but in these moments he would often express his own vulnerabilities as part of the instruction. "A man hasn't got a chance unless. . . ." "The big mistake I made was. . . ."

The upshot of the instruction was always to stay out of the mill, to look ahead, get an education, and find a job you didn't hate going to every day. But he would also tell me incredibly complex stories about his relations with various foremen and industrial engineers (some of whom I had gotten to know by name from previous stories, like characters in a soap opera) and about union grievances he was working on. From the time I was about eleven or twelve years old till I graduated from high school, I also helped him fill out his grievance reports. He was a "lousy speller," as he said, and his grammar wasn't too good either.

These stories of everyday interactions with "the boss" were the kinds I could most relate to, and he was ingenious in drawing lessons that related to my experience. Not reacting too quickly to a foreman's provocation was like waiting for a good pitch in baseball. Fooling an industrial engineer who was trying to time your job was like running the deck in playing the card game hearts. These microlevel stories were the substance of most of our direct father-son interactions. But they were placed in a larger historical context by his frequent speeches at family gatherings about "the companies and the union." In these speeches, history was neatly divided between "before the union" and "since the union."

My grandfather, once a skilled turner at one of Bethlehem Steel's Johnstown rolling mills, had lost both his arms to the mill in 1917, when my father was four years old. Both Dad and his sister, my Aunt Ruth, loved to tell stories to us kids of the amazing things that Grandpa, who died before any of us were born, could do with his heavy mechanical arms. He could pick up a dime with his steel fingers, but he couldn't lift his arms to scratch his nose. The basic Grandpa story was about what a strong, God-fearing man our grandfather had been—how every day of his life was a struggle and how he never complained, always did his best, and never lost faith in God. This usually came up when one of us kids had been complaining about something; a Grandpa story was told to encourage us to face and endure our troubles. At least we had arms! But my father could not tell Grandpa stories without getting the companies and the union into it—and with the same freshness and intensity of emotion each time. We had to hear about how the companies treated the men back then, including the lack of safety gear, and about the procedures the union had since forced on them. We heard about the importance of disability insurance and what it would have meant to Grandpa: When better prosthetic arms became available, he could have gotten them for free. He would have been able to scratch his nose. "Imagine what it would feel like if everytime you had to scratch, you had to *ask* somebody to do it for you," they would say.

Uncle Will, Grandma Metzgar's stepbrother, was one of the few of my grandparents' generation who survived to see grandchildren grow up. Uncle Will was a hunchback—and my father never lost an opportunity to tell us that Will's deformity had resulted from his having been forced to carry water buckets for the railroad as a child of "just about your age." A mild-tempered, gentle man with a pixie-like smile and a somewhat amused outlook on life, Uncle Will liked to tease children and to tell us funny stories from his "real life" as a boy (none of which included working on the railroad). But he always went quiet and put on a solemn face when my father would point to his hunched back and angrily denounce "the companies." Will was a bit uncomfortable with the angry edge my father put on the telling, but he was not embarrassed to have his bodily form exhibited as proof of how terrible life was "before the union," though in his case it had been a different union. I wondered, even at the time, how my father could repeat this story over and over—in almost the same words, with the same intensity of feeling—as if none of us had heard it before, as if none of us knew how Uncle Will had acquired a hunched back.

My family respected emotion when it was used to convey the meaning in a story. Actual outbursts of crying, complaining and anger were not otherwise condoned (though they happened, particularly with Dad's bad temper). Our Sunday School teachers, the good ones, were the same way in telling Bible stories. The details of the story had to be clearly conveyed, but only the genuine expression of emotion made their meanings clear and memorable. "Turning it on" was an expression that in some contexts referred to the insincerity of someone's emotions, but in other contexts it was used as praise for someone's ability, and willingness, to express a truth with the appropriate emotion. In the second sense, my father, like a good preacher, could really "turn it on." Everyone in our family, even those who were not strong union supporters (such as my Aunt Ruth and Uncle Bill), knew my father's anger was genuine and justified, and judging by their reactions, they saw what he said about the importance of the union as one of those basic truths, like those in Sunday School, that bore repeating again and again, particularly for children, but not only for them.

By the 1950s, the union was well established in steel, on the railroads, and in the mines. It would have been easy by then to take it for granted —but this was something my father would never allow anybody in our family circles to do. Even as others mellowed, even as others began to wonder if maybe the union had become too powerful, he would hark back to past sins. He knew the contract line by line. He was one of the mill's shop-floor lawyers even before he became a "grievance man." He could patiently explain why this or that provision was important, what it would be like without it—not only to "the men," but even to those of us who had never been in the mill. But though his practical knowledge enhanced his general credibility, it was nothing compared to the broad moral and historical context in which he placed it.

Those who think that labor negotiations and strikes are simply about money have never met anybody like my father. Though he very badly wanted the money, the benefits, the vacations and holidays—and though he would fly into a rage if someone, such as the newspaper columnist David Lawrence, suggested he and other steelworkers didn't deserve them—striking the companies, or even wringing more money out of them without a strike, was as much an end in itself as it was a means to a better life. What mattered to the companies was money, and if you could take some of their money, it hurt them out of all proportion to the *amount* extracted—it hurt their pride; it humiliated them and made them feel powerless over their own destinies. For my father a grand Old Testament justice was being achieved with each penny per hour—a justice somehow related to his father's heavy mechanical arms, to Uncle Will's hunched back, to the fear and vulnerability he was made to feel in the 1930s, and to the indignities he had suffered last week from some snot-nosed industrial engineer fresh out of college.

Not everybody in our family entirely credited this view of things. They knew that Dad's righteous indignation was all mixed up with a calculating self-interest and other base instincts. Some of it was just blind revenge, blowing off steam at the basic frustrations of life as a mill hand. Some of it was about male dominance games, to which my father was fully committed. Some of it was simply the intensity that comes with any us-vs.-them contest. But for many of my father's generation, a lot of the moral intensity of their unionism was about achieving justice for past as well as present wrongs—and that part came with an obligation, a duty that required you to do your best to right the wrongs. One way to measure how you were doing in performing this duty was in pennies per hour. But the basic moral issue was about power. We—our family as a whole and everybody in the valley, not just the men who worked in the mills—not only "owed the union" for the good life we were living, but we also had an obligation to make sure that the power of the companies to control every jot and tittle of our lives was never allowed to return. This, not only for its practical benefits to us, but for general justice's sake.

My father's vision of unionism was even more complicated than this. Increasing the spending power of steelworkers and other workers, it turned out, was just about the best thing you could do to improve everybody's life. Bantley's Hardware, DeFazio's corner grocery, Glosser Brothers' department store, the church collection plate—everybody was "living off the steelworker's paycheck." If the steel companies kept all their profits, the money "left the valley." By keeping some of those profits in the valley, the union made things better for everybody, even the steel companies because workers could afford to buy cars, refrigerators, washers, and all manner of things made out of steel. The companies' greed had caused the Great Depression, my father claimed, and in an ironic twist of paternalism, the union had to keep the companies in line or they'd do it to themselves (and us) again.

There was, it seemed to me, an inexhaustible coherence to my father's view of things. Key to it was the way our self-interest so neatly meshed with social justice, a justice that in his telling couldn't help but have strong religious overtones. The union was not merely a mechanism that allowed us to rigorously pursue our self-interest, though it certainly was that. It was something that required us to pursue what was right and good and in the best interests of *everybody* (not merely the greatest number) at the same time as we made a better life for ourselves.

Of the things you try to teach your children, some "take" and some don't, and who knows how that works. My father grew disenchantened with the union and a lot of other things in the 1960s, but in my growing-up years nothing commanded his belief and commitment, excluding Jesus Christ of Nazareth, like the union. Though he would have much sooner had Jesus make a more lasting impression on me, as the years passed it was "the union" and the belief system that went with it that had the most abiding effect. As I studied the history (albeit haphazardly, never as a professional historian) and then later became involved in the labor movement myself, I was amazed at how apt—how complex, adequate and true—his perspective had been.

It was not really until the 1980s, when the slow decline of union power turned into a precipitous crash and I realized what was being lost, that my father's insistence on not forgetting what life had been like "before the union" took on a practical and moral significance for me like what he had felt and articulated. As what one Steelworker leader called a "creeping holocaust" was devastating the American steel industry, the American Federation of State, County and Municipal Employees (AFSCME) was organizing thousands of new members in Chicago and throughout Illinois, and I had occasion to be involved in the education of some of their new local officers and stewards. Again, I heard people referring to "before the union" and "since the union" with the same combination of practical and reverential terms my father had used. Others reversed the order: Victims of plant closings who had never before worked without a union explained in horror what it was like in their new, nonunion workplaces, "after" the union. As a teacher, I began to hear myself saying things that my father had told me, passing on bits of wisdom and perspective that I hadn't known I'd remembered.

The labor union is an underappreciated and easily misunderstood institution. It's underappreciated first because American culture depreciates *all* institutions as "bureaucracies" that stifle the natural goodness and spontaneous vitality of both "the individual" and that collected mass of individuals we call "the people." But of all our institutions, none (with the exception of the armed services) goes against the grain of our radical individualism like the labor union—not just in its practice, but in its beliefs. Most people have little or no direct experience as a union member, and even members, particularly those who have to join the union as a condition of employment, have little to do with the union unless or until they have trouble. Most union members probably appreciate their union, if they do, like they appreciate the sewer system—they're glad it's there, but they neither understand how it works nor are cognizant *that* it works until it malfunctions. Only those who directly experience the before and after of the union can properly appreciate it for what it is and what it does. My father was one of those, and though nobody else in my family was active in the union and though everybody agreed with Aunt Ruth that "Johnny is too strong for the union," my parents' generation could not help but appreciate the institution as essential to their lives and to whatever prospects their children might have. Johnny was the one who pointed it out, who insisted that they recognize it and not forget, but they all agreed, and not at all half-heartedly.

The CIO Story

The version of unionism I learned from my father was undoubtedly shaped by his experience as an employee of U.S. Steel (U.S.S.) and by the way unionism was won there. The CIO's Steel Workers Organizing Committee (SWOC) was a top-down operation run by officials and staff of the United Mine Workers. The initial recognition of the union in 1937, after a half-century of bitter resistance, came without a fight and before the ranks were really organized. The union was something that "came in" from the outside, not something that rose indigenously from the workers themselves.

Other CIO unions, including some steel locals, had more complicated origins, combining rank-and-file insurgency with CIO "direction." And there were lots of fights, some with pitched battles between workers and police, strikers and company goons; eighteen workers were killed in 1937 in organizing steel alone.[1] But many rank-and-file CIO workers must have experienced the rise of unionism in the 1930s as my father did—as a sort of *deus ex machina* that came out of nowhere.

The CIO story is one of the great social justice dramas of American history—comparable to the Revolution, the Civil War and, in our time, the Civil Rights movement. Usually consigned to but a chapter in the history of the New Deal or the Great Depression (where it is often viewed as one of the "problems" the great man Franklin Roosevelt had to deal with), the CIO shaped those events, and what resulted from them, more than they determined the shape of the CIO, which was substantial. In Johnstown, a classic company town owned and operated by Bethlehem Steel and surrounded by other, smaller company towns owned and operated by coal companies, my father was both a bit player and a self-interested spectator on one of the drama's main stages. But it's not clear to me how much he knew of the larger CIO story.

I do know that nobody in my family, including him, ever referred to "the CIO" as something we were all a part of, or even as a great social movement of the recent past. I remember that, sometime between the ages of ten and twelve, I asked what the "CIO" stood for in the CIO Little League, and that I got an incomprehensible, possibly evasive answer—an answer that clearly said it was not important to know. This would have been between 1953 and 1955, at just about the time when the CIO was losing its last shreds of identity by merging into the American Federation of Labor (AFL).

My father's invocations at family gatherings, however, were a version of the CIO story. His version not only did not refer to the CIO, but it also never mentioned SWOC, the Steelworkers, or the labor movement. In his version, there was simply "before the union" and "since the union." And though "the union" referred to was usually his union, the United Steelworkers of America (USWA), his usage was not precise. It could refer to the Mine Workers or the United Auto Workers (UAW), CIO unions not represented in our immediate family or neighborhood, or to AFL unions such as the Carpenters, the Teamsters or the Pressmen, which neighbors belonged to, or to Uncle Will's railroad union, the Brotherhood of Maintenance of Way Employees. In my dad's version, "the union," like Plato's ideal forms, was the reality; particular unions were mere instances of it.

This usage has its advantages, but it leaves out a lot that explains where our *deus ex machina* came from. Unfortunately, if my family's experience is typical, the memory of the CIO disappeared before the CIO itself.

The Committee for Industrial Organization was formed November 9, 1935, less than four months after the passage of the National Labor Relations Act (the NLRA or Wagner Act) on July 5. The NLRA was not simply a piece of special-interest legislation; nor was it just one more of Roosevelt's scattershot, maybe-this-will-do-some-good New Deal programs. It was the centerpiece of a sophisticated economic and political strategy that would transform American society. The purpose of the NLRA was to foster a certain kind of organization, the labor union, that would, by its very nature, redistribute wealth and power, democratize and rationalize production in the workplace, and provide a countervailing force against the stranglehold that an oligarchy of wealth had on the American economy. That same kind of organization would create a disciplined political constituency for the rest of the New Deal program—that is, for the federal government's permanent role in the nation's economic life. The CIO was formed by a handful of veteran union leaders, led by John L. Lewis of the Mine Workers, to take advantage of this mid-1930s "window of opportunity." It succeeded brilliantly.

The NLRA and the CIO did not come from nowhere, of course. They were, as a package, attempts to give form and focus to the effervescent but inchoate rebellions that had been erupting in the American working class once the initial shock of the Great Depression had been absorbed. Labor unions were but one form these rebellions could take—the nation was rife with both leftist revolutionary sects and quasi-Fascist demagogues, such as the radio priest Father Coughlin. But unions were the most formidable of these rebellions, and the most hopeful and manageable from a New Deal government perspective. A few of the old AFL unions, especially the Mine Workers and the Amalgamated Clothing Workers, had taken advantage of previous New Deal legislation (the National Industrial Recovery Act in 1933) to rebuild their ranks. In the year before the NLRA, the Longshoremen in San Francisco and the Teamsters in Minneapolis showed how narrow labor union struggles could explode into citywide class warfare.[2]

For its first five years, the CIO was personified in the singularly distinct personality of John L. Lewis, who threw himself and the money and staff of his union into organizing the guts of America's industrial economy—auto, rubber, steel and electrical goods workers, and anybody else—department store clerks, newspaper reporters—who expressed the slightest interest in forming a labor union. In its first twenty months, the CIO gained 3.7 million members,[3] and won contracts at two of the largest and most important industrial corporations in the country, General Motors (GM) and U.S. Steel. The intensity and urgency that Lewis's CIO brought to this task (along the way playing a vital role in reelecting Roosevelt to a second term in 1936) was fully justified by what happened next—the defeats in the spring of 1937 at Ford Motors and in "Little Steel" (Republic and Bethlehem being the leaders of that virulently anti-union group of steel companies that were "little" only in comparison to U.S. Steel). As the economy stalled in what came to be called "the Roosevelt Recession," so did the CIO organizing drive. But the CIO had established a base from which it could build, a core of members it could develop into real unions and who, in the meantime, would be paying dues to finance the organization of the rest of their industry's workers.

In its first years, the CIO was not really a membership organization. Rather, it was an organization of organizers. Lewis took some of the best of his own staff and those at the other AFL unions that initially formed the CIO (the Clothing Workers, the Ladies Garment Workers, and others). He swept up Socialists, Communists, Trotskyists, and various and sundry freelance revolutionaries—anybody who knew how to organize people for disciplined collective action. Young workers without families who showed leadership ability and were no longer essential to organizing their own workplaces were plucked out of them, put with experienced organizers, and thus "trained" for future organizing. Organizing then did not simply mean recruiting new members, let alone merely signing union cards. It meant *developing organizations* of workers, from shop committees to local unions, that could function on their own. A lot of the most important organizing occurred *after* the union was recognized and had a contract. This is certainly how it happened at U.S. Steel.

Key to this post-unionization organizing was the shop steward system. In those early days, the first contracts had almost nothing in them. The stewards, called "grievance men" or "grievers" in the steel industry, had a lot of leeway in representing the workers in their work areas. And from the beginning these stewards formed an important communications network for the union, collecting dues and educating members as they were themselves being educated in how to be a union.

As the U.S. economy began to improve in 1939, based on boosts in production caused by the war in Europe, the CIO got its second wind. In the spring of 1941, it won contracts at Ford Motors and Bethlehem Steel, completing its successful sweep of the metalworking, auto-dominated core of America's industrial economy. Equally important, the CIO's initial successes in 1936 and 1937 woke up those remaining AFL unions that had been opposed to the industrial (versus the craft) form of union organization. Beginning in 1937, the AFL started doing its own organizing, and its membership grew even faster than the CIO's —often because it had the distinct advantage of being able to offer itself to employers as a "more reasonable" alternative to the "militant" CIO. By the time the United States entered World War II in late 1941, more than ten million workers, 27 percent of the nonagricultural workforce, were union members—more than triple the three million, or 12 percent, just before the Wagner Act was passed in 1935.[4]

The CIO lost some of its distinctiveness when Lewis resigned from its leadership after a colossally vain political gamble on the 1940 presidential election. The transformation of various AFL unions (including the Teamsters, the Machinists, and the Electrical Workers) into organizing machines also dulled the CIO's distinctiveness. And, once

organized as Auto Workers, Rubber Workers, and Electrical Workers
—union members' identification shifted from the CIO parent to the
workplace-related unions, each of which were now formidable membership organizations that dwarfed the organization of organizers that
was still the CIO.

At the beginning of World War II, the CIO and most of the AFL
unions agreed not to strike for the duration of the war in return for
government guarantees of "union security" where unions were already
in place. During the war, both prices and wages were regulated, and by
mid-1942 the War Labor Board had arrived at a cost-of-living formula
that froze *real* (that is, inflation-adjusted) hourly wages at their prewar
level. The formula's design was patently unfair to workers and resulted
in an actual decline in real *hourly* wages for most workers during the war.
But because work was steady and there was extensive overtime (which
the government, under the Fair Labor Standards Act of 1938, required
be paid at time and a half), weekly and annual earnings increased substantially during the war.[5]

There was a lot of debate then, and it continues today among labor
historians, about whether this arrangement strengthened or weakened
the CIO.[6] The union security provision (called "maintenance of membership") merely made it harder for members to quit the union once
they had joined and easier for the union to collect dues in the meantime. The inability to improve real wages and the necessity of enforcing
the no-strike pledge against the numerous wildcat strikes that increased
in frequency as the war progressed made it a difficult time to be a labor leader—and opened all sorts of divisions between membership and
leadership as well as among factions within the leadership.

Nevertheless, union membership continued to grow during the war
—from ten to more than fourteen million members and from 27 percent
to 35 percent of the nonagricultural workforce.[7] More importantly, the
unions that emerged from the war were entirely different, a thoroughly
"new and improved" version of the institutions that had entered it. The
difference lay in their *internal organization*. Not having to fight for their
very existence year in and year out and having a steady stream of dues
money meant that the CIO unions could help their local unions sort out
and develop their leadership structures and steward systems, creating
the intricate and, by the end of the war, highly dependable networks
that could link a blast furnace worker in Baltimore to a rolling mill hand
in Buffalo through a command center in Pittsburgh. The 1945–46

strike wave evidenced a substantially different labor movement than the one that had existed in 1941.

On August 14, 1945, World War II ended. Over the next twelve months, more than a third of all American unionists struck their employers in what labor reporter Art Preis has called "the greatest wage offensive in U.S. labor history." First out were 43,000 CIO oil workers on September 17, who demanded "52–40 or Fight"—a forty-hour week at fifty-two hours' pay, or a 30 percent increase in hourly wages. In the next week, 200,000 coal miners and 44,000 AFL lumber workers joined them, followed in October and November by AFL longshoremen in New York, CIO glass workers in Pittsburgh, a coalition of AFL and CIO machinists in the San Francisco Bay Area, CIO textile workers in New England, and AFL truck drivers in the Midwest. Many of these strikes were long ones, continuing into 1946—the truckers for eighty-one days, the glass workers for 102, the textile workers for 133, and the Bay Area machinists for 140.[8] But these were just the preliminaries.

From November to March, more than 200,000 Auto Workers at GM struck ninety-two plants in fifty cities. On January 15, they were joined by 200,000 CIO United Electrical Workers at seventy-eight plants of General Electric, Westinghouse, and GM's Electrical Division. The next day, 125,000 CIO Packinghouse Workers and 90,000 AFL Amalgamated Meat Cutters struck Armour, Swift, Wilson, Cudahy, and Morrell. Finally, after numerous delays occasioned by jawboning from President Truman and various maneuvers among the companies, on January 21 some 800,000 Steelworkers, all of basic steel and many thousands from steel-fabricating plants, weighed in.[9]

It was an awesome display of labor power. As Preis commented:

> When the steelworkers hit the picket lines on . . . January 21, a total of almost 2,000,000 American workers in basic industries were on strike at one time. In the twelve months following V-J Day more than 5,000,000 workers engaged in strikes. For the number of strikers, their weight in industry and the duration of the struggle, the 1945–46 strike wave in the U.S. surpassed anything of its kind in any capitalist country, including the British General Strike of 1926. Before its ebb it was to include the whole coal, railroad, maritime and communications industries, although not simultaneously.[10]

The strike wave resulted in eighteen and a half cents—the wage increase that President Truman had "encouraged" the steel and auto companies to grant, which then became a benchmark for everybody else. This was about a 15 percent increase, not enough to make up for inflation and the loss of overtime in the immediate postwar years. There was lots of bickering and lack of coordination among the CIO unions (the Auto Workers were said to have struck "too soon," the Steelworkers to have waited "too long"), and not as much solidarity between CIO and AFL unions as the above account might suggest. The strike wave also scared "the public"—not only management, media and politicians, but many of the 90 percent of the workforce that hadn't gone on strike and probably even some of the 10 percent that did. There was now something called Big Labor that could apparently put a halt to daily life anytime it wanted. In November 1946 the Republicans won control of Congress for the first time in eighteen years, and the following year the Taft-Hartley Act was passed, over Truman's veto, in an attempt to constrict the power and prospects of unions.[11]

The 1945–46 strike wave—tactically and strategically, politically and economically—was not an unqualified success. But organizationally, looking back to 1941, it was an incredible achievement. What is most amazing is the coordination and the discipline of the members—the tight internal organization of the individual unions.

Take, for example, the Auto Workers—225,000 of them in ninety-two GM plants in fifty cities. It was no simple matter to get all these workers to go on strike together and to return to work together. That had to be organized—not only through leadership statements, directives, and written materials, but also through hundreds of thousands of shop-floor and living-room conversations where small-group leaders debated the leadership's position but made clear that "this time we have to stick together." In 1945 there was a well of pent-up militance in the industrial working class, so there were probably few who had to be talked into striking. But many, millions probably, had to be talked into *not* striking, or into waiting until their leaders said, "Go!" Ford and Chrysler workers, for example, wanted to strike, too, but they did not. And all of the GM workers who had carried the load for nearly four months returned to work together, even those who were not at all happy with their eighteen and a half cents.[12]

That 800,000 Steelworkers would go out and back on cue was by no means to be taken for granted. In the Great Steel Strike of 1919, steelworkers in Johnstown were among the best organized and most militant elements in that nationwide effort, but seventy-two days into the strike, almost two-thirds had crossed their own picket line.[13] Likewise, in 1937 Bethlehem was able to defeat the SWOC strike in Johnstown (part of "the Little Steel" debacle) by pulling a large part of the workforce across the union's picket line.[14] Going out together and going back together—that is to say, disciplined collective' action—had been by no means a tradition among steelworkers before 1946. But in 1946 they waited an interminably long time to go, were out only twenty-eight days, collected their eighteen and a half cents, and returned to work having gained an exhilarating lesson in the meaning of the union slogan "In unity there is strength."

The potential of the labor movement, based on this demonstration of solidarity and militance, caused expectations to race, particularly among leftists and radicals (of which there were many then), but also among many rank-and-file workers like my father. The CIO's ambitious People's Program of 1944, incorporated as an "Economic Bill of Rights" in FDR's 1944 campaign platform, envisioned a sweeping postwar expansion of the New Deal.[15] The CIO unions' bargaining agendas envisioned not only a dramatic increase in their members' standard of living, job security, and general welfare, but also a thorough transformation of workplace power and national economic decision-making through "industrial democracy." Yet few of these expectations would be immediately met, and many would never come to fruition, as the Cold War and a politically conservative consensus gradually developed in the postwar years.

The dashing of these expectations, and the eventual isolation and crushing of the political Left, has caused many progressive historians to see everything that followed the strike wave as a defeat.[16] But in 1946 a conservative consensus meant conserving the New Deal, including the very powerful labor organizations that had established themselves through the previous decade. What were killed in those years were all varieties of broader social and economic visions of a just and democratic society, which the CIO unions carried for the Left. Lots of fruitful proposals and exciting possibilities were lost as collective bargaining became a narrower and more private process, both politically and economically. The New Left generation of labor and social historians recovered some of these prospects and possibilities so that we could mourn their loss, but in the process they covered over, as a groundvine covers an old walkway, the real impact that Big Labor had on working people's lives and on our society as a whole.

For the purposes of working-class memory, though, the CIO was gone by 1946, dispersed among its constituent parts, lost in the confusion of different leaders and organizational initials that only the most astute rank-and-filer could keep straight. In its initial years, the phrase "the CIO" had an almost magical quality. Signs and posters invoked that magic, proclaiming "CIO is here" or "The CIO has come to town." Individual unions were identified by the CIO initials, as in "the CIO Auto Workers," not just for organizational clarity, but as a totem that could strike fear in the hearts of giants such as General Motors and U.S. Steel. But by 1946 two of the primary unions that had first formed the CIO (the Mine Workers and the Ladies Garment Workers) were back in the AFL, and John L. Lewis, the embodiment of the CIO in its early years, changed institutional affiliations like a vaudeville comedian changing costumes.

By the 1950s, when my father was instructing me in the basic pattern of world history, the CIO had been tainted with the charge (not entirely without justification) of being Communist. Though my father could never have believed that, he was probably not prepared to argue against such a charge, either. Unlike any existing union, let alone any federation of unions, for my father "the union" had few imperfections, and he would not tolerate such negative talk. Though, as we'll see, the CIO was alive and well in the memories of organizers and radicals in the 1950s, it was just another set of meaningless initials to the industrial working class by then. But the CIO had worked a revolution in our lives, and before it disappeared, it left us an institution that we could use to protect and even better ourselves.

Before the Union and Since

Johnny Metzgar entered the mill in 1930, shortly after graduating from high school. He was seventeen years old. He got his job as a molder's helper, a good job because you learned a skill, through a combination of family connections and persistence. His father knew somebody in management who passed on a good word to a man in the plant's personnel office, and then Johnny badgered that man every day for three months until he got a job.[17]

Johnstown Works of U.S. Steel was a relatively small plant, employing only about 2,000 in good years; its basic function was to produce equipment for other U.S.S. mills and mines. According to my father, he could have had a job at the much larger complex of Bethlehem Steel because it had a policy of hiring the sons of its disabled workers, but he wouldn't "give them that satisfaction after what they did to my father." He was referring to Bethlehem's meager ($30 a month) disability payment and its general indifference more than to the accident itself.

Evidently there was work in 1930 and into 1931. He worked six days a week, from eight to ten hours a day. He got paid for sixty hours a week, but on any given day he could leave after eight hours if his work for that day was completed; on the other hand, he could not leave until the day's work *was* completed, even if that took more than ten hours, though that happened rarely. But those long weeks didn't last. In 1932 he had only fifty-two days of work; in 1933, only eighty. "Work picked up after that," he said.

He learned the molder's trade from a friend and second cousin of his father's, Runt Espey, and enjoyed the work at first along with the camaraderie among the men, though not the dusty conditions that left you "still coughing two or three hours after you left work." He transferred out of molding in 1940 to the Lower Shop, where he eventually worked as a machinist making rolls for U.S.S. rolling mills. He remained in the Lower Shop until he retired in 1969, at the age of fifty-six. In good times, when there was lots of work, he was a machinist; when work was slack, he bumped down several job classifications to become a "hooker," the person who attached things to an overhead crane for delivery elsewhere in the mill.

He joined the union at his first opportunity in 1936, having been signed up by Runt Espey and in turn signing up others among the younger men, including my Uncle Stan. Runt, who was short and cocky like my father, had some job security and not a little shop-floor power through his craft skills. There were certain molds that only Runt knew how to do correctly, and many others that benefitted from his skills and knowledge. In addition, in my father's words, he was a "crafty bugger" who "had something on everybody, or could make you think he did," and most foremen or superintendents had to solicit Runt's cooperation if they were to get production. Runt, therefore, could openly advocate for the union without fear of losing his job. Others could not.

If the company had found out he had joined the union, my father would not only have lost his job at U.S. Steel, but he would also have been put on a do-not-hire "blacklist" at Bethlehem and at the various smaller fabricating plants in town. Before the Wagner Act, the companies made sure everybody knew about the blacklist and were very demonstrative in using it. After Wagner, which made such practices illegal, they were more subtle about it, but according to local legend, once you got on the blacklist, you *never* got off. Once, sometime in the 1950s while we were out shopping together, my father pointed to a man who had been fired from Bethlehem before the union and explained that the blacklist was why "even today" that man had to work as a grocery-store clerk.

I once asked my father if he had thought, when he first joined, that the union would accomplish all that it had. Without hesitating, he answered, "No. That's not why I joined. I didn't really think it would do any good. But I didn't care. I was young, single, and I hated my job, and . . . I just couldn't live with the fear. I was just rebelling. I knew the company hated the union, so I joined. I don't know what I'd have done if I'd had a family then." The fear, he explained, was the fear of losing your job, and some foremen used that fear like a whip. He told numerous stories to illustrate how this worked, none of which involved him directly. "I was young, and I really didn't care if they fired me or not —I hated the mill—and they knew that. It [not caring] protected me. They went after the guys with families, the guys who couldn't afford to lose their jobs. If you let them know you were afraid for your job, they owned you. They owned your job, and that meant they owned *you*." The worst of these stories, which he and others told me several times over the years, went like this.

When work was slack during the Depression, before the union, foremen were in control of who worked and who didn't on any given day. In 1932, for example, my father had to report for work every morning six days a week, even though the company needed him only fifty-two of the more than 300 days on which he reported. To get work, workers would vie with each other to curry favor with foremen and superintendents. One fellow who had a reputation as a particularly good worker had been employed steadily during one period; to ensure his employment, he cut his foreman's grass in the summer and shoveled snow for him in the winter without pay; he also brought homemade kielbasa and other goodies to the foreman on a regular basis. One day the foreman ran into this worker while the worker was with his sixteen-year-old daughter, a particularly beautiful young woman, as the story goes. The next day at work the foreman, a married man with a family and himself only slightly younger than his employee, asked the worker if he could arrange a "date" with his daughter. The worker said he'd see and would let the foreman know the next day. The next day the worker arrived with a particularly large supply of freshly made kielbasa, but told the foreman he would be unable to arrange the date. At this point he was summarily fired and was subsequently without work for the better part of a year—at a time when there was no unemployment compensation and "relief" was a breadline.

This story got told and retold because it was so extreme. Most foremen would not dream of doing anything like this. Most foremen were, in fact, good guys, people you could reason with. But they all had this power over your life and the life of your family, and most of them used it in both big and little ways, sometimes with a purpose, sometimes just out of meanness, but always with the same humiliating result. The worst part of this story, for my father, was not the man's being without work for so long. The worst part was that he didn't, that he couldn't, just say no—that even in refusing the foreman's request, he couldn't "stand up to him," couldn't maintain his dignity.

As my father used to say, "If the union didn't do anything else, it put an end to that." Though it didn't happen all at once, the union eventually stripped not only the foreman but even the company of this arbitrary power.

At first, in 1937, it just gave a guy like Runt Espey something additional to work with, a way to extend to others some of the protections he enjoyed based on his craft skills. The grievance procedure in those early years didn't take away much of the foreman's formal power, but it meant that a union griever could go over his head to a superintendent, and then the union could go over a department superintendent's head if a complaint seemed justified. This immediately eliminated the worst excesses of foremen, which (as in the story above) violated existing company policy. And, with a little imagination, a crafty bugger like Runt, who was the molders' first grievance man, could use the formal power of the union contract to extend his informal power in the labor process. Pretty soon the guys on the molding floor were going to Runt asking, "Can he [the foreman] do that?" and Runt almost uniformly would say, "Hell no!" and then go have a talk with the foreman. The foreman needed Runt's craft skills, and now his leadership, to get production; besides, many foremen, like most rank-and-file workers, were none too sure what the new system required of them. In this context, Runt was able to give the union a power and a presence on the molding floor all out of proportion to what had been agreed upon in March 1937 by John L. Lewis and U.S.S. head Myron Taylor in a hotel in New York

City. To my father, who was twenty-five then, it was indescribably exhilarating to observe this process.

In these first years, Runt gained some of the arbitrary power the foremen used to have, and though Runt could be mean, both to foremen and to workers who didn't support the union strongly enough, he never, according to my father, used his power "against the men." Though I never met him, I have a clear memory of Runt Espey from the stories my father told me when I was very young. Besides the company-and-the-union stories, Runt figured in most of the stories my father used to instruct me in how to be a "little guy" (a phrase that referred to both height and strength) in a world of big men. Runt had a mean streak, and he would sometimes humiliate others just for the satisfaction of doing it; he particularly liked making a fool out of big guys who were soft, which could hurt a lot more and a lot longer than a punch in the face. Runt was also vain—he liked to be recognized as a leader and to be deferred to. My father both gloried in and was ashamed of Runt's negative qualities, with which he clearly identified, but in his scheme of things these qualities were necessary and justified if, in general and for the most part, they served a larger purpose. "We needed a guy like that in those days," he said. Speaking as much about himself as about Runt, he would say, "Not everybody can be like your mom and Stan [who we all recognized as models of the quiet, selfless Christian humility we were supposed to strive for]. We needed a guy like that at the time. Otherwise, we'd still be slaves."

Runt, in today's jargon, was my father's role model. But nobody's perfect, even role models, and that's why the union wouldn't really be a union if it had to depend on the consistent righteousness of the Runt Espeys. The idea was to eliminate arbitrary power itself, not just to shift it from one person to another. Though it didn't happen all at once, that's exactly what the union contract eventually achieved.

Assigning work, firing, disciplining, even warning a steelworker— by the 1950s nobody—not the foreman, the company, nor any union leader, from the shop floor to international headquarters—had much discretion in doing any of these things. The rules laid out in the union contract determined who got laid off and who worked during bad times, who got overtime and who worked night shift, who worked in Job Classification 10 and who worked in Job Classification 15. If you had the seniority and could do the job, it was yours by right. Nobody *gave* it to you. It was yours according to the rules everybody had agreed to.

Though you needed the union to ensure that the rules were followed and, indeed, to get the rules written down and agreed to in the first place, you didn't need to be in anybody's good graces; you didn't need to bring anyone kielbasa, not even the union.

This system of rule-making and rule-observing is the essence of bureaucracy, and it has its disadvantages for both workers and managers. But it is also the essence of industrial democracy in the American system. Today, as labor historian David Brody has shown so clearly, both the Left and the Right attack this "workplace rule of law" with little sense of its role in liberating workers from arbitrary authority and all the indignities, the humiliation, and the fear that come with being directly subject to the unlimited authority of another human being.[18] Bureaucratic work rules, and the legalistic grievance system designed to interpret and enforce them, take away a lot of management discretion that may be desirable for competing in a more fiercely competitive world. They also bind workers as well as managers, restricting them from taking things into their own hands with wildcat strikes and other spontaneous job actions that might oppose injustices allowable under the contract; in the long run, this may undermine worker militancy and the very capacity for concerted action. Both the Right and the Left have a point. But the easy use of "bureaucracy" as a broad perjorative with rich negative connotations allows them to avoid the issue of what the alternative to living by impersonal rules might be.

Sometimes complaints about "bureaucracy" refer simply to the *excesses* of the impersonal observation of rules and regulations. Such complaints are directed simply at "bureaucrats" who lack common sense or a human touch in applying the rules to specific situations. But the casualness of current attacks on bureaucracy and bureaucrats often includes a weariness with democracy and its requirements, a weariness with the rule of law itself, and a dangerous yearning for leadership unrestricted by the results of previous generations' struggles, outcomes, and decisions. This is certainly true of the free-market Right with its deep belief in Great Men operating unfettered in the marketplace, but it was also true of a large part of the New Left with its attraction to the style and drama of revolution more than to its substance.

In my father's view of things, the very impersonality of the labor contract as a binding document was the foundation of his freedom and dignity, and a great deal of peace of mind as well. He believed in what was called then "the sanctity of the contract": "You have to live by the contract. It binds us as well as them [management or the company]. But it's *our* contract. We were bound before. They weren't." The union itself, not anything that it did or didn't do; the contract itself, not anything that was in it; these were the fundamentals, "the big thing," as he said. The rest was gravy.

Which is not to say he was indifferent to the details, just that he knew that neither God nor the Devil were in them. Specific work rules and working conditions were crucial to him, and he had a way of dividing them from wages and benefits, a way that coincided with the split between work and family that was so much a part of 1950s culture. The wages and benefits were for the family; the working conditions, for him alone. The money for both "came out of the same pot," he would say, and we should not expect him to degrade his working conditions (or fail to improve them) so that he could bring a little more home to us.

Not that it seemed we ever had to make that choice. Indeed, it was in the wages and benefits that the rest of us could see the revolution "since the union." And unlike so many other Americans, who just saw "prosperity" improving their lives, we saw the union doing it. Take 1946, for example. The union wanted twenty-five cents (most other CIO unions wanted closer to thirty cents), but the company allowed it could afford only a dime. The government recommended eighteen and a half cents, and that's what we got. Into the 1960s, the Steelworkers' wage-and-benefit package was always bargained and reported in cents, not in percentage-increase terms. This was done to benefit the lower pay grades, but it also had the effect of making the impact of wage bargaining more clear and meaningful to Steelworker families like mine. Through ten sets of negotiations and five strikes from 1946 to 1956, the steel companies fought every advance the union sought—and did so in a highly public way. It was pretty simple to figure out that without the union we wouldn't have gotten eight and a half of those eighteen and a half cents in 1946, and only a little more complicated to reason that without the union the companies would never have offered that dime in the first place.

From the time my father joined the union in 1936 until the 1959 strike, the average *real* wage of steelworkers increased 110 percent, with the bulk of the increase coming after the war.[19] Think of that a minute. Think what it does for a family's well-being to have more real spending power year after year, to experience a steady, relentless improvement in its standard of living for more than two decades. And, though they were often in the forefront, it wasn't just the steelworkers who experienced these benefits: The average real wage of all manufacturing workers increased 89 percent during the same period. This was not gravy. This was the very basis of life for a wage worker in a capitalist society. It meant, first, that you could routinely cover the basic necessities of life. Then it meant you had something very few workers had ever had up until then —discretionary income, income that in a sense you didn't need, income that you could *decide* how to spend. Eventually, and this had happened by 1959, it meant an upgrading in what counted as necessities. In 1946, we did not have a car, a television set, or a refrigerator. By 1952 we had all those things, and I can remember vividly the excitement of the day when each arrived. And by 1959 these were all necessities, without which we could not have imagined living.

But the real wage increase doesn't cover the half of it. In 1949, the Steelworkers struck the companies for forty-two days in order to get them to fund a pension plan and to partially fund health insurance. These were nothing to brag about at first. The pension formula committed the companies to supplement Social Security so that a steelworker with enough service could receive $100 a month in retirement (at a time when it took at least $250 a month to live). Likewise, health insurance only covered certain hospital costs and major procedures by doctors, and the company only paid half the premium. But they were a big deal at the time, and the companies at first resisted them on principle as "un-American and contrary to the most cherished ideals of self-reliance and personal initiative."[20] After forty-two days, the companies gave up on that principle, and the union then improved on the substance with each negotiation in the 1950s.

In 1952 when my mother had her first heart attack and spent quite a while in the hospital, most of our costs were covered by the health insurance. Still, Mom's heart attack set us back. We had to sell the frame house we were buying and move to a government housing project (very nice then). My mother had more heart attacks, but we all just kept plugging along. According to a mantra my father repeated almost until the day he died, "Without the health insurance, our lives would have been wrecked."

And the pension eventually turned out to be a wonder. The idea of retiring at the age of fifty-six and being able to live comfortably, if frugally, was unimaginable in 1946. Though the "winter shack" he rented with his second wife in Florida was a decidedly modest dwelling, it allowed him to avoid more than a decade of northern winters when he "should have been in the mill aching and freezing"—and yet to return to the glorious spring, summer, and autumn of the western Pennsylvania hills. What is it worth for a man to have thirteen years of contentment like these—when *everything* he hates in life is avoided?

But the life, health, and disability insurance and the pension the Steelworkers won in 1949 were more than just themselves. Besides the peace of mind they provided, by taking away the need to save up for hard times they released savings for other things and made buying on installment (and credit in general) rational and feasible behavior. This made for more discretionary income. This process was further aided by the union's winning of Supplemental Unemployment Benefits (SUB) in the fifty-eight-day strike of 1956. SUB supplemented government-funded Unemployment Compensation to pay about 80 percent of a steelworker's wages when he was laid off (by the 1970s it was paying as much as 95 percent). In a brutally cyclical industry like steel, this gave a security and predictability to life that allowed steelworker families to pursue long-term goals and investments (whether buying a house, expanding the one you had, or saving for children's education). All this meant more discretionary income, more discretion itself, more freedom to develop your life in relation to your own values and choices.

The perception and remembrance of the 1950s as a time of repressive conformism and spiritless materialism might relate to the middle-class organization man, the white-collar professional and managerial worker of the time. It did not relate to us. All the discretion that the foreman and the company were losing was flowing right into our home. There were choices. There were prospects. There were possibilities. Few of these had been there before. Now they were. And because they came slowly, year by year, contract by contract, strike by bitter strike, they gave a lilting, liberating feeling to life—a sense that no matter what was wrong today, it could be changed, it could get better—in fact, by the late 1950s, that it was quite likely that it *would* get better. Hang in there. Stick with it. These moral injunctions to daily fortitude made so much more sense then when there were so many visible payoffs for doing so. And as my father would find out, my mother, my sister and I—like nearly everybody else in American society—were learning to tolerate less and less repression from anybody or anything, including him. If what we lived through in the 1950s was not liberation, then liberation never happens in real human lives.

What we did with it—that was another thing. Many times when Aunt Ruth or someone else wondered whether "maybe the union has become too powerful," their comments reflected a concern that life was getting too good for us. The pundits and columnists that Johnstown's only newspaper brought into our homes and whose writings all the adults read and discussed (above all, those of the conservative Republican David Lawrence), meant something different by this standard worry about Big Labor—something that had to do with business conditions, inflation, the national economy, and the decline in the power of Great Men. But for us, as evangelical Protestants who saw great value in suffering "in this life," the steady improvement in our material conditions might also have been undermining the progress of our souls. My father, though he was prepared to combat David Lawrence point by point, shared *this* concern. But he insisted on knowing the practical implications of restricting the union's power. "What should we give up?" he'd ask, and then he'd go around the room referring to something that he knew was important to each person—Aunt Bettie's curtains, Stan's hunting vacation in Potter County, Frommy's first car, and always "that full collection plate" that allowed us to keep up and improve our church. His point was supposed to be something about how we used our money and our freedom, but the way this technique silenced everybody one by one, and the looks on their faces, made it palpable that these material things, though they varied from person to person, were more than just themselves. Each was a token of freedom and enjoyment that nobody was prepared to give back or to really believe was undermining any souls.

It's important not to exaggerate how well we and other steelworker families were living in the 1950s. Labor historian Mark McColloch has carefully tracked the progress of the "average steelworker's" standard of living in "the union era." The increase was not quite as steady as I remember it, and by the middle-class standards of the graded family budgets of the Bureau of Labor Statistics (BLS), the average steelworker family did not move out of poverty until 1953 and did not arrive at a "modest but adequate" standard of living until the late 1960s at the earliest. As Germans and Protestants, my family was perched near the top of the ethnic pecking order in the mill and in town, and all of the men had at least mid-level skilled jobs—so our standard of living was somewhat above the averages McColloch uses. Still, his description of the

BLS's minimum budget of the late 1940s almost perfectly describes my immediate family's situation in 1959:

> This budget envisioned a family of four, living in a rented apartment, consisting of a kitchen, bath, and three other rooms. The family had hot running water and owned a washing machine [a wringer-washer, not an "automatic"]. On the budget "it should be possible to serve meat for dinner several times a week, if the cheaper cuts are served." Each child could have a bottle of pop every other day, and one beer a week could be consumed. Three shirts and two pairs of pants could be purchased each year for the growing boy. The family did not own a car and there was no money in the budget for any vacation ever, but every three weeks the family could afford a movie, if they bought no food at the theater.[21]

By 1959 we differed in three ways from this description. We, and almost everybody in our neighborhood, had a used car throughout the 1950s—in our case, a 1936 Dodge from about 1950 to at least 1955, a 1949 Chevy after that, and by 1959 a (breathtaking) two-toned 1956 Chevrolet. We had taken a vacation—a week's long drive through New York and into New England—sometime in the mid-1950s, not to mention my father's Canadian fishing trips, which according to him "paid for themselves" with the two portable freezers of fish he brought home. And finally, we didn't need that money for one beer a week!

There was one other important difference—not only between us and the BLS minimum budget, but between us and nearly every other steelworker family I knew. We had enough savings for both my sister and me to begin college, which she did in the fall of 1959. Maybe it was not drinking that one beer a week. Maybe it was our ethnic and skill-level advantages. Or maybe it was the initial savings my mother had brought to her marriage from her former life as an old maid school teacher. But it was also definitely related to the fanatical commitment my father made, and which he insisted the rest of us make, to "saving for an education." In any case, that opportunity existed, though we both messed it up, at least initially.

But even the minimum budget described above, without the extras my family had, doesn't sound as "harsh" to me as it does to McColloch. Take those three shirts and two pairs of pants every year. In junior high and high school, that many changes of new clothes clearly differentiated the steelworkers' kids from the kids whose fathers did not work in the mill; they, like the girl who would become my wife, were lucky to have one set of new clothes a year. Two bedrooms for four people didn't seem too bad either (though I hated rooming with my father at the time) if you compared it to three bedrooms for nine people, as was the case in my wife's family. We often seemed "middle-class" because we were so obviously better off than a lot of our friends—and when you figured in the health insurance, the SUB, and the pension, we were a lot better off. To my wife, when we first met in junior high school, I was "a rich kid." I hated that category and rejected it out of hand, but I knew what she meant—we all did.

The trick to understanding people's nostalgia for the 1950s lies not in remembering how we actually lived then as compared to now. By most objective measures (per capita income, real family income, home ownership, poverty rates, infant mortality, and life expectancy, not to mention racism, sexism, and general intolerance—though not crime rates) life is still dramatically better today, even after substantial erosions. What was better then was the direction we were going. We expected less, appreciated more, and were much more likely to get what we strove for. Then, a rising tide *was* lifting all boats, raising everybody's prospects and expectations—not like today, when having any expectations at all often seems difficult, even unnatural, for younger people.

The final piece of the union revolution, the reduction in work time and the increase in leisure time, was possibly the most important one for my father, if not for us. For us, his being home was a double-edged sword. Because he interfered with and dominated everything, and because he had a quick temper, whenever he was home there was almost always a tension in the house, a tension that, it's not too much to say, lifted from our hearts, and our stomachs, when he left for work. On the other hand, he was the one who carried the action in the family— things got done, decided, or at least talked about when he was home —and we never doubted either his dedication to us or his willingness and ability to help us solve our problems. For me, all things considered, I liked having him home, but I enjoyed his leaving as well.

I don't think most steelworkers hated their jobs and the mill as much as my father did. If they did, they didn't express it as often and as passionately. Because he hated it so much, he seemed to savor every minute of reduction in work hours—and the reductions were substantial. When he joined the union in 1936, the standard work week in steel was sixty hours across six days. There were no paid vacations, no paid holidays, and no possibilities for retirement. The very first contract with

U.S. Steel granted a week's vacation; a year later, the federal Fair Labor Standards Act established forty hours as the standard work week, requiring employers to pay 50 percent more for each hour worked after forty. After the heavy overtime during the war, he actually worked a forty-hour week throughout the 1950s. By 1952, my father was entitled to three weeks' vacation and seven holidays. Before he retired, he had at least one of the thirteen-week vacations ("the steelworker's sabbatical") that the union won for high seniority workers in 1963. And in the 1960s, the union worked hard to get pensions and rules good enough so men in their mid-fifties could retire; it won thirty-and-out in 1965, allowing someone with thirty years' service to quit work forever.

Getting paid for not working always amazed my father, even in the last years of his retirement. I think he even felt a little guilty about it. In his speeches about the union, he never justified shorter work weeks, vacations, holidays, or even retirement on their own—though he gloried in them. These were justified because they opened up work for others; they "spread the work around." And because he never felt fully entitled to being paid for not working, he could make something like "paid vacation" sound almost magical. It was one of those things he had never expected from the union—which, in his version, was primarily about balancing power on the shop floor and guaranteeing fair wages and benefits. If these vital details were already what he considered gravy, then paid time off was a garnish—but a garnish that in many ways surpassed the meal itself.

At the very beginning of the modern American labor movement came the demand for "eight hours for work, eight hours for sleep, eight hours for what you will." As the weekend and the eight-hour day finally became standard in the wake of the war, 1950s sociologists took to worrying about whether workers were spending their newly won leisure time in a way that advanced the species—which was what the labor movement had always claimed would result.[22] A weighty question this, open to various kinds of judgments.

As far as its results in our family were concerned, my father was not one to sit around doing nothing or watching television. He hunted, fished, gardened (strictly vegetables, no flowers), and enjoyed fixing things, mostly in cars and houses. For him, the worst part of our living in a housing project from 1952 to 1955 was that nothing needed to be fixed, and even if it did, he had to call somebody else to do it. He always had a hobby—fiddling with ham radios when he was younger, tying flies for fly-fishing later. He coached Little League baseball. He read the newspaper, *Reader's Digest*, and the union's monthly paper, *Steelabor*, regularly, and occasionally he read a religious book (sermons and essays by Billy Graham or Daniel Poling, not the religious novels of Thomas Costain and Taylor Caldwell that my mother and sister read in the 1950s).

He also fulfilled Daniel Bell's high-faluting definition of a "leisure civilization" as "one with a fixed task of exploring and extending a specific cultural heritage."[23] He taught Sunday School three Sundays a month and built the Young Married Couples class from a handful of regulars to the largest and most active class in our church. He worked on his Sunday School lesson most of the week, and then intensively for a couple of hours on Saturday night. The national church, Evangelical United Brethren, which later merged into the United Methodists (against my family's wishes), designated a biblical passage of eight to twelve verses each week and provided some supplementary materials to help in the interpretation. But it was up to the Sunday School teacher to develop his or her own interpretation in relation to a specific audience. Dad would pore through the multivolume *Clark's Commentaries on the Old and New Testament* for help, but he also fully utilized his gift for analogies based on our common experience. And he took very seriously his role as a spokesman for the union; even before he became a griever in the early 1950s, fellow workers, their family members, and neighbors sought his perspective on and explanations of union matters. As a child accompanying him as he did shopping and chores, I waited impatiently through many of these exercises in exploring and extending the culture of unionism.

The church and the union, along with our immediate and extended family (which blended more or less seamlessly into them), formed the coherent core of my father's "eight hours for what you will." Both were the kinds of "mediating institutions" that William Greider has so poignantly shown were necessary for our oligarchy of wealth to erode so that the working class could become alienated and powerless again.[24] Both were national institutions that provided uniform educational materials that gave very specific direction about how to think and act while allowing, in fact counting upon, thousands and thousands of local leaders to give them the specific, face-to-face interpretations that made them vital and real. In church this was called witnessing, and it involved more than just expressing yourself. It required putting yourself on the line, making public a personal commitment to practice what you preach as you were demanding it of others. This working-class hermeneutics was something my father was particularly good at, and something he enjoyed immensely, though it was not as relaxing as fishing or fixing the car.

My guess is that few steelworkers used their increased leisure as productively as my father did, but no matter how open neighborhood and family life were then (and they were much less private than now), there's no telling for sure. Our neighbors, for example, would never have guessed at the effort and creativity he put into those Sunday School lessons. And few of them appeared to be engaged in anything like the pathological dialectic of "wildly aggressive play or passive, unresponsive viewing" that the sociologists were worrying about at the time.[25] In any case, the free time was there to be used for good or ill, and the union was continually expanding it.

Shop-floor power and dignity; a steadily increasing standard of living that not only made life more secure, but kept increasing chances for discretion; an explosion of free time for what you will. The 1950s saw an amazing transformation of daily life that fully justifies, depending on where you sit, dividing the American Century into before the union and since.

Being a Griever

In the 1950s, unions were very powerful institutions that commanded the public's attention. All the steel strikes, and many others, were front-page national stories in a time much less saturated with national-news reporting than ours. One of every three families were union households, as opposed to about one of seven today. Yet "the public" (which C. Wright Mills once defined as the 60 percent that was in neither union nor management households)[26] likely saw the inner workings of unions as David Reisman did in his best-selling 1950 sociology book, *The Lonely Crowd:* a relationship of "union officials to an indifferent mass of nominal union members."[27]

Indeed it often seemed this way. The press covered the doings and sayings of John L. Lewis, Jimmy Hoffa, Walter Reuther, David J. Mc-Donald, and other national leaders, and it seemed the members simply did what they were told. Though often excoriated as "labor bosses," the leaders were seen as powerful, accomplished, and, above all, successful men. The workers were simply followers, "an indifferent mass." This image may have been enhanced by CIO leaders' use of public media to communicate with their members. Unions used radio broadcasts, press releases, news conferences, and full-page newspaper ads to articulate their positions to both the public and their members, and they were well practiced in addressing these dual audiences. Sentences beginning "Steelworkers think," for example, simultaneously informed the public about what steelworkers thought, informed steelworkers as to what they were supposed to think, and encouraged steelworkers to think that way.[28]

The press supplemented its reporting of official views with man-on-the-street interviews with rank-and-file workers, deliberately bypassing local leaders, who they expected to simply parrot the national leaders' views. This was easy to do in steel towns, where a reporter could simply hang around a mill-gate bar during shift changes. In 1959 the *New York Times* periodically printed entire pages of such reports from steel centers around the country. Perusing these pages would have disabused the sociologists of the notion that the union functioned simply as a relation between a national leader and a mass of indifferent members.

It is rare for members to feel an intense personal loyalty toward a national union leader who they know only through the media and occasional mass gatherings. Reuther had a loyal cadre like this in the UAW, Hoffa in the Teamsters, and John L. Lewis not only in the UMW, but also among many industrial workers like my father. But though this kind of relation can be a major asset for a union, it never constitutes the principal relationship between member and union. David J. McDonald, for example, inspired no such loyalty among steelworkers, but this didn't stop them from following his lead. Rather, the principal relation between member and union, then as now, always involves face-to-face relationships, relationships between people who know each other and make commitments to one another, and who either live up to those commitments or don't. For most workers, this relationship is with their shop steward or griever. Yet not many people, even many in union families, know what a steward is or does. And, by not knowing, they can easily misunderstand what exactly a union is and what effect it has on people's lives.

A labor contract is a living document, in the sense that it is a text subject to various interpretations. The griever or steward must learn the contract inside out and make sure that it is followed "to the letter" by management. Where management errs (for example, in laying off, promoting, assigning work to, disciplining, or discharging a worker), a steward first talks with the foreman involved, urging him to correct the error, which—once it has been pointed out—the foreman sometimes does. But the foreman may not agree with the steward's interpretation of the contract, claiming that there has been no error. Sometimes this convinces the steward, but when it does not, he files a written grievance describing what management did wrong and citing the specific contract clause violated. This initiates a process, from the department to the plant to the company level, in which higher levels of union and management meet to resolve the grievance, and which in instances of ongoing disagreement ends with a neutral arbitrator deciding what exactly the contract requires in this specific instance. These higher-level decisions often set precedents for what the contract means, precedents that go well beyond the particular department or plant where the grievance was initiated.

But the process begins with a worker complaining to his steward about something management has done, and with the steward deciding whether management's action was a contract violation. Management perpetrates lots of daily injustices that workers resent and rebel against but that are not violations of the union contract. This was particularly true in the 1940s and early 1950s in steel, as the contract was being built clause by clause to restrict more and more of management's discretion in dealing with its workforce. A good griever has to educate his workmates on a case-by-case basis about what is and is not in the contract— the difference, in the jargon of traditional stewards' training, between a gripe and a grievance. But a good griever also needs to be creative in stretching contract language to apply to any "gripes" that could possibly be construed as grievances under the contract.

Good stewards or grievers are what makes a union a union. By gaining a reputation for diligence, toughness, and fair dealing with both workers and front-line supervision, they can settle many disputes on the spot, whether the disputes involve a violation of the contract or not. By regularly attending union meetings, reading the national or local union newspaper, and keeping informed about what's going on, they *are* the union for most of its members, providing leadership to their immediate workmates on everything from presidential elections to the local union picnic. This requires skills in reasoning and formal argumentation, but it also requires less tangible skills in cajoling or intimidating, soft-soaping or avenging, and in knowing when to "stand up" or "back down" to either a foreman or their fellow workers.

Most stewards, in my experience, complain of being "in the middle," trapped between apathetic and unreasonable members on the one side and unresponsive or wrong-headed leaders on the other. This is more or less the natural condition of the steward, full of frustrations, no matter how involved and reasonable the members or how responsive and right-minded the leaders. But where there is a strong union culture, which there was in basic steel in the 1950s, being a steward is something you can take a lot of pride in as well, something that can engage your imagination and bring out the best (and sometimes the worst) in you. The people you work with look to you for answers, and the people you work for respect you and maybe even fear you a little. There's a lot of satisfaction in "winning a grievance," especially when it puts a fired worker back to work with back pay or requires upper-level management to admit that it made a mistake. And there's the sense that, as one of thousands of grievers, you are a part of something as large and powerful as a steel company.

Johnny Metzgar was one of these grievers. He watched the steward system grow in basic steel, and when he came of age in his early forties (in about 1953 or 1954), he took on the responsibilities, frustrations, and joys of being a griever. Despite his set speech about "all of us" being the union, he really believed that this middle part between members and leaders was the core of the union. He was cynical about leaders, even elected local leaders, and assumed that they were in it for themselves. Though he recognized lots of exceptions, anybody who drew a full-time paycheck from the union was, in his words, unlikely to "really care about the men." Rank-and-file members, on the other hand, weren't that great in his estimation, either. Many were too easily influenced or intimidated by the company. Many were too quick to complain about the union, expecting the union to do *for* them without *them* doing anything but pay dues. "They don't even *look* at the contract," my father would explain. "They won't read the [union's] paper. They don't come to meetings." There were, of course, "good union members," the ones who at least browsed through the contract, looked over the paper, and always did what he told them to do. And there were a few who knew their contracts, provided leadership to their immediate work group, and helped the grievers in innumerable ways. "They didn't get anything out of it," he said. "They just knew their responsibility and did it." It was out of this group that future grievers came.

The public image of unions as consisting of a relationship between national leaders and rank-and-file workers was, to my father, nothing but "a face on a body." The real guts of the union for him lay in the way it linked the grievers and their allies in thousands of small work areas in dozens of huge steel mills. Even though grievers knew only their own immediate work area, somehow they all thought and acted as one. Without them, the leadership couldn't lead and the membership wouldn't follow. The quality of stewards and grievance systems varies greatly from union to union, place to place, and time to time. But when it works well, a union steward system is a wonder of workplace democracy that blends thousands of face-to-face, grassroots encounters into a powerful national institution for collective action.

Grievance systems became progressively more bureaucratic and legalistic after 1946. In the early days of the CIO, no distinction was made between a gripe and a grievance; something did not need to be in the contract to count as a grievance. As contracts grew more complicated, a lot of the discretion that had at first belonged to both the foreman and the workers was removed to higher levels of the company and the union, and even, in crucial instances, to a third-party arbitrator. The complex process of solving disputes came to center on the interpretation of the contract, not on what was fair in itself. To many of the current generation of labor historians, the grievance system as we know it today is a bureaucratic encumbrance that saps the militance of rank-and-file workers. Instead of leading direct action at the workplace, slowing down or stopping work (which was common in the CIO unions during World War II), the steward "files" a grievance, which then gets lost in a complicated bureaucratic process that eventually "issues" a decision. Historian Nelson Lichtenstein, for example, sees "the rigidly defined system of work rules and seniority rights" that developed after World War II as "a conservative turning point in the evolution of workplace power relations . . . [that] sharply circumscribed the promise of a more fluid and robust industrial democracy."[29]

There is undoubtedly some truth to this evaluation, but it's important to see the system at its best as well as its worst. The system in which my father participated through the 1950s and 1960s was a fully mature contract administration system of the kind scorned by Lichtenstein. It virtually eliminated the possibility of direct workplace action in the form of wildcat strikes and job actions—though "quickie" strikes still occurred into the 1950s. But the formal power vested in the contract could, with a little imagination, expand as well as circumscribe the power of rank-

and-file workers and their stewards. The key issue in the 1959 Steel Strike involved the cornerstone of the "rigidly defined system of work rules" in basic steel, Section 2-B. 2-B contained a deceptively simple provision inserted in the 1947 contract that the union built into a very powerful weapon for saving jobs and restricting management's right to reorganize the labor process. The power 2-B gave workers was based on both the imagination of the unions' lawyers, who talked arbitrators into expanding its restrictions on management's discretion, and the imagination of grievers and other local leaders, who convinced foremen and superintendents that 2-B was even more restrictive of their actions than the arbitrators had ruled.

Though much more sweeping in its impact, 2-B was typical of "rigid union work rules" in the 1950s because it not only gave workers formal power, but it also allowed them, with a little imagination, to expand their informal power as well. The very rigidity of the formal rules required management, particularly foremen, to negotiate on the shop floor for "flexibility" in specific instances. The cat-and-mouse games involved in this shop-floor bargaining was something my father thought he excelled in, and he loved to tell me about them. I don't remember many of the specifics, and I didn't understand much about them at the time, but I know they could involve techniques such as "doing it by the book," using "the silent treatment," and strategically placing dead rats (and in one instance a live one). One standard ploy my father used involved enticing a foreman into routine violations of the contract and then flooding the grievance system with valid grievances that cost the company money and embarrassed the foreman. My father delighted in these activities—some of which were simply *mano-a-mano* contests in his decades-long battle with the evil foreman I knew simply as "Yock," but others of which required him to organize his fellow workers to maintain or establish informal operating procedures they saw as important to their work lives. A cooperative foreman, on the other hand, could count on my father not only never to embarrass him, but also to occasionally rally the men for extraordinary production efforts that would make the foreman look good.

In my father's telling, creative shop-floor dueling like this went with being a griever, and as good as he thought he was at it, he never claimed to be anything special. In subsequent years, I would learn to judge a local union and its grievance system by whether its stewards could tell good shop-floor bargaining stories like the ones he told. In many unions, the steward is nothing but a messenger who carries a worker's complaint to a union staff representative, who decides whether it is a gripe or a grievance and then does whatever is appropriate. In such situations, stewards will typically not have sufficient understanding of the contract to use it to enhance their own and their workmates' informal power; the union's paid staff will have all the power, formal and informal, and only they will have the opportunity, at some distance from the specific work setting, to exercise imagination and creativity—if their workload allows time for it, which usually it doesn't. Though it's hard to say with any certainty, my impression is that my father was a fairly typical CIO steward of his time. The CIO unions focused their educational efforts on steward training in the immediate postwar years, and they defined the steward in broad terms as a shop-floor leader with responsibilities well beyond mere grievance handling.

A typical steward's training then emphasized that grievance handling was only one of four basic functions of the steward. The others were *organizing* (winning support of members for union programs and recruiting new members if there was no union shop), *educating* (explaining union goals, encouraging members to read union publications, and providing a steady stream of union information), and *being politically active* (encouraging members to register and vote and informing them about the union's legislative program). Stewards were the eyes and ears and the voice of the union on the shop floor; they were the *organization*, as described in the following panegyric addressed to stewards:

> [L]ike the framework of [a] house, the steward system often goes unnoticed—yet it's the most important part of the union. Remember—the company has an organization: managers, then supervisors, then foremen. Policy decisions are made at the top and handed down in the form of orders. Information about what's going on in the plant is sent upstairs—[moving from] foremen to supervisors to managers.
>
> With this organization, the company operates like an army—with communications flowing both ways. The men in the field (the foremen) know what headquarters wants them to do. And headquarters knows what's going on in the field, because the foremen pass the word back to them. This is what the union must deal with—and the union cannot deal with management on equal terms unless the union has a similar organization of its own.
>
> The union must have an organization—and the steward system is that organization! The steward system gives the union its strength.[30]

I doubt my father ever had any formal training in being a griever, but he must have gotten a pamphlet from the Steelworkers that said something very similar to the above. He used both the housing and military metaphors in explaining the system to me, and he surely had taken to

heart this conception of the role of the steward. The analogies to corporate and military structure make it clear that, while communications
should flow both ways, the top-down dispersion of the message from
"headquarters" is the most important. But the grievers' function of
spreading the message required more than just passing down orders
from headquarters. It, like enforcing the contract, required interpretive
activity, and this made it an important enhancement of democratic life
in the industrial working class, regardless of how unresponsive leaders
might be to the upward flow of information about "what's going on in
the field."

As a griever in basic steel, my father was a spokesman for the union
in all its aspects. But there were many messages coming from headquarters (mostly through the national union newspaper *Steelabor*), and
a griever had to select which messages to push and how to push them
to different audiences. After 1948, for example, Johnny Metzgar did not
push the union's political endorsements for national office and often explicitly rejected them, as in 1960; but he pushed the union line hard on
our state representative. Likewise, he not only never defended Steelworker president David J. McDonald but actively denounced him as a
"silk-stocking" who was too close to the companies. On contract issues
and general union principles, on the other hand, he adopted the union
line with vigor, adding his own interpretations and analogies while freely
borrowing from printed union materials and from what he'd been told
by other grievers and local leaders.

All of this was stimulating intellectual activity infused with immediate practical significance, particularly during negotiations and strikes.
There was no contradiction, to my father's way of looking at things, between thinking for yourself and following the union line. Indeed, the
two reinforced one another. The union, like the church, was a mediating institution that provided a broad framework of belief and practice
that you shared with others. Each individual was too limited to understand everything on his own. Each needed guidance, direction, clear
messages and explanations. But the process of absorbing these messages
and passing them on to others required thinking for yourself, relating
the messages to your own and others' direct experience. It was modest but noble work that, if done well by enough people, could make an
enormous difference in what happened in the larger world. I think this
is why he enjoyed, even gloried in, strikes. A strike was when all the
grievers' organizing and educating, all their chatter with their work-

mates about union principles, came together in one great, unified action that had palpable force and weight. "Sticking together" was the basic union principle, and what brought and kept people together was the everyday activity of the grievers. That's what the union's educational material said, and my father believed it heart and soul. It was one more of the union's benefits: the pride and satisfaction of being such a vital part of something so much larger than himself.

The Labor Movement in 1959

The power and continuing promise of the labor movement in America in 1959 is hard to imagine today. There was a general view then, as now, that unions had become part of "the establishment" by 1959, that leaders were complacent and members, fat and happy. And there's some truth to this. The Steelworkers, for example, was no longer a movement but an institution, and the CIO's larger visions of industrial and social democracy were nearly extinct.

The 1945–46 strike wave, besides initiating a political and public-opinion backlash against Big Labor, had firmly established that, though future union growth might be constrained, there was little possibility of dismantling the power that unions had already gained. On the other hand, Big Business had also been reinvigorated by the war. It would fight to retain as many of its management perogatives as it could, and it was still capable of mobilizing political, economic, and cultural forces to define the rules of engagement.[31] After 1946, it became clear that the class struggle in America would result in a negotiated settlement. The struggle would be about the terms of the settlement, not whether there would be one.

In steel the battles would be fierce but civilized. From the first nationwide steel strike in 1946 to the last one in 1959, the Steelworkers would assist the companies in achieving orderly shutdowns, including allowing some workers to cross their own picket line to maintain furnaces that could not be simply turned off. In return, the companies would not even think about trying to breach the line by operating with scabs. Rather, both sides would engage in a battle of words, numbers, and ideas, seeking to win public opinion and, through it, the favor of the federal government—which always played a role in steel negotiations. From 1946 to 1956, the companies resisted every improvement the Steelworkers sought, but each time they yielded bit by bit until, in

1956, they finally gave the union everything it had wanted, even the union shop.

By 1959 unions had established the basic principles of what some labor historians have called a private welfare system, most of which was in the process of spreading to many nonunion workplaces as well.[32] Besides real wage increases, this system included vacations and holidays, pensions, health insurance, sickness and accident and disability insurance, and a huge measure of job security in the form of seniority systems with bumping rights up and down a ladder of job classifications. For more and more unions, it included automatic cost-of-living adjustments (COLAs) that protected workers from inflation, and for a few, a "guaranteed annual wage" in the form of supplemental unemployment insurance (SUB)—both of which the Steelworkers won in 1956. To those who could remember 1936 and 1946, as my father could, all this *was* a social revolution—a fundamental transformation of the conditions of daily life. Though many of the details of this fundamental transformation were nothing to brag about yet (a Steelworker's pension combined with Social Security, for example, still left a retiree close to poverty), the principles had all been established.

But it is important not to exaggerate *how firmly* these principles were established by 1959. As labor historian Ronald Filippelli has shown, management's acceptance of unions in the 1950s was tactical, not strategic: "American labor history has been marked by conflict—not primarily over contract issues but over the labor movement's right to exist. . . . Unions in America have always been fragile institutions trying to survive in an inherently hostile and unstable situation."[33] Looking back from what labor economist Richard Edwards calls the "post-union era,"[34] the USWA in 1959 doesn't look very fragile, and it wasn't, but the situation was indeed hostile.

Though even during the immediate postwar backlash better than two-thirds of the public were favorable toward unions,[35] the drumbeat of antiunion propaganda coming from the National Association of Manufacturers, the conservative press, and some Republican politicians never ceased. As Melvyn Dubofsky has pointed out, the laws designed to constrain union power—Taft-Hartley in 1947 and Landrum-Griffin in 1959—ended up firmly within the basic New Deal framework of the National Labor Relations Act, but the rhetoric around these efforts "dripped with antiunion venom . . . persistently associating unions with coercion, intimidation, violence, corruption, and crime, and their leaders with greed, tyranny, and communism."[36]

The late 1950s provided a particularly hostile environment. The public image of unions took a beating through widespread publicity, including television coverage, of the McClellan Committee Hearings, which exposed racketeering and corruption in a handful of (mostly AFL) unions and undemocratic practices in many more. The McClellan Hearings, which eventually focused on Jimmy Hoffa, dragged on from 1957 through 1959, when they resulted in the Landrum-Griffin Labor-Management Reporting and Disclosure Act. More importantly, there was a substantial recession in 1957–58, followed by a weak recovery in 1959 and general sluggishness after that. A lot of economists and employers thought this condition meant the end of the postwar boom, something that might jeopardize the American Century before it was over.[37]

This set of circumstances caused employers to mount what Mike Davis has called "The Management Offensive of 1958–63":

> It is generally forgotten how close American industrial relations came to a raw re-opening of the class war in those years. . . . In industry after industry, the management attack on work rules and wages provoked long strikes. The meat-cutters battled Swift, the Western miners fought the copper bosses, the rubber workers conducted the most bitter industry-wide strike since 1937, and the East Coast longshoremen were restrained only by Taft-Hartley. Union strikers in Kentucky were shot, while in North Carolina eight leaders of the textile workers were imprisoned.[38]

In 1958 the Auto Workers absorbed the indignity (and risk) of working without a contract rather than striking during a recession. The Big Three automakers, after flirting with the idea of a general lockout, took advantage of the situation by speeding up work and trashing work rules, particularly at Chrysler. In 1960 General Electric broke a strike of its unions by maintaining production and encouraging back-to-work movements; more than half the locals of the International Union of Electrical Workers (IUE), the largest of the GE unions, broke ranks and returned to work before the union officially gave in.[39]

In 1959 labor leaders could not afford to be complacent, though undoubtedly some were, and a fat and happy membership was highly vulnerable to being torn apart, as they were at GE. But outside the South and with the exception of the GE strike, unions turned back the management offensive of 1958–63. Looking back with more than a little nostalgia, we can see that unions were very powerful institutions then and that unionism as a culture of beliefs and behaviors was too strong in the hearts of millions of men and women to be easily cast aside.

Nor was the *promise* of unionism yet extinguished. As a percentage of the workforce, unions would never get any bigger than they were in 1959, when they still represented nearly one of every three nonagricultural workers. With the merger of the CIO into the larger AFL in 1955, there was a definite narrowing of the CIO's social and political vision, a more cramped and timid attitude toward organizing new sectors of the workforce, and, indeed, a widespread complacency concerning the possibility of future growth—a complacency that actually sat pretty well side by side with a fierce determination to "take no backward steps." But there were still elements within the labor movement bent on providing workers with the experience of before the union and since.

Beginning in May of 1959, for example, something called Local 1199 struck a half-dozen hospitals in New York City for seven weeks, lost the strike, but initiated a decade of inspiring interracial organizing among health-care workers.[40] The explosion of public-sector unionism was still in the future in 1959, but with the groundwork laid in the mid-'50s, AFSCME would grow by a factor of ten over the next thirty years, from less than a hundred thousand members to more than a million. In the fall of 1960, a one-day strike by New York City teachers initiated two decades of teachers' organizing and strikes, often with union leaders spending time in jail for violating local laws or court injunctions. With President Kennedy's Executive Order 10988 in January 1962, federal government workers got collective bargaining rights, and the American Federation of Government Employees organized nearly a half-million members by the end of the decade. And in 1970 the postal unions faced down National Guard troops in an illegal two-week strike that won them *de facto* collective bargaining.[41]

The American labor movement still had a future in 1959. It also had a well-remembered recent past; the steel strike occurred in a world still soaked with the CIO story. From 1936 into the early 1950s, the CIO had cultivated an organizing culture in working-class communities across the country, not excluding the South. Organizing then was not simply about signing union cards. It was about breaking through people's fear and lack of confidence and working out the nuts-and-bolts organizational details to inspire them to collective action. It was about developing local leaders, forming committees, and *uniting* people for struggle. Stories of CIO victories, as well as creative analyses of various CIO tactics and strategies, informed both the Civil Rights movement in the South and the community-organizing movement in the North. Most people over thirty in 1959 could remember when labor was a "movement"; in fact, the CIO was *the* example of what a movement could accomplish. Activists under thirty were regaled with stories, which many would eventually come to resent, that began with phrases like "In the labor movement" and "The CIO used to."[42]

A version of the CIO story, then, was still fresh in the minds of most steelworkers in 1959, since a high proportion had been in the mills for twenty years or more.[43] Though nobody spoke of the CIO as such, dramatic before-and-after terms were common points of reference. The industry's chief negotiator, U.S. Steel's R. Conrad Cooper, stirred up those points of reference when he declared early in the negotiations that the industry's aim was to reverse "the mistakes of the past eighteen years."[44]

This was a deliberately provocative reference to 1941, when the union was first officially recognized throughout the industry but had not yet done much to change our lives. "The mistakes of the past eighteen years" could include just about everything worthwhile the union had won. As it turned out, Cooper didn't really mean quite all that, but coming from the official spokesperson for one of the world's largest and most powerful corporations, such a statement was more than an idle threat.

The final result of the 1959 Steel Strike would be measured in pennies-per-hour, but that's not what it was about. It was about defending the life and prospects that had been won through two decades of struggle on the shop floor and at the bargaining table. If the Steelworkers' union had worked a revolution in our lives, 1959 was management's Thermidor, its attempt "to turn back the clock." In 1959, to mix the metaphors used then, there would be "no backward steps."

2

No Backward Steps

The Biggest Strike in U.S. History

I agree. My life is narrow. From one perspective or another, all lives are narrow. Only when they are placed side by side do they seem larger.

—D. J. Waldie, *Holy Land*

My father was one of more than 500,000 Steelworkers who did not report for work on July 15, 1959. This was close to 1 percent of the entire labor force in the United States at the time. It would take the president and the Supreme Court to get them back to work 116 days later on November 6.

Many strikes have been longer—particularly since the 1980s, when "scabs" returned to labor disputes after an absence of nearly three decades. And a few have involved as many or more workers, including other steel strikes. But no other strike in U.S. history compares when you combine length and mass, a figure that labor-force statisticians capture with the now-quaint term "man days idled."

A lot of other things seem quaint about the world in which the strike took place. No one questioned, for example, the centrality of steel to the U.S. and world economy. It was right at the heart of metalworking, which was at the heart of manufacturing, which was, without doubt, the heart and soul of the economy. Today, while about the same amount of steel is shipped in a year, it takes about one-fifth the number of workers to do it, and the national economy is three times larger.

Getting steelworkers on strike was a simple matter then. Union president David J. McDonald told the Associated Press, "We're on strike," and half a million people at a dozen steel companies from coast to coast, many of whom did not want to strike, refused to work. No one even thought about crossing their own picket line, let alone doing it. This is in stark contrast to today, when many unions bet their existence by striking. It was also in stark contrast to twenty years before 1959, when in its organizing days SWOC had to agitate, educate, and organize each and every steelworker before sustained collective action was possible.

McDonald's power to snap his fingers and shut down 90 percent of steelmaking is what earned him and others the sobriquet "labor boss." But beneath McDonald's snap was a complex series of local and regional organizations, with 1,200 paid staff and thousands of local leaders and grievers who had earned the respect of their fellow workers in face-to-face dealings.[1]

The international union's monthly newspaper, *Steelabor*, was mailed to the homes of all USWA members. It included, by today's standards, incredibly sophisticated economic analyses of the basic steel industry, and detailed data and arguments for the union's points of view on all sorts of things. If nobody else read these long articles, the grievers did, at least while negotiations were going on. Some selection of the facts and arguments would then arrive on the shop floor via the griever, along with some badgering to "read the paper."

During negotiations for a new contract, particularly as a strike loomed, this communications infrastructure would become very intense and animated. But by 1959, after five strikes in thirteen years had won a series of highly visible improvements in people's lives, even those who did not want to strike, who had thought it through and concluded that striking was a bad idea, did not need to be convinced that acting in concert with their fellows was the only option. The belief in the power of collective action was so deep and strong that everybody took it for granted. Not once during more than eight months of negotiations did McDonald trouble himself to ask if the troops were behind him. He didn't need to. They were—but not without millions of daily conversations on shop floors from Baltimore to Oakland, Buffalo to Birmingham.

Pre-Strike Negotiations: The Long Strike as a Management Strategy

Negotiations in steel were very public events in the 1950s. Beginning shortly after the first of the year, even the most bland and predictable statements by either the companies or the union made front-page news. And almost every presidential news conference included some comments about the "steel negotiations," even before they officially opened on May 5.[2]

Though President Eisenhower had an official hands off policy, the government was expected to play a role in steel negotiations because the price of steel reverberated throughout the economy, affecting the prices of all sorts of products that everybody wanted—automobiles, refrigerators, stoves, steel beams for buildings and bridges, reinforcing bar for highways, and special alloys for missile bases, not to mention paper clips, tin cans, and thumb tacks. Since World War II, when the federal government directly determined steel wages and prices, a firm link had been established between these "private" economic variables and the public welfare. If wages were increased too much, this forced an increase in steel and steel-related prices, a situation that was considered inflationary. This inflationary effect was compounded because the Steelworkers was a bargaining leader then; what happened in steel affected other labor-management negotiations, a few directly and many more indirectly.

The USWA routinely argued that since productivity and profits had increased, a substantial boost in wages was not inflationary. The companies marshalled evidence to the contrary, and in 1959 for the first time introduced the threat of foreign competition, which had not been a problem until the late 1950s and was not much of a problem then. The government and the press tried to play the role of neutral fact-finders in all of this, with minor nuances in the president's statements being picked over to see which way they tilted. There was lots of gamemanship in this process, but also a lot of thorough and interesting analysis. The American Iron and Steel Institute (AISI), the companies' trade association, gathered massive amounts of highly reliable data. The Steelworkers' Research Department pored over this and other data and developed sophisticated interpretations, which it presented in several forms. Independent academic, stockbroker, and government studies contributed as well, and the national press—primarily the *New York Times* and the

Wall Street Journal—covered it all in substantial detail, as did the steel-town press.

Beginning in March the companies ran full-page ads in these papers, giving their interpretations a public-relations gloss. The Steelworkers answered with some full-page ads of their own, as well as with detailed presentations on their fifteen-minute monthly TV show that aired only in steel towns. Both the companies and the union sent letters and pamphlets to steelworkers' homes, and while these included overheated rhetoric, they also included the basic outlines of each side's economic analysis of the industry.[3]

It's easy to be cynical about this battle of economic analyses, though my impression is that people were much less cynical then than they are now and that all the players were much more earnest in trying to determine "the facts" than they are in comparable public debates today. Though there was lots of hard data, what it all meant, particularly what it meant for the future, was *very* hard to determine. Profits, for example, might be "high" now, but could they be sustained in the future? Productivity varied substantially depending on "operating rates," meaning that the higher the demand for steel, the higher the productivity; thus the Steelworkers could legitimately argue that the overall state of the economy affected industry productivity more than their work effort or work rules. Both sides were scored for misleading and one-sided "propaganda," and it was undoubtedly frustrating for the public that "the facts" seemed so unclear.[4] But at its core, the disagreement over basic economics did not reflect a lack of integrity on either side so much as it reflected a basic difference in class interests, which resulted in a different weighing of the facts and a different interpretation of the relations between one set of facts and another.

To steel executives and the business class generally, workers are primarily a *cost*. If you increase costs, you either have to cut profits (which are, of course, necessary for investment in economic expansion) or increase prices. Both reduced profits and increased prices choke off demand and thereby hurt economic growth. To steelworkers and other workers, increased wages are not a cost but a *benefit*, and the higher the wages, the more spending power they have; this stimulates economic growth. Yet each side recognizes the logic of the other. Higher wages across the economy, while causing an immediate increase in costs for a steel producer, might result in more auto sales, which means more demand for steel, which means higher operating rates and thus higher productivity, lower unit costs, and higher profits. Likewise, the steel-workers were well aware that they might "price ourselves out of a job." Though each side could see the other's economic logic, it is extreme naivete to expect them to have weighed these counterlogics equally—a naivete that leads to cynicism.

The difference between 1959 and twenty years before or after 1959 is that because unions were so strong in the '50s the "spending power" argument got equal time in the public debate. Before the upsurge of the labor movement in the 1930s and since the Reagan revolution of the 1980s, the notion of wages as an economic cost seems to far outweigh that of wages as an economic benefit. In 1959 this was not the case. The September issue of *Steelabor*, for example, carried the headline "Remember: The More You Earn—The More You Buy," and there was not a steelworker in the country who needed to read the article to understand what the headline meant. Likewise, the steel-town business class—though aware that a steelworker wage increase put upward pressure on other wages as well as on a host of prices—had direct experience of what a positive effect an increase in steelworker spending power had on their business, whether they ran a tavern, a car dealership, a hospital, or a bank.

Steel negotiations in 1959, then, played before a large and complicated audience. The detailed debates about wages, profits, productivity, work rules, and operating rates did not occur without a lot of phony p.r. spins, but in their essence they were a symphony (or at least a cacophony) of *democratic discourse*—a heartening example of American pluralism and its countervailing powers at work. Public opinion, through its effect on politicians if not in any other form, played an important role in these negotiations. When the steel companies, for example, could not produce convincing evidence to back up their extravagant claims about "featherbedding," it hurt them.

Outside the court of public opinion, "the industry" and "the union" were not nearly so unified and simple as they often seemed on the surface. Both McDonald's and Eisenhower's accounts of the negotiations focus on one aspect of the scene behind the scenes: who said what to whom where and when in the various meetings between the public figures—R. Conrad Cooper and Roger Blough from U.S. Steel, Ike and Richard Nixon, and David J. McDonald, the only labor leader worth a mention in either of these accounts. According to them, the strike was finally settled in these meetings in hotels, on airplanes, in the White

House, and at Nixon's home. In reality, there were many more key players in the drama than the great men allow.[5]

The 1959 Steel Strike was a battle of endurance, testing solidarities
on both sides. On the companies' side, U.S. Steel was not loved and
honored by the other eleven major steel producers, nor did U.S. Steel
require that, so long as the other companies obeyed. Within the industry's Coordinated Bargaining Committee, the labor relations chiefs
from each of the twelve companies met regularly to discuss strategy, but
with more than two-fifths of the industry in its control, U.S.S.'s was the
dominant voice. Though it had to reconcile its approach with the interests of the other companies in the details, U.S.S. alone determined the
broad strategy—in 1952, 1955, 1956, and 1959.[6]

In 1959 the industry's strategy was devised by U.S.S. labor relations
chief R. Conrad Cooper, a handsome and articulate former University
of Minnesota football star who spoke bluntly and carried a big stick.
Cooper answered to U.S.S. chairman Roger Blough, a humorless corporate lawyer who had worked his way up through the industry's financial side. Industry solidarity required that Blough and the other corporate presidents give free rein to Cooper and the other labor relations
chiefs. Thus McDonald's job was to bypass Cooper and get to either
Blough or any of the other presidents. The immediate objective was to
undercut Cooper and weaken industry coordination and solidarity. The
longer-run objective was either to weaken Big Steel's resolve or to get
one of the smaller companies to settle independently and then to use
that as the pattern for the others. Cooper's job, on the other hand, was
to open a gap between the union's leadership and rank-and-file steelworkers. His strategy for doing that was a powerful one.

A clear pattern had developed in the postwar steel strikes. Prior to
negotiations, steel users (particularly auto companies) began buying and
stockpiling steel; then, after a relatively brief strike, demand fell pre-
cipitously as the users drew down their stockpiles. Previously, the companies had tried to avoid this boom-and-bust cycle, but Cooper proposed to use it to their advantage. The Steelworkers had never been
tested in a long strike (the fifty-eight days in 1952 being the longest),
and there was widespread and very well-publicized rank-and-file opposition to McDonald within the union.[7] Why not stimulate buyers'
stockpiling, really rev up the industry in the first part of the year, and
then force the union out on strike? With sufficient stockpiles, it would
take quite a while before the industry began to lose orders, and mean-

while they'd have earned enough profits in the first half of the year to cover the entire year. Steelworker savings might stretch across sixty days, but the rank and file might get pretty testy with their leadership in ninety or 120 days.

The industry's ad campaign early in the year helped stimulate stock-piling in anticipation of a strike. So did Cooper's rude treatment of McDonald and the parrying back and forth in the press before negoti-ations even opened. The industry's initial proposal, on the other hand, though obviously unacceptable to the union, was fairly moderate as an opening gambit: a one-year wage freeze. The interpretation of this offer —which, according to McDonald, Cooper never put in writing—varied as time passed; in one of its versions it seemed to be something like a one-year extension of the status quo, and in late June McDonald seemed willing to accept that, depending on whether an "extension" included continued cost-of-living adjustments, which in late June it did not.[8] From May 5, when negotiations formally began, to June 10, no real negotiations occurred. The one-year extension, if that was what it was, was dubbed the Minus Zero Proposal by McDonald and rejected. The union was even more vague, demanding a "substantial wage increase" without specifying an amount. The war of words in the press focused on the economics lessons referred to above, not on specific bargaining proposals.

On June 10, with only twenty days left before the contract expired, it was time to get down to serious negotiations. Instead, Cooper dropped his atom bomb: an eight-point proposal that sought a series of dramatic changes in "the workplace rule of law." It was the kind of proposal that became familiar in the 1980s, when union-busting law firms wanted to push a union out on strike in order to break it. The eight points zeroed in on work schedules, seniority, the scheduling of vacations, and man-agement rights to set incentives and work standards—all items that were firmly detailed in past contracts and all of which protected work-ers from arbitrary harassment (or special treatment) by supervisors. As it turned out, management wasn't serious about most of this stuff; the proposal was designed to make sure the union went out on strike, and the companies would eventually give up seven of the points if the union agreed to the eighth.

The eighth was the previously mentioned Section 2-B, which gener-ated a complex of issues that got summarized as involving "work rules," "local working conditions," or "past practices." To the companies, 2-B amounted to a universal right to featherbedding, and allowed the union to interfere with management's organization of production, keeping them from achieving maximum efficiency. To the union, 2-B protected workers from speed-up and the unhealthy and unsafe conditions that went with pursuing "maximum efficiency" at the expense of workers. The dispute over 2-B also involved a job security issue, since the reason the companies wanted maximum efficiency was so they could eliminate thousands of steelworker jobs.

Though he would later deny it, McDonald was stunned by the eight-point proposal.[9] Cooper's strategy was proceeding brilliantly. For the first half of the year, the industry was operating at 90 percent of capacity; despite the 116-day strike that was about to begin, the operating rate and total after-tax profits for the entire year would be higher than they had been in 1958.[10] For two months prior to June 10, polls and informal interviews by newspaper reporters showed that steelworkers, while getting ready to strike, had little stomach for it. Younger workers had experienced long layoffs in the 1957–58 recession, and they were just getting back on their feet. Older workers said they were pretty happy with things as they were. One survey of ten steel-producing cities in five states found "five of every six [steelworkers] were against a further wage increase at this time."[11]

My father notwithstanding, then, few steelworkers wanted a strike. But once the eight-point proposal had been issued, they had to strike. The union cranked up its membership communications machinery, sending letters to each steelworker's home to supplement a two-page spread in *Steelabor*. These explained briefly what each of the eight points meant, labeling the package a "Break-the-Union" proposal and the strike that now loomed a "Battle for Survival."

It is unlikely that Cooper had any notion of busting the union. Though when the strike finally came he threatened to run scabs, no preparations for doing so were actually undertaken.[12] Nor did McDonald fear such a thing. But Cooper was clearly out to reverse the momentum the Steelworkers had gained in postwar negotiations, where each new contract had added some new benefit as well as a steady string of real wage increases, while at the same time the workforce built up its shop-floor power day by day. The long strike was a key tactic in the management offensive of 1958–63. Just prior to the steel strike, Pittsburgh Plate Glass had experimented with it, forcing the United Glass and Ceramic Workers out for 128 days. During 1959 coal miners in

Kentucky and West Virginia were out for 129 days, New York City wholesale and retail bakers for 102 days, and copper workers for 173 days at Kennecott Copper and 238 days at Phelps Dodge.[13]

Though Cooper was deliberately forcing a long strike, he could not say so publicly, where to both the White House and the public he had to make a display of reasonableness. But *Iron Age*, a steel management publication, was less constrained. It expressed the exuberance steel management was feeling in early July: "There is a new type of collective bargaining in the steel industry. . . . The goal of this new type of bargaining is to regain some of the ground lost in recent years. . . . The steel side has said 'no' to everything the union said or asked. This was a calculated move and is the core of the new type of bargaining. . . . This is an apparent effort to make up quickly what has been bargained away in the past eighteen years."[14]

The long-strike strategy involved an economic war of attrition. With about two months of steel stockpiled at steel users around the country and the year's profits already largely in hand, it would be months before the steel companies had any economic incentive to bargain with the union. Meanwhile, by October, with no paychecks coming in, savings depleted, and mortgages jeopardized, steelworkers would see things differently—maybe not all, maybe not even a majority, but enough of them to split the ranks and put pressure on their leadership to give away some of what had been won in the past eighteen years—most importantly, 2-B.

The Private War

David Brody, in his book on the 1919 Steel Strike, neatly divided the dynamics of that losing strike into two parts—the "public event" and the "private war." The public event was the battle for public opinion that might force the federal government (the progressive Democratic administration of Woodrow Wilson) to intervene on the side of the union. The private event was the strike itself. Brody is clear on which he considers to have been more important: "The great steel strike pivoted on external events, on the response of public opinion and political authority. Waged on a grand scale in America's steel centers, the strike itself really was in the nature of an historical detail. For, once public intervention was ruled out, the outcome became a foregone conclusion."[15]

I'm in no position to argue with Brody about 1919—though he shows clearly that, in the private war, the fragile coalition of unions that had organized the steelworkers was divided, weak, and unprepared for that strike and that the companies in most places had virtually absolute control of everything from the state police to the press. Had the private war been better organized then, Woodrow Wilson might have acted differently.

But in 1959, in a long-strike war of attrition, the relationship between the private and public battles was reversed. Though public opinion and federal government intervention would be important in the final outcome, they reacted to rather than determined the result of the private war. The 1959 strike was fought in half a million homes like mine. It involved getting by with very little, which required persistence and endurance.

Steelworkers and their families were not particularly adventurous people. Whether living in geographically isolated mill towns like Johnstown, city neighborhoods in Chicago, or industrial boroughs in metropolitan Pittsburgh, we were stay-at-home kinds of folks, focused on our families, our neighborhoods, our immediate environments. There was little of the pioneering spirit among us, that spirit of striking out on your own to see what's over the horizon. But persistence and endurance, "sticking to it" and "holding your ground," were exactly what we were good at.

The private war in 1959 started at home, but it reached out to and was sustained by a set of institutional arrangements the union had built over the previous twenty years. All it required of us was persistence, endurance, and loyalty to the union. So long as those were there, we could bend the wills of giant corporations, stand up to the dictates of Congress and the Supreme Court, and eventually persuade the president of the free world to enlist himself in our cause. But it started at home, for as the steel companies were building their stockpiles, so were we.

The strike as a whole couldn't have been that difficult for my family, and that's probably why I don't remember much about it. My mother was a substitute teacher, and thus a paycheck was coming into our home. My father was a mid-level skilled worker and a fanatical saver. He had been in the mill for twenty-nine years, and the seniority system would have protected him from layoffs through most of the 1950s. Like other men in our family and neighborhood, he could build, fix, or grow all kinds of things in and around the house. And my mom, like other women in our world, could can all manner of fruits and vegetables in large glass jars, and was highly skilled at making low-cost macaroni casseroles.

My best friend, Denny Dishong, lived down the alley from us. His mother and father remember the strike as the absolute worst time of their lives.[16] With four kids, including one preschooler, Mrs. Dishong didn't work outside the home. Mr. Dishong was a little younger than my father and had not entered the mill right after high school, as my father had. As a result, he had a lower-paying job and less seniority protection. Less income and more children meant less savings—and a harder strike.

The Krenzes, down the other alley from the Dishongs, had only two kids, both in junior high school, but Mr. Krenz had made the mistake of quitting the mill and trying to start his own business. When his business failed and he returned to the mill, he had lost his seniority—meaning long layoffs during the 1958 recession.

Each home was different. The younger you were, the more kids you had, the less continuous your work record, the harder the private war was for you. But there were few hapless victims among the steelworkers in 1959. Our fathers were among the best paid industrial workers in the world, averaging $3.03 an hour—compared to $2.78 for oil workers, $2.65 for auto workers, and $2.19 for all manufacturing.[17] If those additional pennies an hour were husbanded well, they could make a big difference in an economic war of attrition. And our families were experienced strikers. Well before R. Conrad Cooper started talking nasty, steelworker families had begun to prepare for the strike—simply because strikes were a natural part of labor negotiations then.

The Steelworkers union did not pay strike benefits in basic steel. It couldn't. To pay each striker as little as $10 a week would have cost $5 million, and the union would have depleted its entire treasury (not just its strike fund) in just six or seven weeks.[18] Though practices varied among local unions and in the union's thirty districts, the basic principle was to provide only for hardship cases. What constituted a hardship was determined by the local union, but the international union trained hundreds of local leaders and volunteers to be strike counselors, who then returned to their locals and trained hundreds more. For this purpose, the union produced a clearly written, thirty-two-page pamphlet, *Beyond the Picket Line: How to Organize a Strike Assistance Program.*[19]

The pamphlet instructed counselors to meet, before the strike, with public and private "social agencies" (local welfare departments, the Red Cross, the Salvation Army, and Catholic Charities) to determine (and influence) their policies and procedures. Then, during the strike, the strike counselors took phone calls and met with troubled steelworkers and their families, advising them about sources of public and private aid. The counselors would call merchants and bankers to ask about the possibility of extending credit or allowing partial payment of a mortgage. If none of this worked, the local union might write a check to cover a steelworker's mortgage. Or it would issue food, drug, fuel, or clothing vouchers good at local businesses. Many locals also established strike kitchens, handed out groceries, and gave out meal tickets good at local restaurants. All this was paid for by the local union. If a local got low on funds, it asked for relief from the district office, which might eventually ask for help from the international union. A fully operational local union's strike assistance program also set up fundraising and job-finding committees.

By 1959 this was a well-established system in many local unions and steel communities. The local business classes often wholeheartedly cooperated with the strikers, and seldom unreasonably resisted helping them. A spokesman for the Chamber of Commerce in Gary, Indiana, for example, explained why local merchants were willing to extend credit to strikers, some even offering prestrike sales under the slogan, "Buy Now and Pay after the Strike Is Over": "The steel worker no longer lives out of a suitcase in a furnished room. He is a home owner with a bank account and roots in the community."[20] Though the local business class often had more in common with the steelworkers than they did with U.S. Steel, there was more to it than that. A well-organized local union could simply put out the word about a local merchant's failure to cooperate, and that merchant would immediately see a decline in his business without ever facing a consumer picket. Some merchants and banks even declared moratoriums on debt and mortgage payments for the duration of the strike. One explained, "No matter what you think about unionism, you have to go along with these fellows in a strike."[21]

A month prior to the strike, a township relief official in Gary made clear that strikers would get relief checks and federal surplus food. During the 1956 strike, his office had given out $400,000 in relief to about six thousand strikers—money that came largely from property taxes on the U.S. Steel Gary Works. Surplus food, which was part of the federal government's price-support program for farmers, was given to states and communities that requested it; it was up to these communities to determine who was eligible for assistance. In most steel towns, strikers were eligible.[22] Steel-town politicians' vision of social justice was likely influenced by the Steelworkers' well-oiled political action machinery.

This had not always been the case. In 1919 in western Pennsylvania, the local business class and local governments were literally owned by the steel companies and made sure police beat up strikers (and their families) who dared defy local ordinances forbidding open-air meetings or rallies.[23] In 1937 in Johnstown, the local business class, with the co-operation of Johnstown mayor Daniel J. Shields, organized the citizens' committee that started a "spontaneous" back-to-work movement that broke the Little Steel Strike there.[24]

But the world had changed since then. Even the private charities had local Steelworker officials on their boards, and local unions routinely raised money for one cause or another. A steelworker on strike, even on the 116th day, might live better than many Johnstown workers who were not on strike, but the steelworker had a claim on the Red Cross and Catholic Charities that unorganized workers did not. As the *Wall Street Journal* commented before the strike began, "Union leaders have been encouraged to participate in community activities, such as welfare agencies, school boards and civic committees and often carry heavy weight in local steel towns."[25]

I do not mean to suggest that the widespread local sympathy for striking steelworkers was simply a product of subtle coercion and influence politics. It was not. There was little love for U.S. Steel and Bethlehem Steel in Johnstown, for example, and lots of genuine support for the steelworkers by people from all walks of life. But what changed the world from 1919 and 1937 was not a spontaneous upsurge of sympathy and charity. Rather, these attitudes were cultivated over time by the power of the Steelworkers—by Steelworker money and Steelworker organization. That's important to realize because when the power waned, so did the support.

In addition to this union-cultivated support network, most steelworker families had their own networks and strategems for getting by. The idea was to avoid the local union's Strike Assistance Center, not to mention public aid or private charity—to do it on your own. My father was proud that he had "never taken a penny of government money" (he didn't count Unemployment Compensation or Social Security because he considered them "insurance" that he had paid for). To convey how terrible the strike was for them, Mr. and Mrs. Dishong simply say— still with a mixture of fear and shame—"We had to go on welfare." Surplus food was a different matter—the government was just going to throw it away anyhow; at one point, Democratic congressmen from steel districts even protested that the surplus food was unconscionably bland.[26]

The union expected its members to do a lot on their own before they got a handout. One local union official predicted that in the early days of the strike he'd be busy "clearing out the poor mouths who flock around our office twenty-four hours after a strike claiming hardship."[27] The general rule was that if you still had a savings account, you didn't have a hardship. This internal and external discipline was essential to Steelworker strength. My father often talked contemptuously of "the poor mouths," and he would have been one of those who made sure anybody who took a handout felt shame in doing so. Yeah, we had our advantages, he would have said, but we were still renters and had yet to own a new car—in contrast, according to him, to "all the poor mouths who were owned by their mortgages and car payments."

Due to steelworker stockpiling, it would take a month or more before most local union Strike Assistance Centers had much to do. Even six weeks into the strike, USWA district director Eugene Maurice reported that not one request for relief had reached his level from the 27,000 strikers in his district (14,000 of them in Johnstown).[28] The one-month steelworker stockpiles had been built on three bases. First, most workers hadn't gotten checks for their last weeks of work until two weeks into the strike. Second, the majority had, like my father, scheduled their vacations for the second half of the year, and thus had those checks to look forward to. Finally, with the industry working at 90 percent of capacity, there had been a lot of overtime available since the first of the year; many workers had grabbed all the overtime they could get to build up their savings.[29]

Before the strike, merchants reported that steelworkers were "coming in and paying up their accounts so they won't have those debts hanging over them."[30] A banker in the old company town of Midland, Pennsylvania, reported that one borrower had already paid two monthly installments in advance "so I'll have that done if we go on strike."[31] The first month of the strike was just like vacation for most steelworkers. In the third week, hardware stores in northwest Indiana and western Pennsylvania reported increased sales of paint and hardware supplies, as "a growing number of idled workers were turning to paint-up and fix-up tasks around the house to help pass the time."[32] Like many others, Johnny Metzgar had done his work before the strike, so he went fishing—bringing home, as always, two large, portable freezers full of walleyes, lake trout, and northern pike.

R. Conrad Cooper's strategy was based on increasing the number of "poor mouths" as the strike started to bite steelworker families. This would divide the rank and file and weaken the leadership. But these things never happened. In fact, something close to the opposite occurred. Going into the strike's third month in late September, all the relief agencies—private, public, and union—had all the work they could handle. Steel towns had sunk into economic depressions, with retail sales disappearing and small businesses and local governments laying off their workers.[33] But reporters found a "hardening attitude" among the strikers: "Grassroots union opinion on [the work rules] issue seems much more vociferous than when the strike began."[34]

All through that summer, before the strike and in its early weeks, reporters had found steelworkers "resigned" to striking, but far from eager. In May a thirty-year veteran at Allegheny Ludlum's Brackenridge, Pennsylvania, mill told the *Wall Street Journal*, "I think if it was put up to a vote, the men wouldn't go out."[35] In June the *Journal* reported that "it seems mainly a case of 'going along' with a union which has done a lot for the men in the past."[36] But by the end of September, the steelworker quotes reporters were gathering had both an anger and an élan that had previously been absent. One Pennsylvania striker declared, "I don't care if we don't go back for a year under their conditions." A California striker cockily predicted, "We'll be picking grapes before this one's over."[37]

An economic war of attrition must be something like (non-nuclear) aerial bombing. You'd think that driving people into economic desperation, like bombing, would cow and demoralize them, gradually sapping their wills—and for a while it may do that. But past a certain point, the very opposite happens. On the other side of desperation is anger, vengefulness, determination, even a heightened sense of humor—and a growing sense of solidarity among those who are being bombed by people they cannot see.

The thirty USWA district directors, grizzled union bureaucrats to the man by 1959, were amazed and inspired by the strike spirit as it developed in their areas. The district directors were well aware of the growing economic stress among their members and the deepening problems of trying to relieve it. The number of poor mouths *was* increasing, but so was "the spirit of the men." In early October, District Director James Griffin of Youngstown, Ohio told his fellow district directors about one newspaper in his town that had tried but been unable to find a single steelworker who was "opposed to the strike and how it was being handled." Griffin had recently held a series of meetings with local union officers and grievers in his district, and he related: "We must have talked to some seven hundred of the key leadership in my district and . . . I want to report to you as an actual fact, that when we got through with those meetings, you would think that we had just started the strike yesterday; the morale is just that high, and our people are determined not to take one backward step."[38]

In mid-October a few of the district directors were thinking about agreeing to Cooper's offer to take the dispute over work rules to a neutral arbitrator, something that even its advocates saw as a giant backward step, regardless of whether the union was to win or lose in arbitration. Griffin and the majority of district directors opposed this route. Carmon Newell from central Pennsylvania, where Bethlehem Steel was the major producer, said, "the Bethlehem membership would be *sickened* by such a proposal and would feel that the Union had let them down." Albert Atallah, the district director from Baltimore, pointed out that while he had lots of problems in his district, "the spirit of the people is good . . . and any suggestion to arbitrate the issues would kill that spirit."[39]

By its third month, the strike had built a momentum of its own. Cooper's strategy—a long strike focused on work rules—had mistakenly tapped into the Steelworkers' strength in 1959. Work rules were something about which rank-and-file workers tended to be inflexible. To effectively fight back the company's demands required a sturdy conservatism of steelworkers rather than a utopian idealism. And even the psychological dynamics of a long strike played into the "I don't eat shit for nobody" machismo of workers with more than two decades of unionism under their belts. The companies were losing the private war. And unlike what happened in 1919, in 1959 this meant they would also lose the public event.

The Public Event

After Cooper's June 10 Break-the-Union proposal, there was no movement in negotiations until October. There were, however, lots and lots of public events. As the June 30 contract-expiration date approached, President Eisenhower asked the parties to extend the contract for a couple of weeks. McDonald and Cooper agreed to extend it to July 15, both knowing that nothing would be changed by then. McDonald told his executive board—the union's thirty district directors, some of whom didn't like the idea—that the fourteen-day extension was "merely to put us in the best possible light with the press." [40]

The White House exerted various kinds of pressure on the parties to settle their differences. The president suggested they use federal mediators to help, so they did, and it didn't help. Secretary of Labor James P. Mitchell appointed himself a one-person fact-finder in the strike's first week, and then took a month finding the facts. There were sporadic talks between August 20 and September 25, but they produced nothing, even though the press reported various rumors of movement. McDonald told his executive board, "Nothing is going on. These reported fifteen-cent proposals of ours are non-existent. Everything is absolutely dead." [41]

After talks broke off September 25, Eisenhower called both sides to the White House for separate meetings. Ike threatened to abandon his hands-off policy and told them "it would be exceedingly unwise for them to force the government to intervene directly in the struggle." [42] A few days later Cooper put forward what Ike called the industry's "first money proposal," which the union promptly rejected on October 5.

By the first week of October, the strike was finally having noticeable effects on both sides. Both industry and steelworker stockpiles had been drawn down, and their hurt was beginning to affect the broader economy. According to Ike, "[I]ndustrial consumers were beginning to buy up the backlog of warehoused steel at increased prices, to use uneconomical sizes, and to cut the work week further. Mass layoffs were becoming imminent. Shortages threatened to delay the construction of new units of the Polaris [missile]. Imports of steel were increasing." [43] On October 9, Eisenhower declared that this amounted to a "clear threat to the country's security," and he invoked the Taft-Hartley Act's "eighty-day cooling off" provision, which would force steelworkers back to work. The machinery of the act required the appointment of a fact-finding board, which ten days later reported that "the disputants were unlikely to reach a voluntary settlement." Ike then had to seek a federal district court injunction, which he got October 21. The Steelworkers appealed that decision all the way to the Supreme Court, arguing that

the government had not proven a "clear threat to the country's security." On November 7 the Supreme Court decided otherwise, and
steelworkers returned to work.[44]

Some steelworkers must have been glad, or at least relieved, to get
back to work, but there wasn't much evidence of that. Instead, there was
outrage, most of it directed at the beloved World War II general who had
been president since 1953. Workers at Wheeling Steel returned to work
with armbands labeling themselves "Ike's Slaves."[45] Walter Reuther of
the UAW suggested that Ike refrain from playing golf for eighty days
to see if that cooled *him* off. Other labor leaders and many Democratic
presidential hopefuls (including John F. Kennedy) denounced Ike's use
of "the slave labor act" that organized labor had always and everywhere
opposed. There were nasty suggestions that Ike's invocation of Taft-
Hartley was a "pay off" to financiers and industrialists who had bank-
rolled his 1956 presidential campaign.[46] And at their November 12
meeting, the USWA district directors complained that McDonald was
not being tough enough with Eisenhower, reporting that the members'
anger was directed at Ike while McDonald refused to denounce him by
name, preferring instead to score "government intervention."[47]

Though capable of incredibly stupid gaffes in relations with his own
members, McDonald's greatest strength as a labor leader was in public-
relations manuevering—in wheeling and dealing, through the press
and in private, with the powerful. He knew how to play with the players, and while he encouraged the district directors to say anything they
liked about Eisenhower, he would not denounce Ike by name because,
at the end of the day, a deal would have to be done with the White
House.[48] Labor leaders outside of steel, like Reuther, undoubtedly knew
that it was their job, not McDonald's, to put the heat on Eisenhower.

The intensity of the anger among steelworkers at Ike's use of a Taft-
Hartley injunction requires some explanation. It's unlikely that their
outrage was caused simply by the principle of the thing, as it was for
all full-time labor professionals, who opposed any use of Taft-Hartley.
Rather, though steelworkers and their families were hurting by the
first week of October, they felt like they were in the driver's seat, as
the strike had finally begun to hurt the companies. But just as soon as
the companies began to lose orders, just as soon as the strike was visibly costing them profits, Ike weighed in on their side. The interrup-
tion of the strike, though objectively giving both sides time to rebuild
stockpiles and gather strength, broke the strikers' momentum and re-

turned the advantage to the companies. Though Eisenhower's rhetoric was still neutral, not casting blame on either side and certainly not denouncing the union, nearly everybody saw the injunction as favoring the companies.

Thus, the injunction hurt Eisenhower and Nixon politically. A presidential election year was just months away, and the last thing the Republicans needed was an angry and mobilized labor movement, out to refurbish the GOP's image as the party of Big Money. The Republicans didn't need, or expect, to win a majority of the "union household" vote, but the size of that majority (the difference, say, between Adlai Stevenson's 53 percent in 1956 and JFK's 64 percent four years later) was crucial to their prospects. Eisenhower had worked carefully to appear a reasonable-uncle type, fair-minded, nonpartisan, moderate, and above the passions of the contestants. The angry reactions of union workers and labor leaders helped strip this image away.

Yet it was Eisenhower's intervention that got the negotiations going. As the Taft-Hartley process was unfolding in October, the two sides began trading proposals. Then in mid-October, there was a break in the companies' ranks: Kaiser Steel, based in California and always a bit of a maverick among the majors, gave up on getting any contractual changes in work rules and agreed to a monetary package the union valued at twenty-two and a half cents over twenty months. Economically, this defection would not have much impact on the other majors, as Kaiser was not a big enough producer to put the remaining eleven companies at a disadvantage. But psychologically and politically, it was a big blow. Henry Kaiser and his son, Edgar, were heaped with praise by the press for their industrial statesmanship. And McDonald now had a pattern contract to trumpet in the press and take to the other companies.[49]

Still, though both the politics and the psychological dynamics of the bargaining situation now favored the union, the eighty-day cooling off period was a potentially dangerous time for it. U.S. Steel and the other majors had by no means given up. They meant to take at least one more run at the membership to see if they were as strong for 2-B as their leadership was. It was an unusual and uneasy situation for the Steelworker leadership.

Unlike in most unions, Steelworkers in basic steel then did not vote on their contracts, nor did they get to vote on whether to strike or not. Formally, these matters were decided by the union's Wage Policy Committee (WPC), which consisted of 136 elected delegates from all parts of the union as well as the thirty district directors. But WPC members rarely even asked questions as they approved whatever the leadership proposed. The district directors, assembled separately as the union's executive board, might challenge McDonald on this point or that, and if they all agreed on something, they would have had the power to overrule him through their influence on the WPC delegates. But because they met infrequently and with an agenda and a format controlled by McDonald, they were not really able to call the shots. Even if the Executive Board and the Wage Policy Committee had functioned as open-ended democracies, however, nobody could be sure they really reflected rank-and-file sentiment, particularly if the ranks were voting in the atomized privacy of a secret ballot, unaffected by the peer pressure of local union leaders and grievers.

This kind of vote is exactly what the Taft-Hartley process required. It stipulated a specified time period, at the end of which the companies had to designate their latest proposal as a final offer. Then the National Labor Relations Board would conduct a secret-ballot vote, yes or no, on that proposal. Though the law did not require the union to abide by the vote, even a weak majority for the union's position could force it to settle on company terms.

On November 15 the companies put forth a final offer that they valued at thirty cents an hour over thirty months—an offer consisting of two six-cent wage increases, COLA increases of up to eight cents, seven cents in increased pay due to the elimination of workers' paying 50 percent of their health insurance premiums, and three cents in pensions and other fringe benefit improvements. On work rules, they dropped seven of their eight points and proposed to submit their case for modifying Section 2-B to a neutral arbitrator.[50]

This was a long way from the Minus Zero and Break the Union proposals of the spring, but it was substantially inferior to the Kaiser agreement that had become the union's pattern. On the money side, the union valued the companies' "final offer" at twenty-two cents, not thirty because it didn't count the COLA increases, which nobody would get if there were no inflation. In a point-by-point comparison with the Kaiser pattern, the difference was this: Kaiser workers would get twenty-two and a half cents over twenty months, whereas the other eleven companies' workers would get about the same amount over thirty months.[51] When you do the arithmetic, this makes a substantial difference, and most steelworkers would have realized that with just a little explanation from grievers like my father. But whether they would resume their strike over that difference was another matter.

Submitting 2-B to arbitration was an even more complicated issue. Many union professionals thought the Steelworkers would win in arbitration, but they opposed it on principle because it undermined the power of the union in collective bargaining; labor leaders outside of steel were particularly fearful of the dangerous precedent it would set in bargaining over work rules. How strong the members were on this principle is anybody's guess. I know it would have been important to my father, who loved to fight over the principle of the thing. But my guess is that rank-and-file steelworkers had a lot less faith in the Steelworkers' arbitration system (which was top of the line, by common agreement among labor professionals) than those who were better informed about its actual workings. To the rank and file, submitting 2-B to arbitration, simply *because* it was a gamble, was just as bad as, or maybe even worse than, giving it away of their own free will. Rank-and-file steelworkers in 1959 were not gamblers. Two decades of unionism had taught them to expect slow but steady progress and had encouraged them to build their lives around careful husbandry and stick-to-it-iveness. No matter what the odds of winning, submitting 2-B to arbitration was clearly a giant backward step. It would count as, in the language of the time, appeasing an aggressor. Give them an inch, they'll take a mile. Let them have Czechoslovakia, and they'll take Poland. But that's just my educated guess. There were lots of much-better-educated guesses to the contrary at the time. Nobody could be sure how the workers would vote.

The companies' strategy was to give the workers the Mr. Nice Guy treatment when they returned to work November 8 and then to sell a proposal directly to the rank and file, over the heads of the union leadership. One company, the union learned, called in its foremen before work resumed and told them, "We want all of you boys to understand that these people have been out on strike for four months. They're soft, not accustomed to working hard. We don't want nobody to be pushed. Take it easy with these boys and we will get along fine." The district directors reported, "They are buttering our people up," "they are kissing their ass."[52] As Tom Shane explained, "If [the foremen] think they need a crew of five they make sure they call seven or eight. The result is that pipefitters and millwrights are standing around with their arms folded and there is nothing to do yet."[53]

On December 1 the companies initiated what the *Wall Street Jour-*

nal called "an industry electioneering drive." Great Lakes Steel, for example, mailed each of its employees a seven-page letter extolling the virtues of the industry's so-called final offer. Though this was longer than previous letters, sending company propaganda to workers was standard procedure in the industry. But this time the companies sent a version of the letter to civic leaders and merchants as well, in what the *Journal* described as an "industry strategy of drumming up support for contract proposals not only among the steelworkers themselves but among their neighbors and friends in mill cities."[54]

The union countered with its own electioneering, predicting that the companies would soon have "Christmas caroling in the mills" and warning its members not to "fall for this red carpet guff." Page one of the December issue of *Steelabor* consisted of only one sentence, printed in very large red and black letters against a backdrop of pictures of Steelworkers on picket lines and at strike rallies: "If the companies get their way, 110,000 Steelworkers could be knocked out of their jobs with a twenty percent speed-up." The rest of the issue detailed the companies' proposal and what was wrong with it.

Though some of the district directors had flirted with the idea of accepting arbitration in October, and though a few of them thought the wage proposal was in the range of the acceptable in November, neither McDonald nor the district directors wavered after the injunction forced the steelworkers back to work. Nor is there any evidence that the rank and file did much wavering. The indigenous anger at being "Ike's slaves" carried people back to work with a certain amount of innoculation against "the red carpet guff." Some workers responded to management's overstaffing, for example, by taunting foremen to give them something to do quick because they had only X number of days before they'd be on strike again. And being back at work had its advantages for the union, as the grievers had the whole workforce to badger and chatter with, not just the folks doing picket duty. In mid-November the district directors inspired, and competed with, each other by relating stories about "the spirit of our people."[55] Soon newspaper reporters were finding something similar. The *Wall Street Journal* informally polled 211 Steelworkers in Chicago and East Chicago, Indiana, with the following results: 60 percent firmly against accepting the final offer, 15 percent for accepting it, and 25 percent undecided—and this was before the union had published its case against the offer and the grievers had gone to work with their chatter.[56]

Not wanting to fly blind, the union initiated its own postcard poll of

494,000 steelworkers. Though only 40 percent responded, that 40 percent rejected the final offer by a margin of nine to one.[57] More importantly, there was no organized opposition in the mills to the leadership's stand. Those who felt strongly were arguing for their fellow workers to reject the companies' blandishments and to prepare to resume the strike January 26, 1960.[58]

The rest of the labor movement also offered a lot of support for the strikers. Even though the Steelworkers regularly reported that their finances were in good shape, other unions contributed more than $6 million to the Steelworkers' strike relief fund during the strike, always with a great deal of fanfare and press attention. The AFL-CIO asked every union member in the country to contribute one hour's pay a month. The UAW by itself sent $1 million. Even the West German metalworkers contributed $23,800.[59] Though the USWA would eventually return all this money, passing it around in public not only had a practical effect, but it also lent a certain moral weight to the Steelworkers' cause. One union after another would announce something like "the Steelworkers are fighting our fight," and then USWA local leaders would tell their constituencies, "The whole labor movement is counting on us. We owe it to them to stand fast."

The Taft-Hartley vote was scheduled for mid-January, and avoiding the possible psychological and political consequences of that vote was now putting pressure on all the parties, just as the law's drafters no doubt intended. But neither combatant had flinched by Christmas, and public opinion was basically at a stalemate, with perhaps a slight tilt toward the Steelworkers. It was the government that flinched first. In mid-December Eisenhower privately cajoled U.S. Steel chairman Roger Blough to meet privately with McDonald, thereby helping McDonald achieve his goal of bypassing, and undercutting, R. Conrad Cooper. Though nothing came of this private meeting, it established that Blough —in agreement with McDonald—wanted to avoid a compulsory arbitration law, which Ike then began threatening to push through an "already restive" Congress.[60]

After Christmas Eisenhower left the country for an eighteen-nation tour of the free world, leaving Vice President Richard M. Nixon to broker a settlement, which Nixon did by leaning on Blough to give in. Here's how Eisenhower described the denouement in his memoirs:

> By the 13th of January . . . union members would, under the law, vote on this offer. Every indication was that they would vote negatively and walk off the job once more.

Both sides now knew that, should this negative vote come about, the union negotiators' bargaining position would be stronger than ever. But they also knew that the Congress was returning to Washington, and that, if the steel workers walked off the job again, the result could be new legislation, probably requiring compulsory arbitration; neither side looked forward to such a law.

. . . on Wednesday, December 30, 1959, [Nixon and Labor Secretary James Mitchell] flew to New York City to meet with officials of the steel industry. In a brief conference with the executives[,] the Vice President "laid the issue on the line," reminding them that if the strike resumed, "the country will have no place to go for a remedy but to Congress, which as you know, the Democrats control. In an election year, management won't like the labor-management legislation such a Congress will produce."

That meeting broke the deadlock. The company negotiators agreed that they would voluntarily accept the settlement recommended by Nixon and Mitchell.[61]

By January 5 a settlement had been reached. As far as the money went, the settlement provided an increase of thirty-nine cents an hour over thirty months. On Section 2B, the two sides agreed to form a joint committee to study the matter. The *New York Times* page one headline read, "Strike Ends on Terms Recommended by Nixon and Mitchell; USWA Wins Major Demands." It was a sweeping victory for the union, a humiliating defeat for the companies.[62]

No one was more humiliated than U.S.S. labor relations chief R. Conrad Cooper. Both Cooper and the rank-and-file opposition to McDonald would subsequently point out some imperfections in the money package, but on work rules the companies got nothing—absolutely nothing. The joint study committee went nowhere and, while the union would eventually accommodate the companies in some minor ways, 2-B and all the shop-floor power it represented would remain. Even where the money was concerned, it was clear that the companies could have forged a much better deal had they not forced the Steelworkers to strike. In May McDonald had broadly hinted that the union would settle for about twenty-five cents over three years; in June he had privately offered a one-year extension of the contract that would have frozen real wages. Though subsequent memories would get foggy on the final round of the 1959 Steel Strike, at the time it was correctly seen, to use the boxing analogies common then, not as a decision or a TKO, but as a decisive knockout that left the companies flat on their industrial-relations backs.[63]

Political reaction to the settlement had its comic aspects, as when Nixon and Eisenhower first tussled over who should get the credit for forcing the deal, and then both sought to distance themselves from any blame for such a one-sided "government intervention." On the day of the settlement, Secretary of Labor Mitchell publicly credited Nixon, and the next day Mitchell and Nixon appeared at the union's Wage Policy Committee to receive rousing ovations. This was too much for the White House, so Ike's press secretary James Haggerty announced that "Nixon had [merely] carried out Ike's instructions" in achieving the settlement.[64]

But it didn't take long for the press and public to think they smelled a certain stink in the air. It was no secret that Richard Nixon was slated to be Ike's successor and that 1960 was to be a decisive political year. Nixon had come down so strongly on the side of the union that people suspected he must have made a deal for the USWA's support, or at least its indifference, in the presidential sweepstakes that was about to begin. By January 9, both the union and the White House were publicly denying any such deal.[65] McDonald, in fact, publicly credited Joseph Kennedy, father of the young senator from Massachusetts, with an "important role in settling the steel strike."[66] When Ike finally returned from his trip abroad, he insisted that the "pressure of circumstances, not the Administration, forced the steel settlement."[67]

In the end, Nixon's role in the steel strike probably hurt him in 1960. The steel companies, other business leaders, and conservative newspaper columnists such as David Lawrence and Arthur Krock were bitter and resentful—and this undermined their wholehearted support for him, at least for the first half of the year. Though some steelworkers, like my father, would vote for Nixon, most bitterly remembered Ike's injunction better than they did the government's final forcing of a deal. Few, in fact, credited the government with much of a role in achieving the settlement. *They*, the rank-and-file steelworkers and their union, had faced down the companies and beaten them. All this stuff in Washington and New York was just a matter of the big boys recognizing that fact.

Indeed, if you read Eisenhower's memoirs carefully, that's about how it happened. Nearly four months without paychecks and then two months of "buttering up" had not weakened the steelworkers' commitment to their union and their work rules. They would vote to go back on strike, and then they'd strike again. With that kind of solidarity, the federal government had no choice but to explain "the pressure of circumstances" to the companies. In the end, Ike was little more than a referee making a good call. His call was not about who was right or wrong on the issues. It was not about inflation, productivity, foreign competition, the legitimacy of the steelworkers' desire for a higher standard of living, or its effect on economic growth. Ike's call was purely and simply about staying power, about who could outlast whom, who could suffer more, stick together, and persevere longer. By Christmas of 1959 he had come to see that, though neither the companies nor the Steelworkers were visibly weakening, when staying power was the issue, there was no contest.

II

CAUSE & CONSEQUENCE
Prologue

My initial research on the 1959 strike consisted of reading on microfilm the daily coverage in the *Johnstown Tribune-Democrat,* my hometown newspaper. As I read along, I got involved in the drama of the strike—who could outlast whom, like a tug-of-war, with President Ike and others jumping in from time to time to tug for one side or the other. But as I read I expected an inconclusive result, a stalemate, because that's how the strike's outcome is most often remembered. Instead, I was surprised (and thrilled) at how dramatic and decisive the union's victory actually had been—and perplexed that almost nobody (except some local management types) remembers it that way.[1]

Reading those old newspapers, I often had to stop to allow a flood of memories to wash through me. On the sports page I read Summer Rookie League box scores for baseball games I think I can remember playing—one when I had three errors at shortstop, including one that cost us the game, and the day I went 5 for 5, including a triple I had always counted as my one and only home run (I would have scored even without that throwing error). *Ben Hur* was the blockbuster movie of that fall, and the Saturday night my "steady girl" and I saw it is more vivid to me than most of what happened last week or last year. But I experienced absolutely no memories of the strike itself, other than the ones I'd begun with. Nothing flooded back—and I wondered if I had even been aware of it at the time.

By the end of the '50s, the teen world had seceded from the adult one. Though we couldn't keep them entirely out of our world, we were very successfully indifferent to what was happening in theirs—and, for reasons I've already explained, I was especially well protected from the kinds of hardship during the strike that many steelworker families remember so well. In addition, the 1959–60 school year was my junior year in high school, the year when I finally had to choose the college track, and this began to distance me from most of my friends, who were in the shop or commercial tracks. Though I identified in no way with the "college types" (who were a small and vulnerable group), my head was by that time already beginning to "leave the valley." My mother and father encouraged this attitude. They saw the strike, I now imagine, as their business and none of my concern; my business was "preparing yourself for college." The strike, and everything it meant, was irrelevant to the self I was preparing. As a result, I missed the history that was happening all around me.

A. H. Raskin of the *New York Times,* the dean of labor reporters in the postwar era, lived far from what he called "the soot-singed valleys of the steel strike," but he saw clearly what was going on. To him the strike was part of a dangerous sea change in labor relations—"a struggle over basic power relationships" rather than a "conventional bread-and-butter quarrel." Citing recent battles in glass and rubber and pending ones on the docks and railroads, Raskin saw the steel strike as but the most important of many battlefields in "a conflict profounder than any fought by unions and employers since the bloody strikes of the Thirties."[2]

Of the strike's eventual settlement, a widely quoted but anonymous steel CEO said, "We took a hell of a licking," and Raskin agreed: "The steel settlement marked a rout of the major companies in what they considered a crusade to re-establish the lost prerogatives of management. . . . A management victory would have meant a general reassessment of the bargaining relationships built up in most major industries in the quarter-century since the New Deal."[3]

As the '50s turned into the '60s, Raskin was not alone in fearing that the hard-won "American system of free collective bargaining" was being threatened by new, more aggressive management attitudes. Though management spokesmen usually denied it, knowledgeable labor relations experts feared that steel and other managements had become so thoroughly disenchanted with the postwar system that they would inadvertently fall into all-out class war while trying to transform it.[4]

In retrospect, this view seems overly alarmist, but in the stagnant economy of 1958–63, managers were boldly probing not just the perimeters, but some of the guts of union power. Had they found more weak spots than they did, the subsequent history of labor-management relations— indeed, the history of the United States—would have been very different. Had the Steelworkers' solidarity broken up into bickering among the rank and file, and between the rank and file and the leadership (as R. Conrad Cooper had hoped), more than the Steelworkers would have been affected—particularly as this defeat would have been followed shortly by a major union debacle at General Electric in the summer of 1960. Any sign of weakness in such a major, high-profile industry as steel would have emboldened other (already pretty bold) managements, just as the 1981 PATCO defeat did in later times. A defeat in steel would also have fed the growing strength of right-wing politics in these years, which would in turn have strengthened the management offensive.

I don't want to exaggerate the danger that unions were actually in during this period. The mainstream of American management did not even flirt with the idea of living without its unions. But management was well organized and deeply committed to reversing the momentum of union gains, and it was tightly focused on what appeared to be a realistic goal —in their parlance, regaining the right to manage unrestricted by rigid union work rules. In the spring and summer of 1959, the time seemed right to make a stand against a tarnished Big Labor, and the forces the business class had assembled seemed very formidable by then.

One of the reasons I think it is important to remember the 1959 Steel Strike is the way it can disrupt the standard image of the 1950s as a placid decade during which nothing much happened. Historians who focus on the decade recognize that the image of a placid, complacent people living happily ever after in an affluent society is based on a handful of years when a benign consensus and a deep sense of security finally took hold in the middle Eisenhower years, 1954–57. The end of the Korean War and the death of Joseph Stalin in 1953 and the downfall of Joseph McCarthy in 1954, followed by just plain Ike's new, more hopeful relationship with the Soviet Union's new leaders, ended what two historians of the decade have called The Age of Fear, which they date from 1948 to 1953. But the years of peace and tranquility, of a long-sought "normality," didn't last long. In September 1957, the violent face of southern white racism revealed itself against black schoolchildren in Little Rock, Arkansas—ending hopes that racial integration could be achieved through small steps taken very slowly, under court orders or even through long, bitter, but basically civilized collective economic struggles, such as the Montgomery Bus Boycott of 1955. In October of 1957, the Russians launched Sputnik, ending America's sense of technological, intellectual, and even moral superiority, which had not been challenged since World War II. By early 1958, it became clear that we were in the worst recession of the postwar period, and the American affluence machine began to seem less mechanical. The late '50s were a time, as Miller and Nowak have noted, of "National Reassessment"—though the reassessing that got done seems pretty tame now, compared to the transvaluation of values that came in the '60s and '70s.[5]

An important part of the national reassessment was that big business wanted a new deal of the cards, one that would give it greater freedom in the workplace and a stronger voice in the nation's economy and politics. Yet the business class was far from unified and monolithic. Besides the traditional splits between big and small business, corporate America itself had a Right and Left wing and a very large, vital center. The Right had never accepted the New Deal or the unions, government regulation, and "national economic planning" that came with it and which, according to the Right, distorted the workings of a free market to the detriment of both economic efficiency and individual freedom. The business Left, on the other hand, embraced the New Deal changes as benevolent corrections to a market system that required government oversight and countervailing powers such as unions to avoid the kinds of destructive competition and financial shenanigans that had resulted in the Great Depression. In the vital center, where U.S. Steel and most other corporate giants with union workforces resided, were the "business realists," to use David Stebenne's term. The realists didn't bother taking firm positions for or against the New Deal changes; they simply accepted them as a reality that had to be dealt with.[6]

The Right had had its day right after the war, with the Republican Congressional victory in 1946 and the Taft-Hartley Act in 1947. Harry Truman's reelection in 1948 ended the lingering roll-back dreams of the realists. Though the realists shifted their weight between Right and Left with changing times, they always proclaimed "We Accept" the changes that had been wrought by the New Deal and the war, even as they defended themselves as best they could against further encroachments by unions and government. The ultimate success of the business realists was the election of General Eisenhower, that symbol of national unity and a firm business realist who genuinely sought class harmony on a pay-as-you-go, ad hoc basis.[7] Until the late '50s, the business Left had the center's ear, and you cannot look at the industrial relations literature of the time, or the bargaining histories of most unions then, without seeing some genuine belief (and a lot of hope) that unions might actually be good for business. The Right, in order to win a hearing then, had to accept the realists' "We Accept" consensus, and they did so, even if under their breath they whispered, "for the time being." But as economic conditions deteriorated in the late '50s, the Right came out for air in a climate that the business center had done much to make more seasonable for the Right's point of view.

As Elizabeth Fones-Wolf has detailed in *The Selling of Free Enterprise*, various business groups, beginning in the late '40s, devised a broad, long-term program to reeducate the American public in the virtues of "businessmen" in a market economy. The traditionally reactionary National Association of Manufacturers, the more consumer-oriented Advertising Council, and the stolidly middle-of-the road Institute for Life Insurance, among many others, spent hundreds of millions of dollars (at a time when that was a lot of money) to reshape public perceptions of the role of business in American life. Some of this was crude propaganda, but most was not. Generally speaking, it was a sincere attempt to infuse the business class with a greater sense of social responsibility while convincing the citizenry that this enlightenment had already occurred. As Fones-Wolf explains, "[C]orporate leaders constructed and sold a specific vision of the reciprocal relationship of businesses and citizens. . . . In this vision, corporate leaders claimed the right to control America's economic destiny without significant interference from unions or the state while acknowledging their responsibility to make the benefits of industrial capitalism available to all."[8]

This was no short-term public-relations ploy, though it involved plenty of direct newspaper, magazine, and television advertising. It had a sophisticated workplace relations arm that advocated greater sensitivity by management to human needs, and which in many versions borrowed heavily from the New Deal outlook of labor relations professionals. It also had a community relations arm, with plant managers expected to play a highly visible and benign role in community affairs, including making a systematic effort to shape school textbooks and public education at every level.

By the late '50s the business class was definitely making progress on the ideological front, but as it did so, it was gradually conceding a lot of ground to the unions, both in the economic package and in shop-floor power. With the depth of the 1958 recession, the business class began to reassess things. Building on their renewed reputation for social responsibility, business leaders began to argue that they could not continue to fulfill that responsibility if, in the words of Roger Blough, the "glacierlike forces of a powerful labor movement" continued to force upon them "labor practices which impair the competitive principle [and] are incompatible with a free society."[9] Though management rhetoric had to be carefully trimmed to keep the public opinion advantage business leaders thought they had achieved, the élan of management throughout the country was stirred in the spring and summer of 1959 as behemoths like U.S. Steel, calmly but determinedly went on the attack after more than a decade of retreats. Prior to 1958, companies often (even usually) dug in their heels trying to resist union demands. But coming out of the 1958 recession, one set of managements after another went on the attack to try to win back some of what they had lost. In a reversal of their usual roles, the companies were now making the demands, talking of principles and rights, and the unions were defending the status quo.

While management spokesmen generally avoided rhetorical challenges to the very existence of unions, others were not so constrained. The Wall Street Journal, for example, routinely challenged the antitrust exemption enjoyed by unions since early in the century, an exemption that formed the basis for the legality of unions in the American system. Likewise, Arthur Krock of the New York Times challenged the right to strike: "This Republican Administration has been as one with its Democratic predecessor in declining to attack the root of the union labor monopoly—the immunity from the antitrust laws by which the steelworkers, for example, were able to shut down a nationwide industry by withdrawing its labor force."[10]

The managerial offensive had powerful political allies during these years as well. As the McClellan Hearings, beginning in 1957, systematically undermined labor's public image, Congress entertained all sorts of labor-law reforms, against which the labor movement had to defend itself. Though the Landrum-Griffin Labor-Management Reporting and Disclosure

Act that passed during the steel strike was considered a major political defeat for labor, it was not as bad as many other proposals floated in Congress then. Senators Goldwater and McClellan, for example, had proposed a nationwide ban on the union shop, and when this failed, conservative forces mounted campaigns for so-called right-to-work laws in a dozen states, including Ohio and California, where unions were relatively strong. Labor mobilized pretty effectively to defeat most of these efforts, and unions were the backbone of the Democratic victories in Congress in 1958 and for the presidency in 1960—victories that helped blunt, though they did not end, the management offensive.[11]

How much the American system of free collective bargaining was actually in jeopardy during this period is something labor historians have just begun to assess.[12] Given what actually happened, a Steelworkers' defeat in 1959 is pretty hard to imagine. But U.S. Steel managers Blough and Cooper had reasons to think that maybe steelworkers would not be so resolute as they had been in 1946, 1949, 1952, and 1956—reasons that justified putting the workers to the test. Had U.S. Steel been even partly successful, it would have given a big boost to the business and political Right. As it turned out, the 1959 Steel Strike was, in Mike Davis's apt World War II analogy, the "Eastern Front" of the "Management Offensive." The long, drawn-out struggle in steel undermined the early momentum that right-wing managerial and political forces had gathered and deterred the majority of business realists from further flirting with the grandiose notions of the free-market purists.[13]

The steel companies' immediate bargaining agenda in 1959 had almost nothing in common with the ideological ferocity of editorial writers and politicians who wanted a return to the discipline of the market. The steel companies were a well-disciplined oligopoly, and the industry's entire history gave the lie to the verities of classical and neoclassical economics. The steelmakers were proudly practical men. Labor negotiations, like all other aspects of the business, were about power and money (in that order), and the steelworkers had been stripping them of both. They saw an opportunity to reverse that, and they took it. Had they been successful, they and their business brethren would have found encouragement to roll back other union gains.

The long strike of 1959 established that there would be no backward steps, that "the mistakes of the past eighteen years" were now written in stone. Though the strike established no new principle, it successfully defended all the principles the union had won in the previous twenty years, adding a little to the substance, and it consolidated the basic framework for the next twenty years.[14] There would not be a steel strike of any kind for another quarter century, and there would never be another nationwide steel strike.

The 1959 Steel Strike was the "big one" and the "last one" (the handles most steelworker families use to remember it), and it was the last one *because* it was the big one. Its outcome ensured that the companies would never again make a frontal attack on union power. Even as the Basic Steel Contract unravelled in the 1980s, it was done primarily on the basis of a cooperative response to the industry's crisis, with some steelworkers finding the union all too cooperative. The length of the strike also ensured that steelworkers and their families would hesitate before striking again. Both sides shared an interest in avoiding the stockpiles and imports that steel customers had used to prepare for potential strikes as contract deadlines approached, and avoiding a strike became a primary goal of every negotiation after 1959. Eventually, in 1973, the Steelworkers gave up their right to strike in return for broad guarantees in virtually all parts of the contract, particularly those concerning wages.[15]

For historians such as John Strohmeyer, who traces the crisis of the American steel industry in the 1980s back to 1959, the companies' defeat made it impossible for them to subsequently reshape the industry to allow it to better survive the eventual onslaught of competition from imports and minimills, which would cut the industry in half two decades later.[16] Though I will argue that Strohmeyer is wrong, the view he represents is accurate in its portrayal of 1959 as the year of the companies' last wholehearted attempt to strip the union of its power, and in its assumption that their defeat then had significant consequences for what happened later.

To me, the long strike represents the culminating victory of two decades of struggle by my family and our friends and neighbors to carve out a space for ourselves—a struggle, not without its noble moments, to find a clean, well-lighted place from which we could begin to see new prospects and possibilities. The 1959 strike needs to be appreciated, maybe even celebrated a bit, for what it did in the short term, before we begin blaming it for what it might have done later. But we can't look at 1959 except through the lens of what happened to the industry and its people in the 1980s; past events are continually recast in memory, their meaning always changing as the end of the story changes.

The 1959 Steel Strike was about hard issues of money and power, complicated issues that even in the much more substantive public discourse of the time were difficult to communicate and explain. But without understanding them, we can neither understand the impact that unionism has on real people's lives nor assess the blame that should be assigned to it for the decline of America's economic competitiveness in the 1980s.

3

2-B or Not 2-B

A Battle for "Rigid Union Work Rules"

He believed that faithfulness of a particularly knowing kind could replace moral choices.

—D. J. Waldie, *Holy Land*

The management offensive was directed at the day-to-day workplace power relations shaped by the union contract and the grievance-and-arbitration system through which the contract was interpreted and enforced. In steel, the offensive eventually focused on Section 2-B. In other industries, other contract clauses and union rules were contested: In plate glass, it was seniority provisions; in meatpacking, overtime rules and performance standards; in longshoring and the railroads, management's ability to eliminate jobs when it installed new technology. In every instance, people's jobs were at stake, and though in most industries, unlike in steel, unions were forced to give up some powers in order to preserve others, in every instance the union was able to preserve many more jobs than management thought were necessary.[1]

From management's perspective, each unnecessary job was wasteful and expensive, an abuse of union power, a usurpation of management's right to manage. But each of these jobs was somebody's livelihood and positively affected others who were dependent on that livelihood—not only family members, but whole communities of merchants, churches,

94

local school systems, and many others who benefitted from having more rather than fewer jobs. Union workers fought tenaciously in these years to save jobs. But the unity and tenacity with which they fought was not aimed simply at saving jobs. Most of those who fought were not, in fact, in danger of losing *their* jobs. Rather, the defensive battles of these years were wars of position, fought in defense of what has more recently come to be called the workplace rule of law or simply rigid union work rules.

As was the case in steel, most employers who had been unionized since World War II were not trying to get rid of their unions. They were not even trying to do away with all union work rules. Neither of these were realistic possibilities. But management rhetoric about waste and featherbedding, about the right to manage—let alone careless yearnings for a golden age of management authority—must have stirred the fears of workers like my father who could remember what it was like without the rules.

Johnny Metzgar's version of "the union" emphasized the mere existence of the contract and the rules it contained. "With the union," he would say, "they can't do just whatever they want. One guy can't come in and change things to suit himself. We've got a say in how things are run." After a pause, he'd qualify, "Don't get me wrong. We don't have much of a say. They're still the boss. But if we all stick together around the contract, they have to deal with us as men, not just 'hands.'" This was the most valuable thing about the union, according to him: "Forget the wages, forget the health insurance. If the union hadn't done anything else, it would have been worth it just for that."

After doing my research, I suspect now that a lot of the speeches I remember my father giving about the importance of the union's work rules were made shortly before, during, and immediately after the 1959 strike. Though these were years when arguments were beginning to distance us from one another, I still listened intently to the mill stories he'd tell me. But I don't know for sure when he said many of the things I attribute to him here—and sometimes I can't even be sure *that* he said them. My memories of him are full of tricks and distortions. One of the firm memories I have of the strike, for example, occurs in a house we didn't live in yet. But the biggest distortion is that he was always the same—that he didn't change and develop like other human beings. No matter how hard I try, from my earliest memory to 1968 when Mom died, he is always the same towering, dominating figure (though his actual height was five feet four inches), a know-it-all who was always in control. I don't think he talked to anybody else the way he did to me, and his instruction was full of contradictions that revealed his vulnerabilities even as he sought to hide them. To me he was always learning lessons. His own vision of himself, that is to say, was of a flawed and developing being, but all I saw and can consistently remember is how solid, unwavering, rigidly consistent, and invulnerable he was.

This chapter and part of the next is a defense of the workplace rule of law, of which Section 2-B of the Basic Steel Contract was a particularly strong example. I try as best I can to articulate my father's view of it—a view I just absorbed by being around him as a boy, but didn't really appreciate until the 1980s, when I got to witness the impact its erosion and destruction had on the lives of students, colleagues, family, and friends. I'm not sure anymore where his view ends and mine begins because as I think through many of these issues, I keep moving closer to his view of things—and it's possible, since he is no longer around to argue with me, that I've been moving him a little closer to my view, though I've tried to avoid that. The one clear difference is that he was a ferocious opponent of the notion of productivity, and I am not. Like the union leadership then and now, I believe that without productivity increases, better wages and conditions are probably impossible in the long run. I have made this argument to local union leaders and stewards time and again, and every time I have, at least one "hard guy" spits back at me my father's words from long ago (the hard guys are a diverse group, with none more like my father than several black women clerical workers with strong Baptist backgrounds). The mere mention of "productivity" pushes a button in hard guys, and out pops a speech. My father's went something like this: "Push, push, push—that's what productivity is. They just want to give me that pain in my back. Productivity means working until you ache—every day, day in and day out. They don't really know what productivity is, but if you're aching you must be productive, at least until you're crippled. When you're fifty and can't stand the ache anymore, you're no good to them, and you're out. Productivity? Why would I want to make myself miserable in order to work myself out of a job?"

In my view, productivity increases can be achieved—in fact, they're more likely to be achieved—without the "push, push, push." In the next chapter I offer the history of unionized workplaces as evidence of that. But, where I agree with him is in his defense of the workplace rule of law, which has come under attack in recent years not just from management (who never liked it much) but from labor historians and other Leftists, who are generally sympathetic to labor unions. To them, the complex, legalistic, and bureaucratic grievance system distanced the union from the workers, coopting them into an orderly process that was good for management control but that left them powerless once they had "filed a grievance." To Christopher Tomlins, for example, the whole industrial relations system, of which the Steelworkers were a primary example, provided a "counterfeit liberty" that "offered workers and their organizations . . . no more than the opportunity to participate in the construction of their own subordination."[2]

Workers in the '50s and '60s made similar (if less grandiloquent) complaints about the slowness and bulkiness of the grievance system. Filing a grievance often seemed like putting a message in a bottle and launching it into the ocean; by the time you got a resolution, you'd forgotten what the problem was. My father had little sympathy for these complaints. The mistake, according to him, was to focus on single grievances and what might happen to them without seeing how the whole apparatus slowed management down every day (no matter how well or poorly it performed in a particular instance or even in general). To him the apparatus was a tool that, if you mastered it, could be used to confuse and intimidate management and, if everybody stuck together around the contract, could slowly but consistently erode management authority, put management on the defensive, and put lots of liberty and control in workers' hands, even without their filing a grievance.

As a griever, he was the man in the middle. "We've got some of the smartest lawyers in the world," he'd say, "and if we give 'em a clean grievance, in time they'll make monkeys of the company. But it don't mean a thing unless we make it work down here—me and you and crazy George and lazy Harry." Many foremen and even superintendents didn't understand the contract very well, and management was often at odds with itself. Industrial engineers (IEs) and labor relations staffers were constantly at war with each other, and front-line supervisors didn't care for either set of these "college boys" who often humiliated them and undermined their day-to-day authority (sometimes intentionally, but more often just because of the nature of things). So long as the Hunkies and the Dagos, the Krauts and the niggers stuck together to keep management divided, grievers could shop contract clauses around and make them mean different things to different audiences. They could make the grievance system sing songs and perform surgeries, which Pittsburgh (headquarters of both the USWA and U.S. Steel) would never know about, without ever filing a grievance. Often, it seemed, "shit was pulled" just for the delight of it, but if my father was to be believed, the unofficial shop-floor skirmishes that industrial relations scholars called fractional bargaining were a tremendous source of daily power, control, and even dignity. Plus, the Steelworkers did employ some very smart "lawyers" in those days. Actually, some of them were economists.

Where Are the Examples?
The Search for Featherbedding

The 1959 strike was about work rules and featherbedding. The companies' public relations campaign claimed that union work rules severely restricted their right to manage, and that this made it impossible for them to achieve the kinds of productivity increases that would allow them to meet the increasing threat from foreign and other competition. They pointed to Section 2-B of the Basic Steel Contract as a particularly egregious example of the restrictions the union had forced upon them, claiming it amounted to institutionalized waste, a license for loafing and featherbedding.

From the beginning of the strike, journalists pestered the companies for examples of featherbedding, and the companies could not or would not produce them. At one point Republic Steel chairman Charles White did give reporters two "illustrations of what we're up against." But, according to *Fortune* magazine, White soon had to admit that his "illustrations actually were not really pertinent to the work-rules problem."[3]

According to John Strohmeyer, the companies did look for appropriate examples, but the problem was so "subtle" they couldn't find any. Strohmeyer recounts the recollection of attorney George A. Moore, Jr., one of the negotiators for Bethlehem Steel in 1959:

> "We asked the companies to go into their plants and produce examples of featherbedding," Moore [explained]. One steel company executive complained about a hot metal crane operator—not identified—who originally had been assigned a man to relieve him every two hours because of the heat inside the cab; later, when the company air-conditioned the cab, the union refused to eliminate the relief operator job.
>
> "Dammit, we looked all around the industry for that example and we couldn't find it. What we did find was that the supervisors who had been doing all the complaining kept no records."[4]

In October the government's head fact-finder, George W. Taylor, also asked for some specific cases to help the fact-finders assess the companies' claims. When a spokesman for Bethlehem Steel demurred, saying the industry didn't want the fact-finding panel to "get bogged down in detail," Taylor snapped, "Well, we're sure getting bogged down in generalities."[5]

Many commentators agreed with *Time* magazine that the failure to produce concrete examples of union featherbedding was a major public-relations blunder. It was surely an embarrassment for those supposed neutrals, like *Time*, who wanted to support the companies more wholeheartedly. Indeed, *Time* saw this public relations gaffe as the turning point of the strike: "Taylor's verdict that the industry arguments were 'bogged down in generalities' led to a shift in attitudes of both the U.S. public and the Eisenhower Administration. The President, who had firmly backed the industry's campaign for a non-inflationary settlement, began to see that he was fighting beside allies who were short on both ammunition and marksmanship."[6]

Given the sophisticated public relations apparatus the steel companies possessed, their lack of preparation on this front *is* astounding, but there were good reasons to avoid examples. As *Fortune* explained:

> [S]teel industry negotiators deliberately decided not to be too specific about work rules. It is apparent that the companies believe they are on stronger ground talking about broad principles (i.e., "management must have the right to manage") than about specific cases—in which the detailed arguments are hard to follow. . . . In addition, there is the problem that practices vary widely from company to company and from plant to plant. . . . Some steel executives seem to fear that complaining about the work rules that exist in some plants will only egg on workers in other plants to clamor for the same rules.[7]

Detailed examples are difficult to follow because you must know something, often a good deal, about specific labor processes in order to assess the impact of a specific work rule—particularly when the two sides disagree over the way the labor process actually works and what the rule requires. When issues of health and safety are involved (as they very often are), following the arguments gets even more tricky. But the difficulty with examples doesn't end there.

The public knew about featherbedding through the famous example of the railroad fireman who kept his job beside the engineer in the cab of a locomotive even after there was no fire to fuel. And there is one work rule that provided the quintessential example of union power run amok: that at a union company, only an electrician can change a light bulb. These two examples have long stood for all others and gotten endlessly repeated and referred to, even up to our own time. Mention these examples to a professional, middle-class audience and you will find a deep moral repugnance toward this fundamentally unfair and ridiculous inefficiency (even if there is sometimes concern expressed for the potentially unemployed firemen). Mention them amidst a strong union culture (as in my labor education classes), and you will see a warm, cunning smile of pride in union power's ability to protect workers' livelihoods and to control at least some rules of the game.

And this illustrates the companies' dilemma in going public with detailed examples of the inefficiencies caused by union work rules. Though everybody tends to be for efficiency in the abstract , when we get into the details, few issues better illustrate the dailiness of class struggle in the American workplace. The opposite of "featherbedding" is "speed-up," and thus the opposite of "efficiency" becomes what we typically call (and what my father certainly saw as) unsafe, unhealthy conditions. As people divide along class lines in debating the examples, the larger case against inefficiency tends to lose its purity.

The union had similar problems giving examples. Work rules did preserve jobs that management might justifiably have eliminated—the December 1959 issue of *Steelabor*, after all, claimed that 2-B protected more than a hundred thousand jobs. In other venues, however, union spokespersons denied that 2-B had much effect at all. Marvin Miller, later the founder and leader of the Major League Baseball Players Association, was a Steelworker economist in 1959. According to him, "The work rules issue was a manufactured issue by the industry from beginning to end." Miller was assigned to represent the union on the "joint study committee" the 1959 settlement had required to investigate the harm 2-B was doing to the industry. He gives this account of what happened to it:

> We smoked out the phoniness of the issue very rapidly after the settlement. . . . One of the ways we smoked it out . . . was to suggest that we send work groups into every plant . . . and get from the foremen and the workers what these practices were. Not theoretically, not the kind of nonsense that was printed in the [companies'] ads, but specifically.
>
> Well, the industry could not buy that. They couldn't buy it first, because it would have become apparent that these exaggerations were purely mythical. . . . In the second place, they couldn't buy it because many of the practices which they complained about had been instituted by management, and in

order to get documentation on that you would, in effect, be asking management people—foremen and people above them—to give you the documentation on things they themselves had instituted.

And that was an impossible task. Once we went down that road, the industry had no stomach for that study. It was agreed, very quietly, to write—I guess it was about a one-page report—indicating we had looked into this problem and—I have forgotten exactly what the wording was, but the meaning certainly was—we were putting it to bed.[8]

Miller was right to point to company exaggerations, and his account of the companies' post-strike difficulties in achieving communication between various levels of management on this issue is confirmed by Strohmeyer's interviews with Bethlehem supervisors.[9] But 2-B and its work rules were far from a phony issue for either side. While the search for examples never came up with the kind of crowd-pleaser the companies needed for public-relations purposes, that doesn't mean that 2-B didn't severely restrict management's discretion in deploying its workforce as it saw fit.

What Was 2-B?

Section 2-B of the national steel labor contract outlined the powers of local unions to negotiate work rules for their particular workplaces, and it contained a particularly effective "past practice" clause—2-B (3+4)—that severely restricted management's ability to reorganize the labor process.[10]

SECTION 2-B

(with the most relevant passages highlighted in paragraph four)

Section 2—Scope of the Agreement

B. Local Working Conditions

The term "local working conditions" as used herein means specific practices or customs which reflect detailed application of the subject matter within the scope of wages, hours of work, or other conditions of employment and includes local agreements, written and oral, on such matters. It is recognized that it is impracticable to set forth in this Agreement all of these working conditions, which are of a local nature only, or to state specifically in this

(continued on next page)

(continued)

Agreement which of these matters should be changed or eliminated. The following provisions provide general principles and procedures which explain the status of these matters and furnish necessary guideposts for the parties hereto and the Board.

1. It is recognized that an employee does not have the right to have a local working condition established, in any given situation or plant where such condition has not existed, during the term of this Agreement or to have an existing local working condition changed or eliminated, except to the extent necessary to require the application of a specific provision of this Agreement.

2. In no case shall local working conditions be effective to deprive any employee of rights under this Agreement. Should any employee believe that a local working condition is depriving him of the benefits of this Agreement, he shall have recourse to the grievance procedure and arbitration, if necessary, to require that the local working condition be changed or eliminated to provide the benefits established by this Agreement.

3. Should there be any local working conditions in effect which provide benefits that are in excess of or in addition to the benefits established by this Agreement, they shall remain in effect for the term of this Agreement, except as they are changed or eliminated by mutual agreement or in accordance with Paragraph 4 below.

4. *The Company shall have the right to change or eliminate any local working condition if,* as the result of action taken by Management under Section 3—Management, *the basis for the existence of the local working condition is changed or eliminated,* thereby making it unnecessary to continue such local working condition; *provided, however, that when such a change or elimination is made by the Company any affected employee shall have recourse to the grievance procedure and arbitration, if necessary, to have the Company justify its action.*

5. No local working condition shall hereafter be established or agreed to which changes or modifies any of the provisions of this Agreement. In the event such a local working condition is established or agreed to, it shall not be enforceable to the extent that it is inconsistent with or goes beyond the provisions of this Agreement, except as it is approved by an International Officer of the Union and the Industrial Relations Executive of the Company.

Source: Benjamin Selekman, Sylvia Selekman, and Stephen Fuller, *Problems in Labor Relations*, 2d ed. (McGraw-Hill, 1958), 577–78. The 1960 contract added three paragraphs setting up the 2-B Study Committee, but otherwise this language was exactly the same from 1947 into the 1960s.

2-B (3+4) was probably the best past-practice clause an American union ever got in its contract. By 1959 the principle of past practices restricting what management could do had been pretty well established within the developing case law of arbitration decisions, where it was often called "the common law of the shop." But many unions had obtained clauses in their contracts that required management to negotiate with the union when it wanted to change any "well-established practice" that affected working conditions. Of these, 2-B (3+4) was exceptional. Originally placed in the U.S. Steel contract late in the 1947 negotiations, it had been one of the primary issues in 1952 and a sore point with management ever after. Both the language of the clause and the way the Steelworkers used that language were well beyond what other labor-management agreements allowed.[11]

But the past-practice clause was just a part of Section 2-B. For a while in 1959 it seemed the companies wanted to jettison the whole section—to simply do away with the local union bargaining that followed the successful completion of a national agreement. The companies' original eight-point program had targeted a whole set of work rules, including the workings of the seniority system, and they didn't get focused on 2-B (3+4) until three months into the strike. Even then, their public language was loose. Sometimes "2-B" referred strictly to the past-practice clause, sometimes to the entire section, and sometimes it seemed to stand for *all* the powers the union had to limit managerial discretion.[12]

The past-practice clause was *not* the only problem. Also problematic were all the written work rules inscribed in local union contracts. These deal with all sorts of mundane activities—procedures for scheduling shifts and vacations, setting work incentives and standards, taking coffee breaks, going to lunch, wearing goggles and hard hats, washing up after work, and being relieved by workers from the next shift—anything that affects or even touches upon working conditions. As problems came up, a local union would formulate a specific rule or procedure to cover it and would then try to get it into the next local contract. Once a rule made it in there, it was very hard for management to get it out. Evidently it took management a while to figure this out, and by the time it had, most local contracts contained a hunter's stew of restrictions on their managerial authority.

The past-practice clause greatly expanded these restrictions. 2-B (3+4) simply said that, in addition to all the carefully specified work rules in the local contract, none of the well-established ways of doing things in a given workplace could be changed without negotiating with the union. Thus, 2-B had the potential to transform every existing practice of management into a "rigid union work rule." It forbade management to change anything (without negotiating) unless "the basis for the existence" of a particular management practice was changed or eliminated. The union, both its "lawyers" and its grievers, got pretty creative in haggling over what constituted a *basis for existence*, and thus a full understanding of what 2-B did and did not do gets pretty complicated.

What it could reasonably have been expected to do, however, was to allow management to reorganize work and revise its practices as required by technological changes, but to require negotiation with the local union for all other changes that affected any working condition. If, for example, management installed new technology that allowed it to do a job with sixteen instead of twenty workers, layoffs should be allowed because the basis for existence of the previous labor process (the technology) had changed. On the other hand, if an enterprising foreman or IE, without any resort to technological change, figured a way to reorganize the flow of tasks and materials so that sixteen workers could do what it had taken twenty to do before, 2-B would prohibit management from doing that unless and until the union agreed.

Had 2-B worked exactly like this, it would still have been a very powerful tool in the hands of a well-organized union and a potentially enormous obstacle to management's achieving maximum efficiency and productivity. But the Steelworkers in the 1950s used 2-B as a Trojan horse to march into the area of technological change as well, allowing management to make *some* changes to accommodate new technology, but filing grievances that eventually would require management to negotiate what exactly those changes would be. Marvin Miller's account shows just how far the union had stretched its past-practice clause:

> I had people in the public telling me that it was a terrible issue because it meant that if you had twenty men working on an operation and the company came along and mechanized the whole thing so it required six men, that they still had to employ twenty. Of course, that was complete nonsense. The most that 2B ever did in a situation like that was to give the union a foothold in seeing that the change in manning, from twenty to six in that example, was logical in relation to the change in technology. In other words, it would be possible for an arbitrator to say, "Yes, this technology has changed; you no longer need twenty men, I think you need eleven." Yes, that could have been accomplished under 2B, but it never froze the twenty men.[13]

It's true that 2-B "never froze the twenty men" when a labor process was "mechanized," but neither was it supposed to give the union *any* "foothold" for bargaining over how many jobs would be required when the technology changed. Imagine: Management spends oodles of money for new machinery that allows it, in its best judgment, to eliminate fourteen jobs (and their wages and benefits), but an arbitrator rules, "I think you need eleven." Because the arbitrator thinks management needs eleven rather than six workers, management is stuck with five "extra" workers for as long as that new technology remains in place. This is why there was nothing phony about 2-B as an issue. Management wanted, at the very least, to eliminate that union foothold for bargaining over new technology, but beyond that, it needed to destroy the very idea of its past practices limiting what it could do in the future.

Miller goes on to argue, "Nor did [2-B] freeze any work practice, as long as some relevant circumstances, equipment, methods, changed. If surrounding circumstances changed, 2B was no protection whatsoever." [14] This is true, but disingenuous (and overly modest), coming from one of the economists who made a living by presenting arbitrators with creative interpretations of how "surrounding circumstances" almost never changed enough to make 2-B inapplicable to anything management did.

During the Taft-Hartley cooling-off period in 1959–60, *Fortune* reported on a study of arbitration decisions involving 2-B; this study, by a management-oriented law firm, clearly documented the power of 2-B to save steelworker jobs. *Fortune* selected from the study six solid cases involving different kinds of issues, from holidays and discipline to work assignments and work crews. The one on "crew sizes" relates best to Miller's claims above and illustrates perfectly what was so galling to management about 2-B:

> Ever since it was built in 1931, a furnace at the National Tube Division of U.S. Steel had had a seven-man crew. In 1949 the company, after conducting time studies, decided to reduce the crew size by two men but to raise the pay of the remaining five through an improved incentive scale. The union balked, and in 1953 arbitrator Sylvester Garrett ruled against the company. He said that there had been no change in the original basis for the crew size [i.e., no change in technology], and that "time study merely constitutes an analysis of conditions as they exist," not a new condition. [15]

In an industry where Frederick Winslow Taylor's theory of scientific management had first cut its teeth, where IEs had scoured the mills for decades with their time studies looking for "the one best way" to do anything and everything, this 1953 arbitrator's decision by itself was devastating to management's sovereign control of the production process. "Time study merely constitutes an analysis of conditions as they exist," Sylvester Garrett had ruled, and 2-B froze those conditions, regardless of what the IEs might come up with. The IEs could no longer speed up or sweat steelworkers without resorting to large investments in new technology, and the union had a foothold even there!

Think of a nonunion workplace today, a place full of white-collar professionals, managers, and clerical workers—a clean, well-lighted place with air conditioning and genteel manners. It's probably been downsized, right-sized, restructured, and reengineered. Its surviving workforce is terrorized. Its workers have no protection from even the grandest and stupidest "recommendations" from management consultants, who are free to decide which members of the corporate family are no longer necessary. These workers can be moved around and redefined like pieces in a chess game whose rules have been forgotten. "Please report to Human Resources," they are asked, where you will be stripped of your dignity, your identity, and your livelihood. Such things could not happen in a steel mill in the 1950s. Other things still could—it was still dirty, noisy, and dangerous, freezing in winter and boiling in summer, and the work was still unpleasant and difficult. But you were nobody's pawn to be moved about in endless combinations in pursuit of efficiency. If management wanted efficiency, if it wanted increased productivity and profits, it would have to come to you (or your representatives) and talk about it, negotiate it, bargain over it—and it had better come with some incentives in its pocket; it had better bargain in good faith; it had better be reasonable if it wanted you to be reasonable.

The cases that wound up with arbitrators were only the tip of 2-B's iceberg. In order to avoid that possibility—with its potential for establishing industry-wide precedents—local management often gave in whenever a griever merely waved the flag of 2-B. According to U.S.S. labor relations chief R. Conrad Cooper, it was "thrown into almost every grievance the union file[d]," and while the union won only 20 percent of 2-B arbitration cases, that one-in-five threat created widespread demoralization among local plant supervision. As one of Bethlehem's lawyers complained, "There is so much uncertainty about their rights that the lower echelons of management finally give up on lots of things that should be done." [16]

Section 2-B tied steel management in knots, and the union's grievers and "lawyers" kept adding new knots all the time. Arbitrators were making decisions that should have been—that used to be and, for most workers today, are again—the sole perogative of management. In the 1950s, the companies went to the courts, pleading for them to overturn or modify what they saw as the arbitrators' most outrageous decisions; in 1960, shortly after the final strike, the U.S. Supreme Court closed that door, too. In what came to be known as the Steelworkers' Trilogy, the Court definitively ruled that in the interpretation of labor contracts, arbitrators had the final word, and that henceforth the courts could not second-guess them. Furthermore, one of the Trilogy cases determined that even where unions had not won past-practice clauses in their contracts, the accumulation of arbitration case law had established past practice as a basic principle restricting managerial discretion.[17]

As the 1960s opened, companies were trapped in a maze of rigid union work rules—not just in steel, but almost every place where unions were strong. Management would have been irresponsible, it would not have been fulfilling its obligation to maximize profits for its stockholders, had it not exhausted every possibility for smashing the maze, breaking holes in it, or eliminating it altogether to restore its "right to manage." The steel companies led the fight, in the courts and with a long-strike war of attrition. They had done their duty, and they had lost on both fronts. The only remaining way to get out of the maze was to negotiate situation by situation with the workforce and/or its representatives.

All told, 2-B sure looks like it was a license to loaf. But whether it actually was or not depends on whether the union was willing to be reasonable in negotiating workplace changes. Your assessment of what counts as reasonable is going to vary depending on which side you are on, but it is telling that the companies were not able to produce one example of a clearly unreasonable result of 2-B, an example that could be declared patently unreasonable by almost everybody—something like the locomotive firemen without a fire to fuel, or the union electrician changing a light bulb. The fact that the companies were not able to produce any examples of this sort allows—if it does not require—the conclusion that the union was always at least relatively reasonable in negotiating necessary workplace changes.

I argue for this conclusion in the next chapter. But let's stop first and think about those two guys who arbitrator Sylvester Garrett said the

IEs couldn't take away from the furnace at National Tube. Though their grievance had taken four years to get resolved, they ended up with secure jobs in the American steel industry in the mid-1950s—which, if their families' lives were anything like mine, was just about as good as winning the lottery, given what the union was to win over the next twenty years. Though "going through the mill" was no bed of roses (especially at the hot end), it was a helluva lot better for most folks than the next best option. By the 1950s a job in the mill was a prize worth fighting for, and everybody knew that.

Taking away some of management's discretion and keeping it for yourself was worth something, too. It meant that management at every level had to deal with you—or at least it made it rational behavior for them to negotiate with rather than boss you. The system still allowed for plenty of bossing, but there was a line (actually a whole set of lines) beyond which managers could not go. And if everybody stuck together around the contract, crafty buggers like Johnny Metzgar and Marvin Miller could keep moving that line in your direction.

"There's No Future in the Mill"

It's hard to exaggerate how decisive and important a victory the 1959 strike was at the time. But now that the industry is a shadow of what it was, many people wonder if the seeds of steel's decline weren't sown in the companies' "surrender" then. More generally, the story of steel's decline, more than any other industry's, embodies the notion that for all the wonderful things unions once did, they got too powerful and expensive, and we can no longer afford them.

The union had real power and must bear some responsibility for what happened to the industry. But many false and superficial tales have been told, and many simple truths have been forgotten, about unions in general and the steel union in particular. The union loaded a lot of costs onto the companies, and this may have eventually hastened the industry's decline. But the glory years of the postwar steel industry could not have lasted no matter what the union, or the companies for that matter, might have done. You have to judge the actions of both the union and the companies in relation to the actual circumstances they faced and to what they could see of those circumstances at the time.

1959 was near the beginning of a six-year period of stagnation in steel production and employment. In 1955, 1956, and 1957, production topped 80 million tons, and total wage and salary employment, about 620,000. After 1957, production did not reach the 80 million mark again until 1964, and the industry would never again employ more than 600,000.[18] The years after the 1959 strike were hard ones. The domestic industry faced increasingly serious competition from imports and alternative materials such as aluminum and plastic, and overall consumer demand was not growing with the vigor it had from the late 1940s through the mid 1950s. Many people, including experts in these things, thought that the postwar boom was over and that the rules of the previous decade and a half were no longer applicable. As we've seen, this was one of the main motivating factors in the broad management offensive of 1958–63.

Steel industry profits, after the three wonder years in the mid-1950s, hit a bad stretch. From 1958 to 1964, the industry's best profit year was actually the year of the strike.[19] Wage employment was hit even harder, with about one-fifth of the 1959 strikers having very unsteady employment at best in the early '60s, and probably tens of thousands being permanently washed out of the industry during these years. (It's difficult to tell exactly how many, because many thousands of younger workers returned to the mills after years in other jobs when wage employment picked up again in the mid-1960s.)

Thus, steelworkers and their union were faced with a difficult strategic situation. Jobs were being lost in every conceivable way—from slack demand, from competition, and from what in the 1950s was called automation. Demand depended on macroeconomic circumstances and policy, and the Steelworkers fully supported President Kennedy's fiscal stimulus in these years; but steel was already a mature industry and was unlikely to grow very rapidly even as economic growth increased. The other causes of job loss were more difficult to manage, because one of the main ways to fight competition, whether from imports or plastics, was with automation. If the industry didn't increase productivity and reduce its unit costs, jobs would be lost to imports and competing materials. But the most effective way to increase productivity was through automation, which also eliminated tens of thousands of jobs.

In this situation, the union was in no position to resist automation, and it never tried to. Though 2-B and other union work rules undoubtedly were helpful in moderating some job loss, 2-B itself actually encouraged investment in new technology because it made it difficult to achieve productivity increases without technological change. This was understood at the time and was consistent with the union's basically favorable "you-can't-stop-progress" policy on new technology. But the union did bargain stubbornly over the effects and benefits of automation. The union's basic approach was to protect its existing members as best it could. There was little hope that very many jobs could be preserved for future generations.

I graduated from high school in 1961, and nobody in my class of more than seven hundred went into the mill upon graduating. Many, probably most, of the boys would have wanted to—we all knew it was "the best job in town," and the phrase "the highest paid industrial workers in the world" was occasionally used in the local newspaper and repeated in daily conversation. But none of us had ever expected to get into the mill. Wage employment had peaked in 1953 at 544,000, and by 1961 it was down to 406,000. Our parents, our teachers, the newspaper, everybody agreed: "There's no future in the mill." The Steelworkers would be doing very well if they could protect everybody who was in there already. There was no possibility of preserving enough jobs so that some of us could have them.

The national union's basic bargaining strategy in the early 1960s was to spread the work around by shortening the work year and work life of steelworkers. Increased holidays and vacations (including the thirteen-week vacation every five years for high seniority workers won in 1963) reduced the work year. More money for the pension fund and more liberal rules for early retirement ("thirty and out") reduced the work life. Older workers, including my father and uncles, benefitted from more time off and earlier retirement, and because the older workers worked less, there was more work for the younger ones. This worked out very nicely for the older workers, as we've seen, but it also worked out pretty good for a lot of the younger ones. Dean Bracken and "Doc" Frombach, the president and grievance chair of my father's local union when it disappeared in the early 1980s, both retired when U.S. Steel left Johnstown for good; both had entered the mill in the late 1940s, right out of high school, and had still been "young fellas" during the 1959 strike.[20]

And even future generations did better than expected (for a while at least) as demand picked up in the mid-'60s and as steelworkers like my father began to utilize the early retirement option. There were new hires again in the late '60s and early '70s—including guys, like Chuck Bowser from the Johnstown High School Class of 1961, who left the jobs they had in order to get into the mill. These were the people, including the women and greater numbers of blacks who entered the mills in the early 1970s, who were most hurt by the industry's crash in the 1980s. Many lost their jobs. Others, such as Albert Mikula, who graduated in 1959 but didn't get into the mill until 1964, earned less and worked under much harsher conditions after the crash.

But until the 1980s, the union's basic strategy worked pretty well. It did not resist new technology and even did some things to encourage it, and it tried to be reasonable when dealing with company efforts to improve productivity. On the other hand, it tried to preserve as many jobs as it could. Productivity was a tricky business for the union and the workforce. The union leadership accepted the economists' wisdom that increased wages and benefits could be gained and sustained only on the basis of productivity increases, but they tried to *regulate* those increases —restricting them sometimes, encouraging them others, depending on conditions in the industry. For management, productivity increases were an unmixed blessing, and it resented any and all resistance from the union and the workforce. For the workers, increasing productivity was both a blessing (a potential source of increased wages and benefits and better conditions) and a curse (a source of job loss and potentially worse conditions). The basic principle behind 2-B and most other union work rules was that simply speeding up a job, simply forcing people to work harder and faster, was forbidden, while other kinds of productivity improvements were negotiable.

Sticking Together to Preserve the Work

Though certain aspects of this policy could be implemented at the bargaining table and through the stewardship of the grievance-and-arbitration system, the main way productivity bargaining got done in steel was through the incentive system. Unlike assembly-line work, where management had much more control over exactly how the work was done, many of the tasks steelworkers did were beyond the reach of management control—and managers knew that.[21] Prior to the union, incentive systems were devised to rate particular tasks by the amount of time it *should* take to perform them. If a worker completed a given task in less than the rated time, he got paid for the full amount of time that had been rated. For example, if a job was rated as taking four hours to complete, but a worker actually completed the job in three, he got paid for four hours. Thus in an eight-hour day, a particularly skilled and diligent worker might produce (and be paid for) twelve hours of product—which was known as 150 percent of incentive. Across a week, it was not unusual for steelworkers to be paid 125 percent of incentive—that is, fifty hours' pay for forty hours' work.

Because they could get paid more, workers worked harder, faster, and more efficiently than they would have otherwise, and management got productivity increases, even though it had to pay a premium to get them. As long as incentive rates were reasonable, individual workers had substantial control over their work pace and exactly how they did their work, not to mention their income. Before the union, management would try to set the incentive rate as low as possible, and when a job got "mistimed" (for example, if somebody was making 150 percent of incentive), it would soon be "retimed." The union established certain rules at both ends of the process—rules about when and how a job could be timed by an IE and rules that made it a lot more difficult to "retime" a job once an IE had made a "mistake." But because the union closed off other avenues of easy productivity increase, the companies came to rely more and more on the incentive system. In 1947, a minority of steelworkers worked on incentive jobs, but by 1977, 85 percent of the workforce was covered by the system.[22]

The incentive system involved a cat-and-mouse game on both ends of the process, a game that predated the union. An IE first set the rate by repeatedly watching and timing workers doing a particular task. While being watched, workers, of course, worked more slowly and less efficiently. The IE knew this, and his job was to make an educated guess (complete with algebraic formulae) about how much the worker was "dogging" the job. On the other end, once a particular job had been timed and rated, everybody who did that job had to hide how quickly they could actually do it. The IE, for example, wanted to set the rate in such a way that an able worker working very hard could earn 135 percent of incentive.[23] Workers, on the other hand, wanted the rate set so the same able worker working very hard could earn 200 percent of incentive, but nobody would ever actually work hard enough to earn that much. You might work to earn 150 percent of incentive, but if you worked more than that, you were labelled an "incentive hog." Before the union, when jobs could be retimed at will, incentive hogs endangered the rate itself. After the union, incentive hogs were refusing to spread the work around, thereby endangering somebody's livelihood.

Both before and after the union, worker control of incentive output involved solidarity among particular groups of workers, and the success or failure of these workers varied greatly from plant to plant, department to department, and even task to task. "You can't make money on that job" meant the incentive rate had been set too low, and workers squawked for the job to be retimed. A "fair rate" meant that with average work effort, you could make a little money. A "sweet job" was one where you could make a lot of money without working very hard—and these were the ones that needed to be most diligently protected from incentive hogs. In good times, you could "push the incentive" and earn more money because everybody was fully employed. But in bad times, you were selfish if you didn't "preserve the time," because pushing the incentive put somebody out of work.

If the union leadership's job was to spread the work around by bargaining for more vacations and better pensions, the rank and file's job was to preserve and stretch out as much work as it could within the incentive system. My father delighted in instructing me and others in how this was done. Life in the mill, according to him, was a constant battle with management to determine how much work would be done in any given eight-hour period. According to him, "You don't have a chance unless everybody sticks together," and "everybody in the valley" would be affected by how many jobs you saved.

Preserving jobs was only one of the reasons for sticking together—the one most important to younger workers after the union had won seniority protection for the older ones. To older workers, a reasonable work pace across the life cycle was more important. Though most steel mill jobs by the 1950s did not involve heavy lifting and hauling (as they had in the nineteenth century), most still required substantial physical effort, and just being on your feet all day got more and more difficult as you got older. Jobs needed to be "pegged" so that the oldest workers could still do them—maybe not making a lot of money on incentive, but not being egregiously "out of line" either. Everybody had an interest in not being pushed so hard that they risked their health and safety, but this generally had different meanings for older and younger workers. The job of coordinating all this, according to my father, fell primarily on the middle-aged workers, of which he was then one. What he referred to as "young bucks" had to be educated, and "old-timers" had to be helped to maintain the average.

Telling me about the necessity of sticking together within the incentive system was one of the primary ways my father illustrated to me how selfishness was both morally wrong and practically unwise. You had to "look out for the other guy," not just to fulfill your Christian duty, but for your own good. It was flat out wrong just to look out for yourself, but if you did, your bad behavior would come back to bite you—in *this* world, long before you got to the next one, where you'd also pay a price. As my father painted it, preserving jobs seemed like one of the great moral issues of our time, pitting selfishness against solidarity—though selfishness, it turned out, was not and could never be in your self-interest.

The ability to stick together was something that had to be cultivated and enforced over time. If a younger worker was working too hard or too fast, my father would explain to him that he was working himself out of a job: "If you're going to bust the rate, we're going to have to bust it too, and guess who's going to end up on the street." Or if you were an older worker with solid seniority protection, you were "working some younger fella out of a job." According to his stories, my father would on occasion go up to an older incentive hog with a snapshot of a younger worker with his children, and then loudly explain how the hog was "taking the food right out of those kids' mouths." Sometimes, if an incentive hog resisted, this process could get nasty, as my father would mobilize his fellow workers to isolate, intimidate, and just generally harass the hog. Once what he euphemistically called a "conscience committee" (a small group of large men) went to a particularly recalcitrant hog's home, gently threatening physical violence, and according to my father, "We never had a problem from that guy again."

What I liked about these stories was how he always made sure they meshed with what we were taught in Sunday School—even where intimidation, including the threat of physical violence or other harm, was used. Such tactics were permissible if you had first attempted to persuade by appeals to morality and long-term self-interest. He liked to tell a story about a dedicated Christian who, after being struck in the face, turned his other cheek, as Jesus had instructed us to do, but when his antagonist struck him on the other cheek, the good Christian "kicked the crap out of him." When his antagonist challenged the good Christian, saying, "I thought you were supposed to turn the other cheek," the Christian replied, "Jesus said you only have to turn your cheek *once.*"

In the mill, the opposite danger of "working yourself out of a job" was "pricing yourself out of a job," and my uncles and other steelworker neighbors and friends spoke more strongly about that danger than my father ever did. But everybody recognized both dangers and the necessity for steering between them. "You've got to give 'em production," they would say, "you gotta let them make some money," or there might not be jobs for anybody. There were often detailed arguments among the men at family and other gatherings over where exactly the line was between working and pricing yourself out of a job, and though I could never follow the details, it was clear that these were serious matters, both for those speaking and "for the younger fellas"—that is, there were both practical and moral issues involved in getting as close to that line as possible.

The idea that steelworkers mindlessly sucked the companies dry, never thinking of their own or others' futures, is an illusion. If a *New York Times* reporter could have heard my father gloating about a particularly satisfying victory over an incentive hog (which, of course, my father would never have done in the presence of a reporter), he might have thought he had confirmation for that view. But if to take any one worker as representative would be a mistake, it would be an even greater mistake to rip one worker's view out of its group context. My father didn't expect that any one person could determine where the line was. He knew his war on incentive hogs and his jeremiads against working yourself out of a job needed to be balanced by the other danger; he recognized that others' fears that his approach would go too far were justified. But just as they appreciated his creativity and dedication in working his side of the road, he appreciated his best opponents' arguments and insights as well—not just the vague, unsupported invocation of "we can't be pricing ourselves out of a job," which always irritated him, but the well-reasoned, hard-argued cases for what the companies needed, cases for exactly where the line was in specific situations.

Many times one of these "where exactly is the line" arguments would end with somebody saying to my father something like, "If it was left up to you, the company'd never get a ton of steel out the door." He'd howl with laughter every time. Far from being an insult, this charge of extremism reflected an appreciation of his vital role in the group process, an appreciation of both the strength and the limits of his point of view. He laughed because he recognized himself in the caricature, and because he enjoyed being appreciated for what he was and no more. This group processing, with its easy recognition of the necessity of alternative principles and views balancing one's own, is something I miss in professional, middle-class life—particularly among middle-class men. As professionals we expect a lot more wisdom and perspicacity of ourselves as *individuals*, and we suffer more disappointments and resort to more denials as a result.

Note that none of this complicated group processing in the service of sticking together required Section 2-B or the union. Though they provided a protective framework for it and could enhance it in extreme cases, this kind of group solidarity in regulating production (what Frederick Taylor called "soldiering") predates the union in steel,[24] and it goes on today in non-union workplaces as well as union ones—though probably not with the explicitness engendered by an incentive system that was specifically designed to get workers competing against one another. If, as we'll see in the next chapter, the presence of a union actually *improves* productivity in most workplaces, one of the reasons may be that it allows this netherworld of industrial soldiering to emerge from the shop floor to trade higher and better production for higher wages, benefits, and more time off.

But no matter what the union did or didn't do, it couldn't have eliminated this process, just as the companies never could. Sticking together had deeper roots in working-class life than the union, which depended on it and merely extended it in a practically efficacious direction. Sticking together was one of the things that made growing up in the working class so secure and warm in those days. In contrast to the professional middle-class tendency to subject all personal relationships to a utilitarian calculus, a cost-benefit analysis, in working-class life there were both narrow and broad groups of people to which you belonged whether you liked it or not, and for the most part you could count on these people sticking with you. In your family, your circle of friends and neighbors, your schoolmates or workmates, there were people who were none too bright and others who were not strong or good-looking or articulate or even likable—and yet everybody belonged. It was just in the nature of things that everybody had some disability that needed to be allowed for and compensated for within the group; you recognized that "nobody's perfect" by themselves, and that's why you needed to complement and constrain one another. While all these interlocking groups imposed their own obligations and responsibilities, from which it was nearly impossible to withdraw, being able to take your presence in them for granted lent a stability and a calm, perhaps an integrity, to life that seems rare today. Though these group loyalties could lead to ethnic rivalries and racial intolerance, they also made middle-class solipsism, lonely individualism, and the vulnerabilities that come with them nearly impossible—and the union, implicitly if not always explicitly, worked to broaden group loyalties. If sticking together plays a smaller role in workplaces today, and in American life generally, that may have something to do with the decline of unions, which are virtually the only institutions in modern life that cannot be practically effective without it.

4

When the Wolf Finally Came

Union Power and the Demise of Steel

Management's assumption of sole responsibility for productive efficiency actually prevents the attainment of maximum output.

—Clinton Golden and Harold Ruttenberg, 1942

One of the problems in the mills is that no union man would trust any of the companies. To the average union man, they're always crying wolf. And the wolf finally came.

—Joe Odorcich, USWA vice president, 1983

Though it had been worried over for decades, the demise of the U.S. steel industry came quickly when it came—with a bang, not a whimper. From World War II until 1982 there had never been a net loss across the industry. 1973–75 had been banner years, comparable to the mid-'50s profit explosion, and 1979–81 were boom years as well. Then, in 1982–83, the industry lost more than $5 billion, followed by another $6 billion in losses in 1984–86. More than two dozen mills were closed and some 230,000 wage and salary jobs were permanently eliminated in the 1980s.

A blame game followed the industry's crash, and 1959 caught some of the blame.[1] Generally, however, the game relied on much broader story lines, covering the highly unionized manufacturing sector as a whole and questioning

118

the basic character of American work life. Beginning in the 1970s, middle-class opinion-makers began worrying about the American work ethic, and by the 1980s unions, particularly in manufacturing, were seen not only as throttling economic efficiency but also as undermining the basic morality of work.

In this context, the shakeout in steel seemed to have epic proportions—complete with a tragic fall from the 1940s, when steel tonnage was seen as a key measure of national wealth, military strength, and even character, to the 1980s, when the industry became a nineteenth-century relic in a new "postindustrial" age. Even though an air of post-industrial inevitability hung over all of the narrative frameworks, even though all of the players were aware that the crisis was international in scope and that the outrageously strong American dollar played a huge role in undermining the industry, most commentators labored to shame and blame.[2]

This was a mistake that still reverberates in our national culture today. Much of the industry's decline was inevitable, and if there's a culprit, it is the laissez-faire American business system, which requires much more of its steel industry and is much more careless of its manufacturing base than any other advanced capitalist nation.[3] In the 1980s, our system—now held up as a model for the world to emulate—meant that more of the industry and its jobs were lost and that almost all of the pain of that loss was targeted at steelworkers and their communities. But the act of fingering culprits—even if they're "systems"—in our shame-and-blame culture tends toward simplistic morality tales that demonize somebody: Management was complacent or weak-kneed; the union was narrow-minded and short-sighted; workers were soft, indolent, and greedy. In this mix, "productivity" somehow becomes a moral concept, not just an economic one, and we are urged to work harder and expect less for our effort. People say, "Look what happened to the steel industry," and without further explanation, we know that means buckle down, tighten your belt, and double your effort.

Within this puritanical story line, the union gets much more blame than it deserves. In this chapter I argue that the union got just about everything out of the steel industry that it could have, but that it should be allocated very little of the blame for its demise. On the productivity front, despite rigid union work rules, the overall effect of the union was probably positive. On the cost front, the union undoubtedly hurt the industry, but you have to remember that each penny per hour the union added to the companies' costs was a benefit to workers and their communities, and that those benefits had broad social and economic benefits for others—lots of others.

Did "Overmanning" Kill the Industry?

If you look at all the ways steelworkers had to restrict production and preserve jobs in 1959, you might wonder how the companies ever got a ton of steel out the door. But if you look at actual productivity numbers, the industry and its workforce compiled a pretty impressive record during the era of union power from 1942 to 1982—that is, from the first full year when the union was organized across the industry to the last year before the union granted massive concessions in national and local contracts amidst the most brutal downsizing an American industry has yet suffered.

When you look at the productivity numbers, it is difficult to see how there could have been *any* featherbedding in the industry during these years. But I guess that depends on how you define featherbedding—or the more current and somewhat sexist term "overmanning." Were steelworkers working as hard and as fast as they could every hour of every day? Of course not. But you've got to compare their production to some standard of what could have been produced—some level that would not have counted as featherbedding or overmanning. And there's the rub. During these years, American steelworkers increased their productivity steadily and dramatically, and into the early 1980s *nobody*, no steel industry anywhere else in the world, produced more tons per worker than the U.S. industry. Even when the U.S. industry (temporarily) lost its productivity supremacy in the early 1980s, U.S. steelworkers actually did better with inferior technology than would have been expected. U.S. steelworkers set the standard against which others were measured. If they were featherbedding, then the rest of the world's steelworkers were a lot better at it than they were.

Take a look at Table A, for example. In 1942 about 500,000 wage workers produced about 61 million tons of steel. In 1982 it took only some 200,000 to produce about the same amount. In that forty-year period, productivity in the American steel industry increased 163 percent, from 119 tons shipped per wage worker to 313 tons. That's a productivity growth rate of 2.45 percent year after year for four decades.

Table A. Employment and Productivity in the U.S. Steel Industry

Year	Total Steel Employees (thousands)	Wage Workers (thousands)	Wage Workers as % of Total	Net Tons Shipped (millions)	Annual Tons Shipped per Wage Worker
1940	511	454	89%	46	101
1941	571	507	89%	61	120
1942	583	511	88%	61	119
1943	564	487	86%	62	127
1944	534	457	86%	63	138
1945	515	439	85%	57	130
1946	538	458	85%	49	107
1947	574	489	85%	63	129
1948	592	503	85%	66	131
1949	581	492	85%	58	118
1950	592	503	85%	72	143
1951	638	540	85%	79	146
1952	622	519	83%	68	131
1953	650	544	84%	80	147
1954	582	478	82%	63	132
1955	625	519	83%	85	164
1956	621	509	82%	83	163
1957	624	508	81%	80	157
1958	523	412	79%	60	146
1959	515	400	78%	69	173
1960	572	450	79%	71	158
1961	523	406	78%	66	163
1962	521	403	77%	71	176
1963	520	406	78%	76	187
1964	554	435	79%	85	195
1965	584	459	79%	93	203
1966	576	447	78%	90	201
1967	555	424	76%	84	198
1968	552	421	76%	92	219
1969	544	415	76%	94	227
1970	531	403	76%	91	226
1971	487	367	75%	87	237
1972	478	364	76%	92	253
1973	509	393	77%	111	282
1974	512	393	77%	109	277
1975	457	340	74%	80	235
1976	454	339	75%	89	263
1977	452	337	75%	91	270
1978	449	339	76%	98	289
1979	453	342	75%	100	292
1980	399	291	73%	84	289
1981	391	286	73%	88	308
1982	289	198	69%	62	313
1983	243	169	70%	68	402
1984	236	171	72%	74	433

Source: American Iron and Steel Institute, *Annual Statistical Reports.*

This picture of productivity is much better than what you usually see for several reasons. One is that it relates total production not to total employees (wage *and* salary), but only to the wage workers—the ones protected by 2-B and the rest of the union contract. As Table A shows, the industry loaded up on salaried employees during this period, increasing their proportion of the total workforce from 12 percent in 1942 to 31 percent by 1982. This whopping increase may not have been the "management bloat" the Steelworkers Research Department often called it, but the sheer numbers hurt the industry's cost structure and productivity growth. What's more, the companies had all their traditional managerial discretion over this part of the workforce, and the Steelworkers had none at all.

But if, as you look over Table A, you're surprised and perplexed that that old dinosaur, the American steel industry, plagued by rigid union work rules, outdated technology, and befuddled management, should have achieved such results—your surprise is probably based on having heard years and years of statistics about *productivity growth rates* without ever having seen any numbers about *actual levels of productivity* (which "annual tons shipped per wage worker" represents). Most discussions of productivity in the period of deindustrialization were designed to show that our productivity was growing at a slower pace than that of other economies, such as Japan's and Germany's, and that unless we increased our rate of growth, they would soon catch up to and pass us. For this purpose, annual rates of productivity growth that *never* report absolute levels of productivity make a more dramatic statement. But they also distort the underlying reality.[4]

After World War II, all other countries' rates of growth in manufacturing productivity, but particularly Japan's and Germany's, were always dramatically higher than those of the United States, but that was because they were starting from a much smaller base, and thus their percentage increases were naturally going to be higher. In fact, the overall manufacturing productivity of the Japanese and the Germans, let alone anybody else, *never* caught up to the U.S. level. The closest Japan ever got, through 1989, was 80 percent, and the closest Germany ever got was just over 90 percent.[5] In steel, the U.S. industry (which *was* overtaken by Japan, for a while, in the 1980s) still enjoyed substantial productivity advantages as late as 1978—12 percent higher than Japan and 27 percent higher than Germany, not to mention France (39 percent) and Great Britain (63 percent).

Table B. International Comparisons of Steel Labor Productivity

Hours Worked per Net Ton at Actual Operating Rates

	1966	1969	1978	1982
United States	12.1	9.6	7.8	7.8
Japan	22.4	13.3	8.9	8.0
West Germany	22.5	11.6	10.7	11.1
France	23.8	17.6	12.8	10.8
United Kingdom	25.5	20.6	21.1	13.4

Sources: For 1969 and 1978, AISI, *Steel at the Crossroads: The American Steel Industry in the 1980s,* January 1980, 11. For 1966 and 1982, Garth L. Mangum and R. Scott McNabb, *The Rise, Fall, and Replacement of Industrywide Bargaining in the Basic Steel Industry* (M. E. Sharpe, 1997), 84.

These productivity advantages were actually pretty amazing, given the technological superiority of the Japanese and German industries at the time. Both had much higher percentages of the key Basic Oxygen Furnace (BOF) and continuous-casting technologies that had the highest productivity payoffs in those years. BOFs, for example, took one hour to produce the same amount of steel that an old Open Hearth Furnace needed twelve hours to produce; in 1981, when the U.S. industry still had overall productivity supremacy, only 61 percent of its steel was being made in BOFs, compared to 75 percent of Japanese and European steel. Likewise, only 21 percent of U.S. steel production was using continuous casting in 1981, versus 71 percent in Japan and 45 percent in Western Europe.[6]

These numbers can go against all the story lines the decline of steel conjures in American memory, but they're generally looked at only in ways that preserve those story lines. The numbers raise two questions that go in different directions. One is, How could the American industry have allowed itself to become so technologically inferior? This is the one that has gotten all the attention. The second question is, Given its technological inferiority, how could the American industry have been so productive for so long? This question is almost never asked.

In the early 1980s, as the industry was going down, the public discussion was all about its technological inferiority and the extent to which this resulted from what some saw as a "capital shortage."[7] When I found out then that, despite its technological disadvantage, the U.S. industry still had levels of productivity comparable to Japan's and Germany's and much higher than the spanking new industries in Korea and

Brazil, I began asking steel analysts how that could possibly be. The question didn't interest most of them, and they'd simply reply, "Well, it won't last." But Don Barnett, who was the head of the American Iron and Steel Institute's Research Department then, had puzzled over this a bit himself. Later he and Louis Schorsch would unravel part of the mystery with detailed productivity analyses of specific steel product lines,[8] but at the time he reluctantly offered, as best I can remember, "Well, I guess you'd have to say it's better operations management."

I didn't like this answer at first, and given the conventional wisdom about steel management then (and now), he didn't seem too comfortable with it, either. There just wasn't any other explanation for how the U.S. industry was still able to compete on the basis of productivity (though not, then, on the basis of cost). I then ventured my (humanities professor) explanation: "Couldn't operations management include what sociologists call the tacit skills workers have accumulated over the years, all the metal sense that's in steelworkers' hands and heads?" As I fumbled to explain what I was talking about, he cut me short: "Sure. There's no doubt about it. Why do you think U.S. Steel is still trying to hang on to Pittsburgh [a reference to U.S.S.'s decrepit Mon Valley Works, most of which was being shut down piece by piece]? But how are you going to measure something like that?"[9]

Measurable or not, metal sense was layered throughout the workforce of those twisting valleys in western Pennsylvania, and everybody close to the industry recognized it and valued it—all the intuitions and implicit ways of doing things, based on generations of fathers and sons cooking, shaping, and bending steel, the "things one knows but cannot tell" that Friedrich von Hayek called "tacit knowledge" and claimed no human society could function without. To include this kind of thing in a serious written analysis of the industry would have had about the same impact on an analyst's credibility as talking about UFOs and spiritual healing would, but steel towns were full of stories about steelmasters and steelworkers doing things that no one could explain. My favorite was about an old hand-mill at the Gautier Works of Bethlehem Steel in Johnstown. It made the steel runners for the wooden sleds (like Citizen Kane's "Rosebud") that kids still used in the '50s and '60s. The technology was pre-World War I stuff, a labor-intensive rolling mill where almost everything was done by hand, just like in the nineteenth century. No automated mill could compete with it for quality and production—and nobody could figure out why or how, not even the mill hands, who insisted they weren't doing anything special.

All of Johnstown took pride in that old hand-mill because of its connection with generations of happy children at Christmas, but most of the wonders of metal sense were much smaller and less public than that. Nonetheless, metal sense was there, and it counted for something, even among the number-crunchers and bean-counters at U.S. Steel, who saw their mission as making money, not steel.

Beyond metal sense, there's reason to think that labor-management relations made a substantial contribution to productivity growth during these years. First, steel management should be given some credit. Though the union had substantial powers to restrict managerial discretion, the companies still had a lot of discretion left. They still controlled investment and basic business strategies, and, as David J. McDonald pointed out at the time, they could get around 2-B and eliminate lots of jobs when they rehired workers after extended layoffs.[10] In addition, after 1959 the two sides made valiant efforts to cooperate. In the early '60s, for example, they established a series of company-level Human Relations Committees (HRCs) to engage in dialogue and to jointly solve some of the very substantial problems the industry faced. The HRCs didn't work in practice as well as their public-relations rhetoric about "industrial statesmanship" made people expect, and most of the cooperation achieved at the top never reached the shop floor. But after 1959, the will to compromise and "cut the difference," along with many genuine attempts to address the industry's problems, was predominant—particularly at the top of the union.[11]

Section 2-B had the best past-practice clause in U.S. labor history, and even though the companies couldn't find examples when they needed them, it would have been pretty amazing if in many particular situations 2-B didn't harm productivity. But it is highly unlikely that, all things considered, 2-B and its ilk damaged the industry's productivity in general. 2-B, like other union work rules, gave the workforce and the union a say in all sorts of decisions that management would sooner have made on its own—indeed, that management instinctively felt it had a right to make without "interference." But this interference probably helped rather than hurt productivity in the long run.

Union workplaces usually have higher levels of productivity than nonunion ones. The possible reasons for this are pretty complicated. Expensive wages and benefits give management more incentive to invest in new labor-saving technology, for example. And maybe unions can only be truly effective in workplaces that, for whatever reason, have high levels of productivity and the capacity to increase them.[12] But many students of workplace dynamics and organization find that the very existence of a union is a source of higher productivity: "Union workplaces possess—and nonunion workplaces lack—institutions for serious productivity bargaining."[13] As Maryellen Kelley and Bennett Harrison explain, "Unionization has long been viewed by industrial relations specialists . . . as a system of workplace governance that provides a counterbalance to managerial power. . . . As such, the 'contentiousness' and the give-and-take which characterize the relationship between managers and workers in a unionized workplace may actually be an advantage [in achieving productivity]."[14] Likewise, the stability and predictability of a rule-abiding workplace culture, typical of union workplaces, lead to lower quit rates and thus the retention of huge amounts of tacit knowledge in a workforce over time.[15]

The assertion that unions such as the United Steelworkers of America have a positive effect on productivity is based on empirical research and sophisticated multivariate regression analyses that try to determine the various weights of the many potential causes of any one effect. This kind of stuff does not stand up very well against anecdotes—particularly anecdotes that fit into blaming narratives that suit the moral imagination of the managing classes. But whatever the causes of its productivity supremacy, whatever impact the union had on productivity in steel, look at those numbers in Table A, compare them with Japan and Germany at the time or with anywhere else on this planet, and you can understand why the official U.S. government postmortem on the 1959 Steel Strike fearlessly announced in 1961, "It is a reasonable conclusion that the clause [2-B] does not protect widespread inefficiency because such inefficiency does not exist."[16]

On the other hand, looking at the productivity increases from 1942 to 1982, you might see why a guy like Johnny Metzgar might think he and his union had not done a very good job of preserving the work after all. But what happened in the decade after 1982—a 90 percent productivity increase in one decade—suggests that the union workforce had had its impact on protecting the slack. Though much of the gigantic boost in productivity after 1982 resulted from shutting down the oldest and least efficient facilities, a large piece of it undoubtedly resulted from the union's loss of leverage after the industry crashed.

A guy who graduated with my sister, for example, works in the same mill as my father and Uncle Stan did—though it is no longer owned by U.S. Steel. Before he was laid off in 1982, he ran one machine and tended a heat-treating oven at the same time. After being out of work for nearly three years, he returned to what was considered the same job, but now he had to run as many as five machines at a time while still tending the heat treater. He did that for three years until he finally bidded down to a lower-paying job in another part of the mill. "I just couldn't take it any more," he explained. "My nerves were shot." The job he has now is pretty stressful and speeded up too, but "my standards are lower than they used to be. Shit, sometimes I wonder if I wouldn't be happier delivering pizzas." Are the mills properly "manned" now? [17]

Was there "overmanning" in the mills during the years of union power? Of course there was. But nobody will ever be able to say how much, or how much damage, if any, it did to the industry and its prospects. If we could all agree what is a *fair* day's work, a *reasonable* work pace, and an *acceptable* level of risk to workers' health and safety, then we might be able to say the mills had X too many workers during the era of full union power. But we cannot agree on that. What we can know is that workers' sense of what is fair, reasonable, and acceptable had a greater role in determining outcomes during the period of union strength, and that now it does not. And the numbers show that, in general, workers did not abuse this power when they had it.

"At Least Two Sides to Every Story"

The idea that workers and their unions simply resist all technological and organizational change, fiercely holding on to every job regardless of the consequences, is a blaming myth. Despite the wealth of facts and figures to the contrary, the idea that unions are essentially about featherbedding persists—with the Steelworkers near the top of the list. For example, William Serrin, the *New York Times* labor reporter after A. H. Raskin retired, fingers "overmanning" as one of the primary causes of the industry's demise: "[T]he overmanning . . . had begun at the end of World War II and was steadily worsening. . . . The union was as undisciplined and uncreative, as locked into the corrupted system, as the corporation." [18] No evidence is cited. None is needed when an idea fits into a compelling story that shames and blames. But *to whom* is the story compelling?

You have to ask yourself why nearly everybody in America knows about the locomotive fireman with no fire to fuel but doesn't know a single story, fact, or figure about the millions of more typical instances in which union workers have accommodated new technology and other job-destroying productivity increases, even as they protected their own interests as best they could. You might think it has to do with ruling-class control of the media, and that certainly provides a context. But class relations in America are more complicated than that. The overmanning blaming myth is, as best as I can tell, a middle-class thing—one generated by college-educated, middle-class professionals in industrial engineering and other managerial occupations. Though middle-class social scientists (including management professors at some of our finest institutions of higher learning) have thoroughly debunked the myth with facts and figures, such evidence has little impact on the managerial outlook or on the journalists who rely on the wit and wisdom of middle managers, who seem such good sources because they are about equally disdainful of both top management and the union.

You cannot understand the lore about overmanning in the steel industry without cultivating some sympathy for the bitter sting managers feel when they cannot do whatever they want with "their" workforce. Consider the departmental superintendent, a contemporary of my father's perhaps, who had been brought up in the authoritarian tradition of scientific management, whose whole idea was to gain more and more control of the production process from a recalcitrant workforce that wanted to work as little as possible. To him 2-B was a final insult in a process of degradation of management authority that had inflicted one injury and insult after another "since the union." Today steel towns (and former steel towns) are full of these guys, living comfortably on pensions they would never have had without the union and more than willing to regale anybody who will listen with stories of the shop-floor wars they think they lost and that they're convinced "killed the industry." Journalists like John Strohmeyer and Bill Serrin have been more than willing to listen.

Often journalists *seem* to blame top management and the federal government about as much as they blame the union, but at base the bulk of the blame goes to the steelworkers. Strohmeyer captures this perfectly in the following formulation: "Many now say the steelworkers have gone too far, that their excessive gains are the cause of today's deep distress in the industry. However, that conclusion ignores two other factors. One was the surrenders and misjudgments made by those in an excessively compensated top management. The other was the continued interference of government, which all but forced those surrenders to labor and abetted many of those bad judgments."[19]

This formulation requires a little deconstruction for complete understanding. First, it is obligatory for journalists never to take sides between management and labor, so when blame is being passed out, they have to appear evenhanded. But misjudgments aside (that is, the companies' inadequate investment in new technology), this formulation puts the onus squarely on the steelworkers. Management's principal fault was in surrendering to them, and government shares in the blame because it pressured management to surrender.

This particular view refers directly to 1959 as the culmination of a series of strikes that the companies seemed always to lose and during which the government, whether Republican or Democrat, seemed always to end up on the union's side. The fact that the middle managers who talked with Strohmeyer in the mid-1980s remembered 1959 and attributed such significance to it is itself revealing. The strike was fought, in great measure, on their behalf, in an attempt to restore *their* power to manage. Nobody felt the impact of the full panoply of union work rules like the middle managers. For Roger Blough and R. Conrad Cooper, with their big salaries and cozy offices, the rules were mere abstractions, cost factors on a balance sheet. They didn't have to live day to day with workers and stewards who constantly bullied them with the rules. Cooper told *Fortune* in 1959 that 2-B was particularly demoralizing to "local plant supervision," and on their behalf, he vowed to do away with it once and for all.[20] In the end, after 116 days, he backed down, and then the "arrogance" of workers on the shop floor was even worse than it would have been had top management never declared war on 2-B in the first place. To the middle managers the mills were hopelessly overmanned, and after 1959 they were helpless to do much of anything about it. According to them, overmanning led to a general slackness and moral turpitude that pervaded all levels of the industry and eventually led to its demise.[21]

William Serrin took his bearings on what happened to the steel industry from the same kinds of people Strohmeyer did—a shop supervisor and a departmental superintendent at Homestead Works of U.S. Steel.[22] These two placed the situation in the kind of morality tale that appeals to journalists and their middle-class audiences: Complacency, petty graft, and overmanning led to the industry's demise. For dramatic effect, Serrin invents a level of apathy and complacence that never existed, claiming that "no one paid attention" in the late '50s and early '60s as thousands of jobs were lost, and that as the industry faced new competition from aluminum and plastics, "the men who ran the com-

panies and the union paid no attention to this, either."[23] Far from not
paying attention to these problems, the companies, the union, and the
steel-town press worried them to death.[24] There were even jokes on the
playground mocking our fathers when we drank soda pop from aluminum cans: "You're drinking your father's job away." We were actually
hurting the Glass Workers, not our fathers, but the animus against aluminum was so universal that details didn't matter.

In the 1980s there was a lot of steel-town lore about "the years of
complacency and excess," as if, had we all saved string and paper bags
(which many of our families did during some of these years), the industry could have been saved. Besides overmanning, Serrin thinks the decline of the steel industry was caused by pilfering from the mills ("I
don't think that anybody in the valley ever bought a bolt. If they needed
a bolt, they took a bolt") and by shop stewards misusing "lost time" for
union business (which the union, not the company, paid for). Serrin
once saw stewards at Homestead Local 1397 actually "sitting around
the union hall, feet on the desk, shooting the breeze" when they should
have been working.[25]

This kind of chicken-shit Presbyterianism is common among retired
supervisors and superintendents. Given the massive amounts of capital that flowed through the industry, this concern with petty "extrava-
gance" would simply be laughable if it didn't tap into a larger blaming
myth: If hard work and diligence are the keys to success, then if somebody or something fails, it must be because of laziness and complacency.

Such a sweeping moral judgment works only if one assumes that there
were no substantial and difficult, possibly impenetrable problems to deal
with—or if there were, that nobody was even paying attention to them.
There were such problems in the American steel industry, and a lot
of attention was paid to them. And while neither the companies nor
the steelworkers and their union handled them in exemplary fashion,
there is little reason to think that the outcome could have been substantially different if they had done everything exactly right—whatever
that might have meant. What is most maddening about the middle-
class moralists, with their "early to bed, early to rise" homilies, is that
they never engage the real problems that real historical actors faced—
even in retrospect, when it should be easier to decide what should have
been done. They just assume that nothing bad ever happens to human
beings if they're honest and forthright, hardworking and diligent. For
every human disaster, for all human suffering, there must be a culprit,

a perpetrator, aided by a general ethos of complacency and corruption. Nothing bad ever happens unless there is waste, fraud, and abuse, and merely denouncing it fulfills all one's moral obligations. This naive self-righteousness is probably all that's left of what used to be known as American innocence. But in my experience, this attitude is also peculiarly professional and middle class.

I got the other side of the story from my father and from interactions among him and other steelworkers at family and neighborhood gatherings. On this side of the story, the superintendents, IEs, and other middle managers were usually the villains, and despite all the ins and outs of the workplace rule of law, these villains still had plenty of power to boss you around. I want to make two points about this side of the story. One is that shop-floor wars were almost always about dignity and respect, and managers who granted some of those usually got cooperation from the workers, even from hard cases like Johnny Metzgar, one of whose mantras went something like this: "I want to cooperate, I want to be a 'partner in production,' but they won't let me. They just want to be boss." The other point is that this side of the story is more epistemologically complex than middle-class morality tales, because even know-it-alls like my father knew that "there are at least two sides to every story," and to a remarkable degree they lived that simple truth, day in and day out.

My father had a more complicated view of things than our shame-and-blame culture allows. First, bad things were a part of life; they were bound to happen, no matter what you did or didn't do. If you were smart, you "played the percentages," which meant that some percentage of the time you'd turn out to be wrong. Therefore, it was inevitable that you made mistakes, that you went too far and had to be corrected by others. It was impossible to be too hard on others' mistakes, or on your own, because people were simply reacting to someone or something based on their own (necessarily limited) experience and what they had learned from that experience. What mattered was diligence and perseverance—doing your best and hanging in there. He, like other adults in my neighborhood, liked to quote the sportswriter Grantland Rice's maxim: "It's not whether you win or lose, it's how you play the game." This maxim is interpreted differently today (when it seems to be about the importance of sportsmanship and is usually counterposed, pro or con, to today's much more popular notion that "winning is not the most important thing, it's the only thing"). In my neighborhood, Rice's maxim was about doing your job well, playing your role, holding up your end, pulling your own weight in a game that would be determined by such a complex confluence of actions and reactions that no one person or group could be held accountable for the outcome—while everybody was always completely responsible for how they did *their* job. It's what sportscasters today often call "a blue-collar attitude."

It's an attitude that recognizes that others are the stars and superstars, and that they have more responsibility for outcomes than you do. But precisely because your own role is necessarily more limited, performing it well is all the more important—*because* less is asked of you, you need to strive for steady perfection in achieving the more easily achievable. On the other hand, while your responsibility is less, it still exists, and nobody, not even the superstars, bears sole responsibility for the outcome. In labor-management relations, this attitude meant recognizing that you could never be in control, that the key decisions were made by others, that the ruling class, whether it had a right to or not, was going to rule. The most you could do was stick together with your own kind and apply your weight with as much shrewdness and cunning as you could muster to affect both the overall outcome and the ways that outcome affected you and yours. If you did that and lost, it was both sad and painful, but you had at least done your job.

The moral complexity and potential integrity of this view of things was often illustrated in my father's tales of his battles with industrial engineers. He respected the IEs and their education, and he never failed to mention that he was "just a mill hand" and that in a perfect world, those with superior knowledge and education should be allowed to run things. And even though their basic purpose was to force and entice him to work harder and faster, he didn't object to what they were doing —they had a job to do, just like he did. The basic contest between them was necessary and inevitable, part of the larger contest between workers and management to determine what constituted a fair day's work. Left to themselves, workers wouldn't work as hard, as fast, or as well as they should. But left to *itself*, management would use up workers like they were so many spare parts. But together, my father running his machine and the IE watching and timing, they engaged in a contest of wits that was, according to him, "about as good a way as any" to determine a fair day's work for a fair day's pay.

What he objected to, and what never ceased to amaze and to hurt him, was management's attitude. The IEs he confronted in setting incentive rates were almost always young men fresh out of college, often engaged in their first real jobs. They almost always assumed that all he wanted to do was slack off and do as little work as possible and that, despite his experience, he didn't know *anything* about machining steel. Of course, my father *wanted* the IE to underestimate his abilities—that's what the whole game was about—and he could play the "I'm just a mill hand" gambit to the hilt. The common IE assumption that he was both lazy and incompetent made it easier for him to jack up the incentive rate. But that assumption hurt and humiliated him every time. He never got used to it. Even after retiring, he could tell some of these stories with the same hurt and anger he must have felt but could not express at the time.

But according to him, the most frustrating, perplexing, and sad thing about this situation was that all he could do was his job—which in this instance was to get the rate set as high as possible—and that his opponent's being so outmatched by him meant the outcome was likely to be bad for everybody. That is, the adversarial system in which he believed wholeheartedly required a rough equality of power to work effectively. Though he wanted to win his contest of wits with the IE, he knew that going too far was bad for business, that he needed strong opposition to balance his own strength, to counter and correct his own direction. It wasn't fair, to his way of looking at things, to put all the responsibility for setting the rate on him—only a fair contest of wits could arrive at a fair result. Sometimes he'd express remorse for having jacked up a rate out of proportion to anything close to being fair and reasonable, but he'd point out that it was difficult to do a good job without an adequate counterweight. Usually, he found it difficult to blame the IEs too much —after all, most of them were "just kids." He just wondered what those colleges were teaching them and what management was thinking when they sent these mere boys to insult him, goading him to jack up the rates: "The whole system was cockeyed. It's a wonder the company ever made any money on it."

In such a moral universe, one that is both more narrow and more complex than middle-class universalism, the middle managers have to share some of the blame for not doing *their* job well. Those who insisted on being boss got less, not more, out of the workforce. Those who underestimated the opposition to an insulting degree got more opposition. Those who insisted on controlling everything lost more and more control, sometimes without even knowing it. But, if the numbers are to be believed, across all the companies and their various plants, through millions of boss-and-worker confrontations over those forty years, the clash of opposing principles produced results that neither side needs to be ashamed of.

In almost every conversation about anything, my father would at some point insert the maxim, "There are at least two sides to every story," and everybody would agree. He really believed that, and as fierce as he could be in telling his side of the story, he (almost) never failed to recognize that his own point of view was limited in principle. Because he was so strong and insistent in pushing his own view, he needed to soften his assertions by beginning sentences with qualifications like, "I may not be seeing something, but . . . ," or "I could be wrong, but. . . ." Others who were usually less confident in the essential rightness of their view of things, including Mom and Uncle Stan, would recognize the same principle by beginning sentences with, "The way I see it is . . . " and "I don't know, but I just sort of feel like. . . ." In my family, there was a religious grounding to this basic epistemological relativism, but I suspect it is a general characteristic of working-class thought, regardless of religious outlook.

In my family, God worked in mysterious ways, and only He could see things as they really were. Human beings, no matter how "big" they were (a notion referring indiscriminately to the educated, the monied, and the powerful), are "not given to see" what only the Lord can know. Even the revealed truth of the Bible required human interpretation, and we recognized that "your interpretation might be different from mine." For all of us, even my father, this way of looking at things led to a fundamental deference to those who *should* know better than us—the educated and those in authority, who by virtue of their wider range of responsibility saw things and knew things that we could not see and know. But at the same time (and with so little sense of contradiction that this still amazes me), within that deference lay a solid assurance that *in principle* no one point of view, no one interpretation, could be *the* right one. Thus, no matter how "big" you were, yours was only one side of the story. Even without this religious grounding, working-class thought operates in a universe where it recognizes its general inferiority in knowledge without ever relinquishing the validity of its own point of view. Such an attitude is nearly impossible for the educated, middle-class professional who, while often deferring to another professional's expertise in one narrow area, is much more committed to the notion that *the* truth can be found, *the* right decision can be made, and is therefore much less likely to recognize the limits of his or her own point of view.

For my father, the adversarial concept of unionism in the American system of collective bargaining enhanced this view of things. The foreman or the industrial engineer had his job to do, his side of the story. You judged these people not on whether they agreed with you or not—such a thing was impossible—but on their ability to see your side of things, to recognize it and take it into account. When they did that, they generally got production.

Did the Steelworkers' Standard of Living Wreck the Industry?

In the summer and fall of 1982, I was part of a group of academics and dissident Steelworkers in the Chicago area who mounted a campaign against concessions in the Basic Steel Contract—$2 billion worth of concessions that eventually were granted by the union in March 1983 and that, viewed in retrospect, marked the end of the era of union power. When we gathered right after the defeat to discuss what to do next, I was surprised when one of the most intense and militant of the Steelworkers greeted everybody with a joke: "Well, goddamn, we lost United Nations Day!"

Most of us hadn't known there was a United Nations Day, let alone that it had been an official holiday for steelworkers. Losing it had been the least significant of the concessions, and for that reason, opening a post mortem of the concessions fight by sarcastically lamenting its loss pointed to a couple of important truths. First, it recognized that the steelworkers had indeed overdone it—that during their period of power, they had won some things that were not absolutely essential to a decent way of life. Second, it recognized a defeat, indeed a corruption, in the union's mission of spreading the work around—a mission that had begun with a demand for a thirty-two-hour workweek in the early 1960s and that had then been diverted to an incremental strategy of adding more vacations and holidays with each new contract. This goal had been corrupted because many workers would sooner work the holidays (and even portions of their vacations, particularly the thirteen-week "sabbatical") at double-time pay than take the time off and open up work for others. Nobody took U.N. Day off—if anything, they used their seniority to make sure they got scheduled for it.

By 1982 there were "excesses" in the Basic Steel Contract. The degree of excess and the time when it began are open to different judgments based on what people consider excessive. Certainly, as Mark McColloch has shown, there was little excess in 1959 or for many years after.[26] But 1959 may deserve some blame for fixing basic power relationships in ways that, when the industry made a key strategic error in the early 1970s, deepened the magnitude of that error.

The logic of this analysis goes like this.[27] Looking back with knowledge of the political and economic environment of the closing decades of the century, we can see that the steel companies should probably have begun a systematic downsizing in the early 1970s, gradually ceding market share to minimills and imports and concentrating their capital investments on creating a few good mills with world-class technology. Instead, steel management read the boom of the late '60s and early '70s as a new take-off period of global growth in demand for steel.[28] Thus, the companies adopted long-term investment strategies of saving and "rounding out" existing mills—strategies of incrementally replacing only the least productive pieces of each mill with the latest in technology. Even though this would result in every mill having discontinuities between old and new technology for a considerable period, it was the only way the industry could afford to maintain its size while remaining reasonably competitive in an expanding global marketplace. Though the companies needed all the money they could get to invest in rounding out their mills as quickly as possible, they also needed stability in their relation to the workforce as they did so; indeed, they needed the ingenuity of workers to integrate the old with the new. 1959 had definitively established that the steelworkers could not simply be ordered to cooperate. Stable, cooperative labor relations would have to be paid for, and in the early '70s the companies locked themselves into a wage-and-benefits arrangement that would eventually price them out of the market when the Great Recession of the early '80s required the downsizing of steel industries all over the world.

In hindsight, this explanation makes a great deal of sense. If the companies had foreseen just how deep and damaging the recession was going to be, they could have concentrated rather than dispersed their capital investments, and they probably would have ended up with more mills and more profits than they've had since 1981. Had steelworkers been able to foresee the future, they might have induced the companies to pursue a modified round-out strategy rather than a full-scale downsizing by moderating their wage-and-benefit improvements and thereby providing more capital to round out existing mills more quickly. Had they done so, there might be more steelworkers making higher wages today.

Even with perfect foresight, however, it is hard to imagine either the companies or the union pursuing these options without a more active government than the one we have had. In other countries, the government would have played a role in brokering such a deal, providing investment incentives to speed up the rounding-out process and a predictable level of protection from imports until it was completed. Likewise, only the government, by exchanging its assistance and protection, could have ensured that the companies would not use whatever largesse they got from government and union to exit from the industry and pursue higher rates of profit elsewhere. Such an arrangement, feasible in the abstract, was unimaginable in the early '70s—and became even less so in the '80s.[29]

Even in hindsight, then, it's hard to imagine how there could have been a happier outcome for steelworkers and their communities. There was no government-industry-labor system within which the union could have moderated its wage-and-benefit demands in the interests of preserving more of the industry for posterity. Though the union had proposed such systems in the '40s and again in the early '60s, neither the companies nor the government was interested. Thus in the early '70s, as the companies were committing to their round-out strategy and as profits were rolling in, the union sought to extract as much of those profits as it could, and because the companies still feared the steelworkers' ability to shut the industry down with a nationwide strike, the union was able to continue to improve steelworkers' standard of living for another decade.

Whatever excesses were present in the Basic Steel Contract by 1982 occurred after the 1971 contract restored solid cost-of-living (COLA) protection and after the 1973 agreement guaranteed real wage increases in return for a no-strike pledge. Though these agreements gave the companies the stability they needed during their rounding-out process, they proved inordinately expensive in the inflationary '70s. Though the biggest jump in steelworkers' *real* wages took place between 1952 and

1963 (a 45 percent increase in money wages and a 182 percent improvement in the real value of benefits), the biggest jump in the companies' compensation costs occurred in the '70s—increases of 171 percent in wages and 577 percent in the cost of benefits. The mysteries of real and nominal wages in a highly inflationary environment can be pretty confusing here, but a clear class perspective can help us disentangle what happened in the '70s.

What matters to employees is their real wages, the spending power of their money in relation to the cost of living. What matters to employers is their costs, regardless of what is happening to the cost of living. While steelworkers' real hourly wages increased only 17.6 percent from 1972 to 1982 (less than 2 percent a year), their nominal hourly wage (what the employer actually pays, which is not adjusted for inflation) increased from $5.15 to $13.96. Thus, while achieving a modest increase in their standard of living, the steelworkers imposed a huge increase in their employers' costs. The same phenomenon is seen in the benefit improvements the steelworkers won in the '70s (the steadily improved pensions, health insurance, and SUB; the dental plan begun in 1974; the Employment and Income Security Program of 1977; the improvements in sickness and accident and life insurance), except that the benefit improvements were much more substantial.[30]

By 1982 or 1983, it became clear how terribly out of whack this cost structure was in a world glutted with steelmaking capacity. In response, the companies slashed and burned. They closed plants and forced union concessions; they eliminated more than 200,000 jobs; some tried to renege on retirees' health insurance; others declared bankruptcy, dumping pension costs on the federal government—and still they lost money, more than $11 billion from 1982 through 1986. This disaster led to other disasters. In steel towns, department stores and auto dealerships closed; cops and firefighters lost their jobs; everything was cut back and downsized, and quickly. Unemployment in Johnstown led the nation in 1983 at 25 percent.

Could the Steelworkers have avoided these disasters? Though they might have fought harder for government involvement in the late '70s, and though they might have embraced worker ownership and worker-community initiatives earlier than they did (in 1984), these would have been salvage operations at best. By 1982, the industry was simply too large—and too much of it was too old—to sustain itself in a global marketplace. Indeed, some serious steel analysts have proposed that the union was engaged in an "endgame strategy" in the '70s, extracting what economists call quasi-rents by requiring the companies to provide as many lifeboats as it could for the day when the ship finally sank.[31] Though, given the public record, it is unlikely the union leadership ever consciously adopted a resolute endgame strategy, from the mid '50s forward they had pretty much always assumed that there would be a long-term decline in steel employment (which there was, regardless of the industry's production or profits) and that the union's job was to take as many people out of the mills as it could through pensions (and holidays and vacations) rather than through layoffs and reduced opportunities for young people. Though there were not enough lifeboats for everybody who was sinking in the 1980s, there were quite a few. By the 1990s, the steel industry supported at least four retirees for every currently employed worker—that's more than 400,000 people.[32] Conscious strategy or not, these are some substantial quasi-rents that had positive benefits for many more than 400,000 former steel industry employees. Had the Steelworkers moderated their demands in the 1970s, there would have been far fewer lifeboats.

But let's broaden this picture. The steel industry had its special problems. Even if Steelworkers had been able to save a larger slice of the industry by moderating their wage-and-benefit improvements earlier, this would not have helped other manufacturing workers survive the 1980s. What if all the manufacturing unions had frozen their standards of living in 1973, refusing to improve their real wages and benefits after that? Things had reached a pretty good level by then, and real wages for most workers now are actually lower than they were then. What if all the manufacturing unions had frozen their real wages back then? Wouldn't we all be a lot better off today?

Perhaps there is some calculus that could determine (not ahead of time, but at least in retrospect) exactly where the steelworkers and other union manufacturing workers crossed the line and became "excessive" —a point on a graph where they could be said to have priced themselves out of a job. But even if there were, it is highly unlikely that we all would be better off today. Any such calculus would have to take into account the broadly distributed benefits of the costs that steelworkers and other union workers imposed on their employers. When you do that, the overall picture is rather different.

For the steelworkers themselves, you have to remember that the improvements of the 1970s have allowed many workers (and managers too) to retire early, with their houses paid for and their health insurance intact. Those pension checks get spent on heat and light, groceries, hardware and lawn mowers; they get spent on new cars, restaurant meals, and vacations in Arizona. And a lot of these retirees even have savings that end up being invested in new plants and equipment, in computer companies and hotel chains. Take all that away, or reduce it substantially, and a lot more than 400,000 people would be harmed. Subtract the autoworkers, rubber workers, electrical workers, and all the other union retirees living well off the pensions they extracted from their employers in the good times, and you may get a sense of what a hole there would be in our economy without them and their pensions.

The Steelworkers and other unions still had the power in the 1970s to extract increased wages and benefits from their employers. The exercise of that power may have had some negative consequences by undermining the competitiveness of some companies as we moved into a global economy. But those same wages and benefits spurred other economic activities without which we'd all be a lot worse off today. All through the postwar period, for example, union health benefits constantly improved after the Steelworkers won a breakthrough in principle in 1949. These benefits fueled what is now our major "industry" —health care. In 1950, there were almost 600,000 steel industry employees (wage and salary) covered by the new benefit; at that time there were about the same number of nurses and doctors—375,000 registered nurses and 203,000 doctors. By 1990, when there were only 164,000 steel employees left, there were more than 1.7 million nurses and 646,000 doctors. The greatest growth in these well-paying occupations—far outstripping the growth in overall population—occurred after 1970.[33] Nor were nurses and doctors engaged in "make work." The resources that unions forced companies to pour into health care have had dramatic results—infant mortality, for example, was reduced by one-third from 1950 to 1970 and then cut in half again from 1970 to 1990.[34]

Today, in our employer-dominated political culture, we are focused exclusively on the costs of things—the costs of all those doctors and nurses, of the federal budget with all its welfare expenditures, of what it takes to educate and care for children. In the immediate postwar period, the period of greatest union power and influence, the focus was exactly the opposite—on the benefits of those costs, on jobs and spending power. Look at all those opportunities, they reasoned then, for people to improve themselves and others—as doctors and nurses, as government employees, teachers, and child-care workers. Are any of them paid too much? Well, that's okay, because they'll spend that money to stimulate other activity that creates even more jobs, more opportunities, more spending power.

The point here is that every cost has benefits and vice versa. To focus on one to the exclusion of the other distorts the reality, but you can make yourself dizzy trying to understand all the complex interactions. The union-enforced focus on jobs and spending power during the quarter century after World War II was much too simple—it contributed to inflation and the problems inflation causes, and it led to some costs getting out of control. But it also led to prosperity and dramatically improved standards of living for almost everybody. Though some cost-cutting, downsizing, and restructuring were probably in order for a while, the current simple-minded, mean-spirited dedication to cutting costs is leading to exactly from whence my parents' generation came. Unless we can keep everything—all the costs and all the benefits—in mind at once, which is probably impossible even for computers, we need pretty soon to shift back to that earlier focus. Remembering unions and the role they played in creating the glory days of postwar prosperity is essential to recovering that focus.

Unions and Postwar Prosperity

With each passing year, there are fewer people who can remember the Great Depression and the underconsumptionist economic theory that came out of that experience, that explained it, and that gave so many working people an ideological framework within which to resolve "never again." My father was the chief spokesman for that theory in my family and neighborhood, but even without his explanations and invocations (many of which, I found out later, had come straight out of the pages of *Steelabor*), we all understood it pretty good.

"Underconsumptionism" blamed the Great Depression on an inequitable distribution of wealth: The bottom 80 percent of our society did not have enough money, enough spending power, to buy all the things the economy could produce. Big corporations and rich people had lots of money, but since all their consumption needs were met, they had nothing to spend it on. Ordinarily, rich folks would invest their excess in new products and companies in order to make more money, but because so few people could afford to buy anything, there weren't enough profitable investment opportunities to absorb all that money. Thus, as the poor got poorer, the rich got *less* rich, and everybody was worse off than before. Given this explanation, underconsumptionism provided a clear direction for a solution: Take some of that unproductive money from the rich and give it to the poor and working masses, increasing their ability to consume what the economy could produce, and everything would get rolling again. In the long run, everybody would benefit, even the rich—because increasing workers' spending power would increase rich folks' investment opportunities and therefore their riches.

This was not anything like Marxism or socialism because it didn't aim to eliminate the rich, or even to expropriate their riches. Indeed, in the long run, it would make them richer. In the short run, however, it required some of their money. Some big corporations and rich people saw the logic of this, but most were penny wise and pound foolish. Taking money from the rich was a tricky business because they were not only rich, but they also were powerful. The New Deal revolutionized American politics and government because it figured out a whole bunch of ways to redistribute wealth without pissing off the rich too much.

One way—the way that subsequently got the bulk of the attention—was through government tax and spending policy, what became after the Great Depression a whole new academic discipline, macroeconomics. The federal government could increase workers' spending power by taxing them less and the rich more. It could also borrow from the rich, running budget deficits, and use that money to create jobs (public works projects and national defense) or make "transfer payments" to the poor (welfare and unemployment compensation, for example). The whole idea was not necessarily to achieve a more fair or equitable distribution of wealth, but purely and simply *to increase or maintain the spending power of the vast majority of the population in order to keep the economy going.* During World War II, the government borrowed from the rich big time, running huge deficits; the economy bloomed and blossomed, and everybody was happy, except the Germans and the Japanese. Though taxing the rich played a role in this prosperity, in the long run borrowing from them became the preferred way to get their money into productive uses.

But macroeconomics took a while to affect government fiscal policy fully after World War II. President Eisenhower was famous for resisting the macroeconomic wisdom on budget deficits, even though he and the Republican economists around him accepted many macroeconomic prescriptions.[35] Prior to World War II, the New Deal had installed other ways to maintain and increase worker spending power. After a lot of trial-and-error experimenting in the early 1930s, the New Deal brain-trusters came up with a variety of policies that intervened in the free market to manipulate the laws of supply and demand. Farm policy manipulated supplies and prices to make sure farming was a profitable activity that produced enough food for everyone. Federal Deposit Insurance protected against bank panics and thereby loosened up credit —and along with other policies, such as federally guaranteed home loans, eventually opened up a whole new world of spending power: consumer debt. Hundreds, maybe thousands of projects and policies were geared to ward off the problem of underconsumption by maintaining or increasing worker spending power.

At the very heart of the New Deal solution to underconsumption, however, was its labor policy—a sophisticated web of laws that systematically aimed to increase wages and standards of living over the long haul. The National Labor Relations Act (NLRA, 1935) was the most important part of the New Deal labor policy, but it was only one part; it merely gave unions some basic rights and set up some procedures for enforcing those rights. The professional, middle-class brain-trusters who designed the NLRA realized that in order for unions to steadily improve wages and standards, other policies were needed *to limit the overall supply of available labor*.[36] So long as there were millions of unemployed willing to work for just about any wage, under any sort of conditions, the formal rights and procedures of the NLRA would have little impact. New Deal policies for creating jobs through public works, war, and anything else that employed people reduced the supply of available labor, but more was needed, and on a more permanent basis. Only in tight labor markets—where the supply of labor was about the same as the demand—would workers, even with unions, be able to increase their wages and standards. The other parts of the New Deal labor policy—the Fair Labor Standards Act (FLSA, 1938) and the Social Security Act (SSA, 1935)—sought to get people out of the labor market, or at least to give them incentives not to rush into it.

The FLSA set a federal minimum wage that directly propped up spending power, but it also required employers to pay time and a half for each hour of labor over forty hours a week, thus giving employers a financial incentive to hire more workers rather than to pay current workers the premium for overtime. After the virtual full employment of World War II, the FLSA—enhanced and supplemented by the political and economic action of unions—established the two-day weekend as a fixture of American life. As a historian of the weekend explains, "Shorter hours came to be widely regarded as a remedy for unemployment—people would work less, but more people would have jobs."[37] Shorter hours also tightened labor markets and thereby helped improve wages and conditions.

The Social Security Act is now generally seen as simply a humanitarian policy that helps old people. But in the depression it was viewed more broadly as a whole bunch of ways to reduce the available supply of labor by increasing nonworkers' spending power. The Social Security retirement benefit, for example, was seen as benefiting not just the retiree, but all other workers. By inducing older workers to retire, it would open up jobs for younger people, and as young people took these jobs, the available supply of labor would be reduced, which would raise wages and living standards, which would stimulate more economic activity and keep the economy going.

Other parts of the Social Security Act—a national system of Unemployment Compensation (UC) and what was until recently Aid to Families with Dependent Children (AFDC)—had similar effects. They provided enough income to the unemployed and to single mothers with children to at least temporarily dissuade many potential workers from entering the labor force at any wage or under any condition. This helped existing workers maintain and even improve their wages and conditions—particularly since, as the macroeconomists pointed out, UC and AFDC acted as "automatic economic stabilizers" that increased government spending and consumer spending power at exactly the right times: when the economy was in recession.

By tightening labor markets, FLSA and SSA provided a basic foundation upon which unions could build. But without strong unions, this foundation would have remained an unused hole in the ground. The NLRA was unique in fostering a nongovernmental institution that the brain-trusters figured would by its very nature provide both the economic and the political support for steadily improving worker spending power over the long haul. This policy succeeded brilliantly, because after their initial hopes for a more expansive welfare state were dashed, the CIO unions (and some AFL ones, too) worked steadfastly to improve the details of the welfare state they had.

At the end of World War II, for example, the Social Security system was actually pretty much of a hoax. The retirement benefit was not nearly big enough to allow most of those eligible to even think about retiring. Likewise, the initial pensions that unions won in the late 1940s were pittances—victories in principle that had no immediate effect, as one pittance added to another was still a pittance. But throughout the '50s, unions worked the system—bargaining one by one with employers, winning wages and benefits that had spillover effects on nonunion employers, and providing the political backbone in the U.S. Congress and in numerous leading states for incrementally improving the details of America's anemic welfare state. Moving back and forth between bargaining and politics, the unions agitated, educated, struck, bargained, and lobbied until they eventually got pensions that actually made retirement possible.[38]

The American labor movement is often criticized for its incrementalism, but the New Deal system would have withered and died without it. Without the postwar unions' attention to details, we might never have gained either weekends or retirement. In 1950, for example, fewer than 2 million workers were retired on Social Security, but by 1960 more than 10 million were. Those 8 million additional retirees helped spread the work around to a younger generation, who had more work, steadier work, and better wages, benefits, and working conditions because the retirees were out of the workforce but still had spending power. Likewise, UC and AFDC provided enough income to dissuade many potential workers from entering the labor force at any wage or under any condition; in 1960, this meant that some 3 million potential workers were not completely desperate to get a job.[39]

Unions provided the strongest and most reliable political support for growing the American welfare state. Through collective bargaining, unions both directly and indirectly increased spending power and decreased working time. And most nonunion companies had to mimic these improvements in order to retain a stable workforce. Tight labor markets strengthened unions, and strong unions increased worker spending power and further tightened labor markets. It was, and still is in its much weakened form, a marvelous system that ought to get a lot more credit for postwar prosperity than it usually does.

As a Steelworker shop steward, my father understood all these complicated interactions, and he enjoyed explaining them to workmates and neighbors. I remember him mercilessly badgering our state representative, Cecil, a small businessman who was a member of our church, to vote for improvements in Pennsylvania's unemployment compensation system (sometimes to increase benefits, sometimes to expand eligibility). In the receiving line at church, at Little League baseball games, or while shopping at Bantley's Hardware, always in an embarrassingly loud voice that attracted everybody's attention, he'd explain how Cecil's vote affected everybody, not just the guys who received UC.

Johnny Metzgar was one of thousands (millions, maybe) who was paying attention to the details in those days and who carried a union-inspired spending-power ideology, a form of social Keynesianism, from his workplace to his community. Through people like him, the labor movement spread that version of how the world works into lots of hearts and minds. It's hard for me to imagine this didn't make a difference in how the postwar world actually worked.

People who study these things pretty much agree that the quarter century following World War II—what is known, sometimes snidely, sometimes wistfully, as postwar prosperity—was an extraordinary time, not just in the United States, but in world history. Economists Barry and Irving Bluestone, for example, call it the Glory Days, "the most prosperous quarter-century in American history."[40] British historian Eric Hobsbawm calls it a Golden Age that "achieved the most dramatic, rapid and profound revolution in human affairs of which history has record."[41] But there is little agreement about what caused this extraordinary period of economic growth and improved standards of living. Most interpretations point to particular one-time circumstances following the war—such as huge savings and pent-up demand for consumer products in the United States, or all the rebuilding that was necessary in Europe and Asia. Political scientists and economists often debate the role of defense spending, balanced and unbalanced budgets, and other aspects of fiscal and monetary policy from 1945 to 1970. But all these explanations usually hide the long arm of causation by simply assuming the presence of the New Deal system described above, without granting it any credit for postwar results.

The postwar period was really the first true test of that system—by which I mean the full panoply of ways the federal government consistently interfered in the workings of the free market, from farm policy and FDIC to the NLRA-FLSA-SSA labor policy and lots of other things. Though the laws that first established this system were almost all passed in the 1930s, they had little impact in the late depression years. And it's difficult to determine their impact during the war, because the war and war policies overwhelmed all other causal forces and circumstances. But if you think about it, it's hard to imagine any glory days or golden ages without this system having been firmly in place and working its will during those twenty-five years, regardless of who was in office or what their policies were. And at the heart of this sytem were labor unions like the United Steelworkers of America.

Imagine, for example, if the strike wave of 1945–46 had turned out differently—if autoworkers, steelworkers, and others had fallen into disarray, taken to fighting among themselves, with scabs and militants battling each other on picket lines and eventually being forced back to work with their organizations in tatters. Many labor leaders feared such a thing at the time because that's what had happened after World War I, and the labor movement of the late 1940s was not unfamiliar with workers fighting among themselves (blacks and whites, Catholics and Commies, skilled and unskilled). A decimated labor movement during those years would have put great parts of the New Deal system in jeopardy. And without an engine to drive it forward, constantly and consistently improving the details, working the various mechanisms for incremental enhancements, that system would have remained a structure without substance, a series of pittances with little capacity for increasing worker spending power. Such a thing is hard to imagine, but who would argue now that without the accumulation of those 10 million Social Security retirees and 3 million adult recipients of UC and AFDC, we'd have made it to 1960 as an "affluent society"? Likewise, an economy without the real wage increases, health insurance, and pensions the unions won and others copied—one without all that increase in the spending power of the bottom 80 percent—is very likely one that would have sunk back into depression.

Nor were developments in the United States during these years unimportant for, or untypical of, the rest of the world. In the mid-'50s we comprised 6 percent of the world's population, but we both produced and consumed about one-third of all the goods and services in the world; "three-fourths of all the cars and appliances on earth were consumed in the United States."[42] The world needed our productive capacity in those initial postwar years, but it needed our spending power even more. It is no exaggeration to say that the U.S. economy was the very engine of the world economy then—a world economy that, once it got moving on its own, quadrupled its output of manufactures, increased world trade in manufactured products tenfold, and doubled and tripled its food supplies from the early 1950s to the early 1970s.[43] Though all these goods were terribly maldistributed around the world and among social and economic classes, for several decades the material conditions of life improved for almost everyone, almost everywhere.

All this should be taken into account when assessing how the Steelworkers did during their period of power—when passing out shame and blame. The billions of dollars they extracted from the companies rippled through the postwar economy, doing much more good than harm. Earlier moderation in improving their standard of living might have helped preserve a somewhat larger slice of the industry, but not without a price in doctors and nurses, retirement communities, and even investment opportunities. Now that unions are weak and real wages are down, it's worth asking who exactly is better for that. For most workers, life is worse, and prospects seem a thing of the past.

Irene and Johnny Metzgar with
daughter, Marion, in 1941

Johnny Metzgar and family
in 1945

Johnny Metzgar on strike in 1959

Johnny Metzgar in the
mill shortly before he retired
in 1969

Johnny, Jack and
Judd Metzgar shortly before
Johnny died in 1981

Johnstown, Pennsylvania, and Johnstown Plant of Bethlehem Steel, in early 1960s

First day of 1959 strike at Homestead Works, U.S. Steel, Homestead, Pennsylvania. Photo Associates. Courtesy of Historical Collections and Labor Archives, Pennsylvania State University.

Chicago-Gary area district director Joe Germano addresses Steelworker rally in Gary, Indiana, shortly after strike began in July 1959. Courtesy of Historical Collections and Labor Archives, Pennsylvania State University.

Although there were no strike benefits,
many USWA locals established food banks
for steelworker families — outdoors in
the warmer months, as left in McKeesport,
Pennsylvania, and indoors later, as above in
Clairton, Pennsylvania. Photo Associates.
Courtesy of Historical Collections and Labor
Archives, Pennsylvania State University.

A strike rally, probably in Buffalo area during the Taft-Hartley cooling-off period in December 1959. "Vote No" signs indicate preparation for scheduled January vote on the companies' "final offer." Courtesy of Historical Collections and Labor Archives, Pennsylvania State University.

David J. McDonald presents new contract to USWA Wage Policy Committee (WPC), January 5, 1960. The WPC ratified the new Basic Steel Contract at this meeting. Nate Fine Photo. Courtesy of Historical Collections and Labor Archives, Pennsylvania State University.

Official signing of 1960 Basic Steel Contract. From left are R. Conrad Cooper, chief negotiator for the companies; McDonald; Arthur Goldberg, Steelworker general counsel; and Eisenhower's secretary of labor James P. Mitchell. Nate Fine Photo. Courtesy of Historical Collections and Labor Archives, Pennsylvania State University.

A joint meeting of Steelworker Locals 1010, 1011, 1711, 3127, and 3443 in the East Chicago, Indiana, area shortly after new contract was signed in January 1960. Courtesy of Historical Collections and Labor Archives, Pennsylvania State University.

Orchestrated demonstration against Dues Protesters at the 1958 USWA Convention. McDonald looks on approvingly from stage (center left). Central Studios. Courtesy of Historical Collections and Labor Archives, Pennsylvania State University.

Buffalo area district director Joe Molony (center, with glasses) campaigns for I. W. Abel against McDonald in January 1965 at South Works of U.S. Steel in Chicago. Courtesy of Historical Collections and Labor Archives, Pennsylvania State University.

REMEMBERING OR NOT
Prologue

n 1992 I was present at the dedication of a historical marker in Homestead, Pennsylvania, commemorating
a one-day battle between steelworkers and Pinkerton
guards that had taken place one hundred years before. The dedication ceremony followed several days of
speeches and historical papers about the Great Homestead
Strike of 1892—speeches and papers that had recreated that
time and place, those events and people, in our imaginations.
As a result, we approached the scene of battle with a certain
awe, though it was a dusty, vacant field along a dirty green
river.

The marker itself was a modest affair—an iron pole holding a cast-iron placard with words in yellow on a dark blue
background. It was just like the ones I could remember from
my childhood. When we had first gotten a car, we used to
take aimless drives, and my mother and father would routinely
stop to read these signs along the side of the road—marking
some battle in the French and Indian War or one of the engineering feats on the Pennsylvania Canal. All traces of the past
reality had disappeared, and a few yellow words cast in iron
tried to evoke it. At each stop, my sister and I would roll our
eyes and joke about how boring our parents' lives must be for
them to care.

One of the speakers at the Homestead dedication ceremony
thanked all those who had helped get this marker placed. As

149

modest as the sign seemed standing there, it had evidently required a great deal of time and effort, even some political wrangles requiring the appropriate clout, to get this spot recognized as an official part of Pennsylvania's history.

The Homestead Strike is a seminal event in American labor history, a worldwide news story at the time and one that has been well studied and remembered since. The union in those ancient days was called the Amalgamated Association of Iron, Steel and Tin Workers, and for the most part it represented only the skilled, native-born craft workers, the immigrant, unskilled workers having been thought incapable of the kind of organization that disciplined collective action required. The Amalgamated had been steadily increasing its membership and strength in the years prior to 1892, and it was particularly strong in Homestead, where it had even reached out and won the support of a lot of the unskilled workers. The "strike" had actually been a lockout that Andrew Carnegie used to crush the union as he was gobbling up the various iron and steel works that in 1900 would become U.S. Steel. After 1892 Carnegie and the other steelmasters would remain in near-total control of their workforces for the next half-century, though they or their successors had to crush the union again from time to time.

But on July 6, 1892, the lockout was just beginning, and the entire town of Homestead was unified behind the steelworkers. When Pinkerton guards came down the river to establish a beachhead for bringing in strikebreakers, the steelworkers and townspeople engaged them in a pitched battle, using guns and a Civil War cannon to fend off and eventually capture the Pinkertons. Ten people, three Pinkertons and seven steelworkers, were killed and many others injured, but it was a glorious, heady victory—the workers controlled Homestead and all access to the mill, the most important of Carnegie's holdings at the time. Their victory showed what could be done when everybody stuck together and is still exhibited in labor lore to make that point. That's what we were commemorating one hundred years later on that uncomfortably hot July day—the one-day victory, not the eventual defeat.

But I could not get the defeat out of my head. The whole conference—designed to commemorate the achievements of a century of working-class struggle, to recall how bad things used to be and how bravely working people had endured and fought on—was pervaded by a sense of grief at what had been lost in the 1980s and a sense of gloom at prospects for the future.

I had been in Homestead only one time before, and it had been a memorable occasion. In the fall of 1983, I was part of a group of "outside intellectuals and activists" gathered together by the Tri-State Conference on Steel, ostensibly to help them devise a fight-back strategy to save the Pittsburgh-area mills. Really, it was a shrewd organizing venture to draw our attention to their struggle and to win our support for a strategy they had already devised. Tri-State was a labor-community coalition stretching from Youngstown, Ohio, through West Virginia and into the Pittsburgh area; at that time its strongest element was based in USWA Local 1398 at U.S. Steel's Homestead Works. Though these were depressed and depressing times, the meeting was a wonderful experience. Local Steelworker leaders, clergy, community organizers, serious steel scholars, lawyers, some politicians, and even some production managers gathered together to figure out how to save the mills through some combination of worker and community ownership backed by the federal government.

Though breathtakingly ambitious, this was no Walter Mitty affair. The discussion was serious, hard-headed, and well organized, with people dividing up tasks and committing themselves to both study and action. Collectively, we knew the industry, its economics, its technology, and its politics, and we saw how the industry's crisis could potentially connect local and state politics with a limited national effort, even with Reagan in the White House. The requisite desperation of people in the Pittsburgh area gave the effort a strong popular base that found resonance in the radical deindustrialization occurring in many other parts of the country in the early 1980s. Though not without illusions (particularly when viewed in retrospect), Tri-State's effort was a model of Antonio Gramsci's "pessimism of the intellect and optimism of the will" that I found exciting and energizing at the time.

Nine years later, the rambling, historic Homestead Works was gone. Unlike most of the mills in other steel towns, it had not been allowed to sit and rust. A real-estate developer had bought and cleared the land. In 1992, buses drove us commemorators across a vast expanse of swirling dust where Homestead Works once had been. We walked up to the marker by the river, and one of the historians explained how the topography was different now than it had been in 1892—the steep bank of the river having been a gentle slope then. Looking down at the river, I tried to imagine the assembled throng of steelworkers fighting off the Pinkertons below, to capture some of the exhilaration of winning that day a hundred years ago, even though "we" would lose for the next half-century. I couldn't capture it. All I could see was a dirty green river. All I could feel was the vacancy of the field behind me.

Like those in 1892, we were again at the beginning of another long stretch of losing, and the forty years of union power I had grown up taking for granted seemed pretty meaningless now, a mere episode in the longer, stronger story of working-class defeat. As one of the speakers intoned the standard messages about honoring those who fought in 1892 by continuing their struggle, I almost shouted, "WHY? WHAT'S THE USE?" As I looked away from the speaker, I caught a glimpse of Tony Tomko—a former president of a McKeesport local and a leader of the Dues Protesters, who had challenged David J. McDonald in the 1950s. Now retired, Tomko had the worn-out, rakish look of a honky-tonk singer, but he was tan and healthy, erect, and apparently still full of piss and vinegar. Usually a clownish, boastful character, Tomko was silently attentive and obviously moved by the speaker's words. Then, without shouting, I answered myself: My whole life was the use; what happened to my father and mother and sister, all my aunts and uncles and (almost) all of their children was the use. I and my generation were (almost) all living well—not only materially, but mostly with warmth, commitment to each other, and a good deal of integrity. None of us had had to kiss anybody's ass or to screw over people to get ahead. The younger generation, my nieces and nephews, would not have this kind of a life, but we had. And for a moment there seemed to be a tangible connection between the faceless masses fighting the Pinkertons, my grandfather's mechanical arms, my father's speeches, and the emotion gripping Tony Tomko's face.

I had planned to write a book about the rise and fall of a steel town—a sad story with a tragic ending, full of lessons about mistakes, full of helpless victims of capitalist oppression and their own illusions. The Reagan administration's version of the National Endowment for the Humanities almost gave me a grant to help me do it. I had already written some articles in this vein, and for a few years I was recognized in certain circles as an expert on dying steel towns. On July 6, 1992, in Homestead, I knew I no longer had the heart for it. Sad stories got me down. Pessimism of the intellect was eating away at my will. Instead, I thought of writing a book that would explain where Tony Tomko had gotten that tan, healthy look, how it could be that there was no glint of cynicism or defeat in his eye or bearing. There had been at least one generation of workers who were not noble victims. Once upon a time, in real life, the struggle had paid off, made a difference, a big, earth-shattering, soul-transforming difference.

This needed to be remembered—to be analyzed and evaluated for what was done right, how success was achieved for a while, not just for the mistakes that were made.

The 1959 strike was a natural for this purpose, but when I began to look for it systematically in the history of our times, it wasn't there. And not only was *it* not there, but nothing like it was. It was as if the Joad family had simply turned into Ozzie and Harriet without any transition, without any cause and effect. When I *could* find snatches of references, it was more often than not cast as a defeat or a stalemate—workers were still noble victims. Tony Tomko, for instance, had made it into some history books for getting beaten up by McDonald's thugs at the Steelworkers' convention in 1960, but no regular guy was worth a mention for just standing there, tan and healthy, near the end of a life well lived.[1]

It's more complicated than this, of course. As I hope I've demonstrated, if you look, you can find plenty of material on the 1959 strike. Even broad surveys sometimes make mention of the strike, and if such works make *any* reference to the existence of unions after the 1940s, they are likely to refer to the long strike of 1959. Besides, what's the big deal? We can't remember everything. That's why there are fights over which spots get historical markers.

There are, in my view, lots of reasons to remember unionism in the 1950s. For one thing, success stories, as all Americans know in their heart of hearts, are heartening. They help you believe in struggling on, in delaying gratification in hopes of achieving a future, sometimes hard-to-imagine goal. Remembering the achievements of collective struggle, and all the work that goes into achieving the always fragile unity necessary for such struggle, is particularly important—for everybody, in my view, but particularly for working classes.

This sentiment is, of course, the heart and soul of the culture of unionism. But it goes well beyond that. Black adults whose lives were transformed by the Civil Rights movement tell me, "Nothing's changed, the racism's just more subtle," and they are surprised (and moved) when we study just how bad things were in the past and what it took to get what today we take for granted. Same thing with women—young ones, of course, but even many who have lived through a complete redefinition of what is allowed and expected of them. They've forgotten, and because they have, they underestimate what has been achieved, which leaves them demoralized about what could yet be achieved. They're also unlikely to defend gains effectively if they no longer see them. This was the point of my father's repetitive speeches, stories, and pronouncements about before the union and since. The lesson of not forgetting has a broader application. Disciplined collective action in its many different forms is an important part of American history, and it has achieved quite a lot in the past fifty years. In fact, grassroots action by ordinary people probably gained more in that fifty years than in any other half-century in human history. Forgetting that impoverishes our future and disables us from making it.

PART 3 of this book is focused on what I take to be extreme instances of forgetting. It offers a causal explanation of these instances and some speculation on what this forgetting means about who we are and where we're going.

The 1959 Steel Strike was a huge event that brought into conflict what people saw then as the three main forces in American society, a "triptych of social and economic power"—Big Business, Big Government, and Big Labor.[2] Historians who even lightly peruse the daily press of that time cannot miss this particular round of collective bargaining—it's there day in and day out for eight or nine months; it received ten or twenty (or fifty) times more space than did Charles Van Doren's cheating on a TV quiz show. The 1959 Steel Strike, in other words, cannot be overlooked; it must be actively ignored.

But ignoring this particular event is part of a larger ignorance and forgetfulness. Big Labor itself—even as an abstraction—has been read out of those times. Robert J. Samuelson, for example, in his popular, recent synthesis *The Good Life and Its Discontents: The American Dream in the Age of Entitlement, 1945–1995,* removes Big Labor from the triptych: "The economy did so well for the first few decades after the Second World War . . . that Americans began to assume that Big Government and Big Business could guarantee its performance and, more, that the resulting improvement would effortlessly lead to more social justice, personal fulfillment, and greater world order."[3]

Some Americans in those days may have thought that Big Business and Big Government could do all this by themselves, though none of them lived in my neighborhood, but I'd bet half my pension that Samuelson cannot find a half-dozen references in the written record of the time to any such merely two-headed expectation. The mainstream conception then was clear: Big Labor, for all its faults, was needed to offset the power of Big Business, and Big Government was needed to keep both within the framework of the public interest. The rosy scenario of the 1950s held that the power of all three needed to be limited and that only the sufficient power of each could limit the power of the others. By reading labor out of the 1950s, you not only distort the actual disposition of social forces at the time, but you also misread its *mentalité,* the national political and economic consensus that every nook and cranny of the daily press exhibited in those days.

Predictably, the union workers who are absent from the happy days of Samuelson's 1950s show up in his depiction of later times to be blamed for succumbing to "sloppiness, laziness, or luxury": "In the 1960s and 1970s, [workers in] heavily unionized industries (steel and auto, for example) pressed for huge wage settlements while resisting changes in wasteful work practices. Labor peace was often purchased with lavish wage agreements that ultimately made companies uncompetitive."[4] There's a pattern in remembrances of postwar America: Not around for the credit, unions show up just in time to share the blame.

But the 1959 Steel Strike and Big Labor aren't the only things that have been forgotten. The third extreme case of forgetting is the one with which I began this book: How did my father forget "the debt we all owe the union"—a debt he had once been so repetitively insistent that we remember?

These extreme cases of forgetting are all really about the same thing— the debt my father claimed, and I agree, that we all owe the union. It's just the forgetters who are different. Big Business had an obvious vested interest in forgetting and, as I've referenced, they spent a great deal of money over a long period to reeducate American public opinion. Though they couldn't cash in on their investment in 1958–63, their persistence (and deep pockets) eventually paid off. But they couldn't have done it without our help—that is, without the help of the professional middle and working classes.

Almost completely independent of ruling-class propaganda, forces of forgetfulness were at work within the working class itself. These forces are the subject of Chapter 5. Among participants in the 1959 strike, many vivid memories remain, but only a few remember what it was all about, who won, and what it may have meant to their lives. Part of the reason for this can be found in the political upheaval within the union in the years immediately before and after the strike—the emergence of a democratic life that produced contesting interpretations of every union event. Though this enriched the culture of unionism in the early 1960s, it also turned Steelworkers inward precisely at a time when the cultural revolutions of the '60s demanded that unionists exercise their social-justice leadership on behalf of those who had been excluded. When they tarried and backslid, they got shamed and blamed in ways that would eventually alienate them from their professional, middle-class allies. The transvaluation of values in the '60s turned my father, like many of his kind, into the sort of "forgotten American" to whom George Wallace and then others appealed. In the process, he sometimes forgot his debts.

But in postwar America, capital and labor got pushed to the margins as the professional middle class crowded between them and established a certain independent control over an increasingly national culture. Our sheer numbers are impressive. As a group, professional and managerial workers have more than quadrupled in the past half-century—from about one of seven members of the workforce to one of four. My own occupational group, university teachers, has increased tenfold, with the greatest period of growth coming from 1950 to 1970; along with other teachers and media workers of various sorts, our society has granted us the leading role in interpreting reality, including a say in who gets historical markers and who doesn't.

The lion's share of the blame for *any* forgetfulness must go to the professional middle class because we're the class that produces the national culture, which either nurtures or corrupts all the local cultures. Whether liberals, conservatives, or moderates, we have a vested interest in keeping ourselves out of the picture as a class. We do this by merging ourselves, conceptually, with people who earn half what we do, who have from four to six years' less education, and who are utterly devoid of the kind of professional perogatives and autonomy we take for granted. By subsuming the working class into an amorphous "middle class" that includes ourselves, we middle-class professionals mistake our own values and goals, interests, and strategies for theirs. That is, we disappear the working class, and as a result, we misunderstand ourselves and distort the social pictures we provide of and for our society. This is the theme of Chapter 6.

Postwar America is a genuinely complex and democratic society where a ruling class can lose some of its power when it tries to rule us directly. Culturally and politically, and to some extent even economically, the professional middle and working classes have a great deal of power to control our own destinies. In 1959, and in the early '60s, a strong alliance still existed between the leading elements of these two classes, a vital "labor liberalism" that self-destructed in the late '60s and whose destruction has defined (and confused) our national culture and memory ever since. My father and I played our appointed roles in that self-destruction. Though there are more mundane reasons for forgetfulness in both the working and the middle classes, the ultimate explanation has to do with the complex relationships (and separations) between these two classes. So that we can more fully understand these relationships and tensions, Chapter 5 focuses on working-class memory, and Chapter 6 on that wing of middle-class professionals who make our living interpreting reality for others.

5

Steel Family Memories and the Culture of Unionism

Of all the institutions in their lives, only the . . . Church has seemed aware of the fact that my mother and father are thinkers—persons aware of the experience of their lives.

—Richard Rodriguez, *Hunger of Memory*

Judging from the interviews I've done, Steelworker family memories of the 1959 strike are a diverse lot, ranging from virtually none at all to vivid recollections off the top of the head. My family members were no exception. Uncle Bill and Aunt Bettie couldn't remember much of anything about it, and as they tried, they kept getting it mixed up with other strikes: "No, that was in '56, I think." Aunt Ruth had similar difficulties, but by calculating her son's age in 1959, she was able to recall: "Oh, yes, that's the summer Ronnie was just back from the Navy and we lived at the cottage. That was a wonderful summer."[1]

On the other hand, Irene Mihailidis, whose husband, Nick, had worked at Inland Steel, gave me a week-by-week account of how she and Nick, who had just recently been married then, got by during the strike. Joe Uehlein, an AFL-CIO staffer who was active in spreading new fight-back strategies in the 1980s, had been seven years old in 1959 and recalls the strike as a "defining moment" in his life. His father was a USWA staff representative in Lorain, Ohio, and Joe spent a lot of that summer tagging after him on picket lines.

158

Besides family, friends, and people I just ran across, I sampled steel-worker memory by calling retired steelworkers who are active in local SOAR chapters around the country. SOAR stands for Steelworkers Organization of Active Retirees, and I spoke with the most active members, the local chapter officers. Though a few identified themselves as "just a member," usually SOAR chapters are headed by people who were union activists in their working days. Almost all of these folks had lots of memories of the 1959 strike. William Werkheiser, who'd worked at Bethlehem Steel's headquarters plant in Bethlehem, Pennsylvania, for example, was responsible for running Local 2600's food kitchen in 1959; he was able to recall a load of details about that operation, including the name of the butcher who occasionally donated hamburger. On the other hand, Werkheiser couldn't remember what the issues had been or who won the strike, though he recalled fondly, "We sure were together in those days—just as solid as you can be."

The most common memory was of "the hardship," of how hard it was to live without paychecks for that long. Though some, like Irene Mihailidis, knew exactly what they did to get by, most had to stretch their memories to recall: "I did odd jobs, I think." "I had two brothers, and they probably helped me." "Oh, yeah, I remember now: We moved back in with my parents—boy, was that awful!" An amazing number said something like, "Jeez, I don't know how we did it. One thing's for sure—no way could I do it now. We didn't have so much in those days, I guess." Though short on details, many remembered being scared that they wouldn't make it, that they might lose everything they had worked for.

The second most common memory was of "how together we all were." Ray Pasnick Sr., who was editor of the Midwest edition of *Steelabor* then, remembers emphatically "the best feeling of unity I've ever been able to see." And that's saying something: Pasnick, from a family of union coal miners, started out as an aluminum worker in 1944 and spent most of his adult life as a Steelworker educator and editor. USWA staffers, it should be remembered, were not paid during the strike, though they put in forty hours a week ("at least") just like normal. A few of the retirees, including Pasnick, used the word "solidarity," but most favored expressions such as "together" and "solid." More than a few were also nostalgic for the kind of community support they received back then. "It's hard to imagine nowdays," said Matt Peulen, who worked at Colorado Fuel and Iron in Pueblo, Colorado, "but nobody said 'boo' against the union in those days."

There seems to be a pattern when it comes to who remembers and who doesn't. People who were near the beginning of their work lives and had just recently started families in 1959 remember better than those who were older and better established. The strike was both harder and scarier for them. Likewise, leaders and activists have clearer memories than rank-and-filers who had not been active in their union. For many of the latter, as for most of my family, the strike was something that happened *to* them, not something they *did*.

But those who seemed to me to have the most insightful memories were those who had a concern for the future—and were still active one way or another in making it. One retiree in his seventies, for example, had to delay talking with me in order to drive sixty miles to handbill a Sears store that was selling boycotted Bridgestone tires. Even when they came up short on details, their process of remembering involved trying to place the strike in a larger and longer context.

Yet even among these, only a few remembered the strike as a decisive victory. Indeed, only about one third of those I talked with counted it as a "win" when pressed, and some of those answered with something like, "I guess you'd have to say we won." Many simply didn't remember, others remembered a loss or a stalemate, and several insisted that "nobody wins in a strike." A handful thought the union had lost, but that the strike had been necessary or worthwhile because it "taught the companies a lesson" or because "we won in the long run." Only a few thought the strike had been unnecessary or wasteful. Most simply saw striking as a fact of life that had to be tolerated in order to get all the good stuff they eventually enjoyed.

Though my sampling was both small and promiscuous, it confirmed my suspicion that there is no *shared collective memory*, no single story line around which conflicting interpretations are organized. Almost everybody remembered that it had been the longest strike and the last one, but almost nobody attached any significance to that. Many seemed to think I was a little weird for asking about it; to most it was a discrete event, something that had happened once but that was not a meaningful part of their life's story.

To me this requires an explanation. Steelworker bargaining history has a clear story line to it: 1937 was the breakthrough. 1946 was the first display of disciplined unity, which began a ten-year process culminating in the 1956 contract, by which time steelworkers had won just about everything they had hoped for (and even some things for which they hadn't had the audacity to hope). The strike in 1959 defended all that, ensuring that there would be "no backward steps" for another couple of decades. Why things aren't remembered this way perplexes me.

Part of the explanation has to do with the mistakes of professional historians. As good a one as James Patterson, like most others, remembers the 1930s as the heyday of union militance and organization.[2] It was not. The "placid decade" of the Fabulous Fifties was. I try to account for this error in the next chapter, where I argue that the way American history is written and taught affects steelworker memory in many fundamental and unlooked-for ways. But most of the old-timers I talked with were still living a strong union culture. Though not representative of the much larger group of steelworkers who were not as involved in their union, they are people who have taken it upon themselves to preserve and pass on the culture. They're used to bucking the tide of middle-class public opinion, and they're good at it. Why do they, too, lack a coherent sense of their own history, a clear and compelling story that is easy to pass on to subsequent generations?

If the 1959 Steel Strike were remembered, as it should be, as a decisive union victory that consolidated union power, it would help remind people of the debt we all owe the union. It could remind us how powerful and effective a union can be, what a wonderful experience sticking together is—and, most importantly, how those two things are related.

Internal Union Politics

Joe Perriello started at Jones and Laughlin in Aliquippa, Pennsylvania, in 1933, and he was active in the union from the very beginning in 1937. He was forty-five in 1959. As with other interviews, after getting basic background information, I asked Perriello, "When I say '1959 Steel Strike,' what's the first thing that comes to mind?"

"The Dues Protesters," he said without hesitation, knowing his answer would surprise me.

"Huh?" I asked, surprised.

"Yes, the Dues Protesters. They almost killed us—almost destroyed the union. That's the first thing I think of."

Perriello had been a supporter of David J. McDonald (he called him Dave), and he explained how the widely publicized ferocity of opposition to McDonald in the union had led the companies to think they could divide and conquer it. Without the Dues Protesters, according to Perriello, there would never have been a strike in 1959.

There are at least two sides to every story, and I grew up on the side that thought it was McDonald who almost destroyed the union. But Perriello has a point. The union was divided in the years prior to 1959, and the companies misread the implications of that division. In fact, this is another reason to remember the 1959 Steel Strike—as an example, probably the best in postwar labor history, of how a vigorous democratic life within a union did not undermine its solidarity in facing its employers. The closing of the ranks in 1959 is all the more impressive once you see how tenaciously Steelworkers fought among themselves both before and after the strike. But the infighting also distorted how things got remembered.

The USWA was not supposed to be a democratic organization. Modeled on the Mine Workers' constitution and structure, the Steelworkers was designed to be a top-down autocracy, with the union president in control of everything. Philip Murray, the USWA's founding father, though a saintly type who mixed bargaining and organizing savvy with a religious dedication to workers and working-class ways, didn't care for independence of mind among local leaders or his staff: "[H]is aim was to build an organization that was disciplined, responsive, and above all, loyal."[3] But, like the Mine Workers and unlike almost all other unions, the president was elected by direct membership vote, not by delegates at a union convention. After John L. Lewis had ruthlessly suppressed his opposition in the '20s, direct elections had not been a problem for the Miners. The advantages of incumbency, combined with practical control of staff, ensured that a president could be reelected, usually without opposition, every four years. Direct membership election actually helped centralize authority at the top of the union; unlike most AFL unions, where most of the money and power remains in the local union, the Mine Workers' president could trump any merely local or regional leader, who had not been elected by "all the men." Most other CIO unions (like the Auto Workers) didn't see it this way. They centralized authority in the traditional UMW manner, but eschewed direct membership elections as a potentially divisive source of "membership mistakes." The other CIO unions turned out to be right. Under McDonald's leadership, the USWA bumbled into a genuinely democratic life. (Two decades and three murders later, so did the Mine Workers). McDonald showed that, with a little practice, he could control conventions after they had become unruly, but he could not control elections. His demise started with the 1956 convention, which temporarily got out of hand, and culminated with his electoral defeat in 1965.

The 1959 strike occurred in the midst of this process, and with just a little sense McDonald could have used it to stop the process. Everybody knew—and it was part of the strength of union culture then that everybody knew—that disciplined unity was the source of union power. Anybody who went off on their own challenged that unity and discipline, and that threatened the union and all the prospects and possibilities it might deliver. Bargaining—even of the most civilized kind, done by men in suits amidst the trappings of fancy New York hotels—was war. It required military discipline. As in war, when you were ordered to strike, you struck; when you were told to go back to work, you went back—no questions asked. Unity was the very fount of union power —and that's what Joe Perriello thinks the Dues Protesters "almost destroyed."

In fact, they didn't even come close. During 1959—not only during the strike, but even before negotiations officially began—the Protesters expressed not a peep of protest. During the crucial Taft-Hartley lull leading up to a membership vote on the companies' final offer, not a word of dissent or criticism could be found by reporters combing the mill-gate bars for rank-and-file opinion. 1959 was a year of unity and discipline. But once a settlement was reached in early January of 1960, the Protesters came out like roaches do when you turn off the lights. The Protesters understood, and respected, the seasons of unity and debate.

If my father was representative of the Dues Protesters, and I'm going to assume he was, they had a more sophisticated sense of union democracy than do most middle-class sympathizers, who often assume that unions must always and everywhere strictly follow democratic procedure. For my father, democracy in the union was not a primary value, and there definitely was a danger in having too much of it. Usually, indeed almost always, good union members followed their leaders—from McDonald to the lowest level of griever—without questioning or carping. But there needed to be a time and a place for questioning and carping, not for the sake of some principle, but because such a time was necessary to inform and correct leaders and to be informed and corrected by them. More than that, such a time and such a process was necessary for achieving unity and discipline—that is, for *being* a union. Without that outlet, the union would eventually either burst apart like a balloon with too much air or shrivel for the lack of it.

There was a place, a context, for carping and complaining—a place where management was not present to hear it. "Take it to the hall" was something my father might snap at somebody if they so much as breathed too loudly when he was representing them to management. On the other hand, once you were "in the hall" (which in his case was not an actual place, since Local 1288 had been too small to have its own union hall), you had better listen, and listen carefully. Though members sometimes didn't know what they were talking about, though they often wanted to eat their cake and have it too, you had to "hear them out" if you were going to be able to explain things to them—and occasionally you might even learn something.

Johnny Metzgar was an arrogant know-it-all, but as smart as he thought he was and as much as he disliked David J. McDonald, he saw the wisdom of deferring to the national union leadership. He would have agreed, for example, with the view of Leon Davis, founder and president of the original Local 1199 of the Hospital Workers' Union: "The idea of wisdom emanating up from the bottom is full of shit, not because the rank and file are stupid but because they have a job which is not running the union and knowing all the intricate business about it."[4] The Dues Protesters didn't challenge the union's basic hierarchical structure. They certainly didn't challenge the need for unity and discipline or even for strong leadership. Nor had they spoken out of turn. But there needed to be a time and place for them to have their say if there were really to be a union.

The Dues Protesters did not have a well-defined oppositional program, let alone an alternative vision for the union. They emerged spontaneously as an expression of the high spirits of the mid-1950s and of various disgruntlements that were fed, paradoxically, by those high spirits. They had a kind of "what the hell" quality at first, a sense that they had both a right and a duty to mouth off at the leadership, and not much responsibility beyond that. They had seen a series of oppressions cast aside or seriously eroded, and a complex set of prospects and possibilities opening up. Things they used to suffer and endure without even thinking now pissed them off. Now, if something wasn't to your liking, what the hell, you might as well speak up about it— you never know, it might make a difference. Serious issues about the future of the union would eventually emerge, but in the 1950s the Dues Protesters were more spirit than program.

Their name, which eventually became an embarrassment, derived from an outbreak of protest against an increase in dues at the 1956 convention in Los Angeles. In the context of that boom year, their unwillingness to pay more dues made them seem like ingrates who wanted all the benefits of the union without "paying their dues." Given the context, their disrespectful attitude toward their leadership was in fact stunning.

The 1956 contract was the culmination of the USWA's postwar bargaining program. With a large annual increase in wages, a brand new mechanism for keeping up with the cost of living (COLA), the establishment of SUB, and, at long last, a union shop provision, it was quite simply the best contract the Steelworkers would *ever* win. The thirty-four-day strike in 1956 had basically been about how long the contract would last. The companies had come to negotiations ready to give the union everything they had previously resisted, including a union shop, in exchange for a five-year contract. The idea was that their generosity would be repaid with a predictability about costs and production that had been lacking since the war. McDonald, in his best poker player's bargaining mode, huffed and bluffed, cajoled and wheedled, got all the goodies over three years instead of five, and did it without jeopardizing the "era of cooperation" he and U.S. Steel labor relations chief John Stephens thought they were initiating. The union's Wage Policy Committee, besides unanimously ratifying the contract, jubilantly declared it "the greatest victory achieved by the union in its twenty-year history."[5]

McDonald, according to his autobiography, "was looking forward to a massive orgy of gratitude and good feeling at our convention," and amidst this orgy, he expected to pass a 66 percent increase in dues (from $3 a month to $5) and an increase in his salary from $40,000 to $50,000 a year (along with comparable increases for vice presidents and other union officers, at a time when the average annual wage in basic steel was about $5,000).[6] But instead, many of the 2,671 delegates—rank-and-file leaders with constituencies back home—rushed the microphones to speak against the dues increase. Some pointed out that, though steelworkers in basic steel might be able to afford it, workers in fabricating units and other elements of the union were still struggling; some called for a graduated rate adjusted to wages rather than the same monthly rate for everyone. But when McDonald cut them off with barrages of accusations and threats, wielding a heavy gavel to enforce obscure parliamentary procedures, others rose to speak for the delegates' right to have their say, and something bigger than $2 a month started brewing. Whose union was this, anyway? Cutting discussion off, McDonald conducted a voice vote and, after lots of shouting and commotion, declared that the dues increase had passed by an "overwhelming majority." Delegates called for a roll-call vote, to which they were entitled by the union constitution. McDonald screamed that that would be impractical and gavelled the meeting to a close.[7]

This was a page-one, national story in 1956, and thus the members knew all about it by the time their delegates returned home. All the top leadership, the district directors, and probably even most local union presidents had supported the dues increase. As one district director told labor reporter John Herling, "We departed from Los Angeles thinking, well, it was a bit of a struggle, but it's behind us, thank God. Then the moment we got home we were faced with open rebellion everywhere."[8] Increases in dues are never popular among union members, but McDonald's refusal to allow open debate about the details sparked a wildfire of rank-and-file resentment.

A group of fifty delegates from the Pittsburgh area, led by Donald Rarick, a griever from the Irvin Works of U.S. Steel in McKeesport, formed something they called the Dues Protest Committee, which began to solicit among the district directors for somebody to oppose McDonald in the 1957 election. Though there was some well-known disenchantment with McDonald among the district directors, the Protesters couldn't find any who were willing to rise to the level of outright opposition. Undeterred, the Dues Protesters decided to run Rarick, a man virtually unknown outside his local, against a genuine national celebrity, in the upcoming election for USWA president.

Getting through the union's cumbersome petition and nomination process was a formidable task, especially since the Dues Protesters were men who, for the most part, had not previously known one another. As an organized group, they were pretty much a Pittsburgh-area outfit, with members driving up and down the valleys to meet and get to know one another. Through phone calls and occasional trips, they reached out to other mills, most of which were in a 600-mile radius of Pittsburgh that reached to Baltimore, Birmingham, Chicago, and Buffalo. They found sympathizers everywhere.[9]

Though nobody expected Rarick to make a showing against the formidable communications and organizational apparatus McDonald wielded, lots of people admired the spirit of the undertaking. The mere fact of opposition—even a weak, disorganized, completely outgunned one—unnerved and embarrassed McDonald. First he tried ignoring the nuisance, and then he threatened Rarick—first with formal union charges of "dual unionism," then with darker hints about friends in "the mob"—and finally he tried bribing him. In the end McDonald beat Rarick, in a more or less free and fair election, by a vote of 404,000 to 223,000. As Herling commented, this relatively close call was a whale of an embarrassment: "There was never any doubt that McDonald would outpace a candidate . . . who had emerged brashly from the great anonymous body of grievance committeemen. . . . [But] McDonald had failed to defeat an inconspicuous local leader by even a two-to-one margin." [10]

And the election didn't end opposition to McDonald. The Dues Protesters turned their attentions to local union elections in 1958 and, despite heavy support from McDonald for their opposition, won some stunning victories. Rarick was elected president of his local, 2227, and Tony Tomko took over 1408, making a sweep of McKeesport. Nick Mamula was reelected president of the huge local in Aliquippa, and Frank O'Brien won the historic Homestead local. Even in California, Dues Protest leader Thomas Flaherty became president of Fontana Local 2869.

In response, the union's "official family" rallied around McDonald big time at the 1958 convention and brought charges against the dissidents. Expulsion proceedings were initiated, by convention vote, against Rarick, Mamula, O'Brien, and others. The charges were read by Joe Molony, the district director (DD) from Buffalo, who was widely seen as one of the most disaffected of the DDs; Molony had run against McDonald's hand-picked candidate for vice president in 1955 and would eventually be part of the team that unseated McDonald in 1965. But in 1958 he denounced the Dues Protesters for undermining the union as an institution and declared, "There is no room in our union for traitors." The charges had to be voted on by the Protesters' local unions, where the Protesters had strong support, and nobody was actually expelled from the union—or deterred from their activism. But McDonald had absolute control of the convention, which, after the Dues Protesters had been excoriated, consisted mostly of speeches praising McDonald and his leadership. [11]

This was the way the USWA achieved unity to get ready for the 1959 bargaining round, and it wasn't pretty. Though the official family was in control of the convention, the hateful words they hurled at the Dues Protesters were returned with equal venom—both on the floor of the convention, where Protesters were grossly outnumbered, and when they got back to their locals, where they were not. In the fall of 1958 the steel-town press brimmed with charges and countercharges. There was no keeping this stuff "in the hall," and R. Conrad Cooper would have been an idiot not to have seen an opportunity here. Though in my view the Dues Protesters ultimately strengthened the union (as did the 1959 strike itself), it's hard to argue with Joe Perriello's claim that their protesting encouraged the companies' aggressive strategy in 1959.

The bitterness and rivalries engendered from 1956 through 1958 didn't help Cooper during the strike, but they became a permanent feature of the union. The most active elements remained divided between pro-McDonald and anti-McDonald, with a large group (probably a majority) borrowing a little from each. All sides were concerned with the potential damage to discipline and unity, but they blamed each other for causing it. Though everybody feared and distrusted it, a democratic life was emerging within the USWA.

This democratic development was very much of a piece with the liberatory process that infused the mid-1950s. Repression and suppression were losing their grip on people of every sort. These were the years of rock-'n-roll and the beginnings of the modern Civil Rights movement, the years when Betty Friedan was beginning to resent "the problem with no name." Authority of every sort was beginning to lose its aura of prestige and infallibility—if not yet its legitimacy. Rebels, with or without causes, were becoming national icons. Ten years earlier, in 1946, McDonald's suppression of dissent would have been suffered as one of the facts of life. But there was a different spirit in 1956. Not only did union leaders make speeches about the rights and dignity of workers, but they actually produced some rights and dignity, and then made more speeches about them. Likewise, in 1946, most steelworkers hadn't had telephones, or automobiles, or the discretionary income to pay for gas and long-distance phone calls; by 1956 they had all these tools for getting to know one another, for organizing themselves into a force to be reckoned with. Over time, these things changed what people felt they were entitled to, and this changed their willingness to fight, to risk and suffer to get it. The forces of authority—"the Big Boys"—in every segment of society saw their authority slipping away in hundreds of little ways. They felt the new spirit, and they feared it. McDonald was neither the first nor the last to come down hard on a tentative, well-mannered bit of questioning and to thereby turn it into a monster that would eventually eat his lunch.

By 1959, then, a democratic polity existed in the Steelworkers union. The union no longer spoke with a single voice; now there was the official line, the opposition's view, and lots of room for mixing and matching in between. Before, during, and after the strike, reporters took regular soundings of these views. Their reports—which were not reflected in *Steelabor*, where steelworkers always thought and felt the same thing —informed steelworkers of what other members were thinking and stimulated them to formulate their own views. The very fact of reporters asking them questions enhanced the democratic discourse. After the moment of unity during the strike, no event, no action or outcome in the Steelworkers union would have a single meaning. Within a few months of the decisive victory of 1959, the memory of it would get lost within these conflicting views, and the views themselves changed as they were informed by conditions in the industry and the larger economy.

In retrospect, you've got to have some sympathy for McDonald and the situation in which he found himself in 1960. His key problem was that the strike, a decisive victory for the union, had been a humiliating defeat for the companies—and especially for Cooper and Blough. Rubbing their noses in the defeat would make it more difficult to administer the new contract and would encourage them to focus on exacting revenge in 1962, when a new contract would be bargained. Also, gloating in public (which the union and its leadership did for a week or so in January) fed the image of a greedy Big Labor trampling over everybody else in pursuit of "more." Right-wing Republicans were already pointing to the steel strike as evidence of why the country needed a systematic reconstruction of labor law, not just the tuck-pointing that Landrum-Griffin had accomplished. In broader public opinion, particularly in the middle class but among other workers as well, steelworkers were objects of sympathy and support as long they were underdogs battling heartless corporate giants like U.S. Steel, but they lost a lot of that sympathy when they won, particularly since many people believed they would now have to pay higher prices for automobiles and anything else made of steel.

Thus, after a few days of euphoria at the companies' humiliation, the union's leaders recognized that both future bargaining and current public opinion required a soft-pedaling of just how sweeping the union's victory had been. McDonald began to cast the new contract as a reasonable compromise in which "both sides gave a little" and began making speeches about the need to cooperate with the companies in the future in order to avoid strikes that "no one wins in the end."

By late January he was getting help in advancing this interpretation from both steel executives and his opposition within the union. Both pointed out that the overall package was not quite as expensive as the

Kaiser contract, that the wage increases were not nearly as good as those in the 1956 contract, and that the companies had won an important concession by establishing a cap on the cost-of-living adjustment. The COLA cap *was* a significant concession in principle, though, as it turned out, it had no effect during the life of the contract because inflation remained low. The difference with the Kaiser contract amounted to less than a molehill (it had to do with the differing lengths of the contracts), but everybody had an interest in calling it a mountain. But comparisons with the 1956 contract were irrelevant because of very different economic conditions and bargaining situations. In 1956 the companies had come to the table bearing gifts, not vowing to reverse "the mistakes of the past eighteen years."[12]

Right after the strike, however, steelworkers were clear about the nature of their victory. *U.S. News and World Report,* which was editorially apoplectic about the abject capitulation of Ike and the companies, surveyed "the nation's steel centers to get from the workers themselves their size-up of the strike settlement." The *U.S. News* coverage of the strike was selling the idea that steelworkers would never make up the wages they had lost during the strike, and their survey team found many workers who, calculating their losses, agreed with that idea. Typical was a scarfer from Inland: "I've lost $4,000 in this strike. I lost $2,000 in wages and I've spent $2,000 of my savings. I'll never get that back, with this raise they got me." But *U.S. News* was forced to draw the following conclusions about majority opinion:

- Support for the union remains strong despite losses suffered as a result of the strike. The union managed to convince workers that the future of their union was at stake. . . .
- The strike, as the workers saw it, was over working rules—not so much over wages or fringe benefits. On the issue of working rules, the men feel that the union won a major victory.[13]

As a worker from Bethlehem's plant in Sparrow's Point, Maryland, later explained to *U.S. News,* "You can't measure it in terms of wages won or lost alone, because there are a lot of other angles. We were fighting for good working conditions. You can't measure that against the money we lost. The strike set me back a few months in money, but I don't count only the money angle."[14]

The 1959 Steel Strike was a decisive victory, but it was a defensive one. This may help explain why its triumphs seem to have been so easy to forget. Once the threat of what might have been lost receded in memory, attention to the absence of pathbreaking gains advanced, as did memories of the hardship. And almost immediately after the settlement, the overall economy began to stagnate, putting the industry into recession. Because of this, for something like a third of the strikers, the strike would become just a creek flowing into a sea of hardship that stretched from the 1958 recession through 1963. About 50,000 basic steelworkers who had been working in 1957, before the recession, would either be washed out of the industry forever or not get back in until the mid-1960s. Another 50,000 who went back after the strike would be laid off for most of the time from mid-1960 through 1962 — the life of the contract.[15] Many thousands of others would experience shorter layoffs and many short workweeks. Even those who worked steadily during the early 1960s, as my father did, worked at lower job classifications, thus bringing home less pay. Piling up some extra cash by working overtime was out of the question.

Though things would soon get worse, already in May 1960 *U.S. News* surveyors of steel-town sentiment were finding a different size-up of the strike: "To many the strike was an error. A raise does not have the lure it once had." Though many still held to the earlier perspective, like the Sparrows Point worker quoted above, they were no longer a majority. Now the strike was often seen as having resulted in a "standoff" with the companies. A U.S. Steel worker from the Fairless Works near Philadelphia said, "At the time the contract was signed, I was in favor of it. Now, I'm not so sure." On McDonald, *U.S. News* reported both widespread criticism and lots of loyal support. One of the loyal supporters, from Youngstown Sheet and Tube in the Gary area, mixed and matched: "McDonald is a good man for the union, but he didn't handle the last strike good. It was too long. The men ought to have more to say about strikes and elections. But I don't blame McDonald. I don't know who's to blame."[16]

The Dues Protesters knew who to blame. McDonald was to blame for the long strike, the poor settlement, the recession in the industry, the inability of the Steelers to find a decent quarterback, and just about anything else that was wrong with the world. Eighty rank-and-file leaders from eight states met in Pittsburgh in May 1960 and reconstituted themselves as the Organization for Membership Rights. The new group, still almost uniformly referred to as the Dues Protesters, characterized the 1960 agreement as a "bag of crumbs" and demanded membership referenda to authorize all future strikes. Unlike most other unions, the

Steelworkers did not conduct either strike authorization or member-ship contract ratification votes in basic steel—and demands for these voting rights became powerful after 1959, resonating well beyond the Dues Protesters.[17]

In local union elections in 1960, McDonald took another run at Rarick, Mamula, Tomko, and O'Brien, urging members they repre-sented "to get these bedbugs put out of my hair," but they won again by large majorities. McDonald could still control conventions, however, and the one in September 1960 in Atlantic City was a rerun of 1958. Amidst appearances by Democratic presidential hopeful John F. Ken-nedy and Eisenhower's labor secretary James P. Mitchell, villification of the "Organization for Management Rights" was generously mixed with paeans to "our great leader." Union pioneer Smaile Chatak compared Rarick to the "screwballs" of the 1920s who had challenged John L. Lewis. Without mentioning that a bunch of those screwballs had ended up organizing the Steelworkers in the 1930s, Chatak counseled, "Let's pop them in the nose and kick them out." Tomko got his pops on the convention floor, but in full view of delegates, the four ushers who beat him were relatively restrained. Rarick's beating was more severe. A mountain of a man (six foot four and "built like a steelworker"), Rarick required a whole platoon of "ushers" in the privacy of a lobby leading to the boardwalk.[18]

This just pissed Tomko and Rarick off. Both returned to the con-vention floor the next day for more verbal abuse, and they and their kind kept coming back. The press loved this stuff—nothing like it ever happened at shareholder meetings—and they spread news of the beat-ings far and wide. McDonald disclaimed any responsibility for the beat-ings, as he did for the verbal abuse and for the paeans to himself by "my steelworkers." Nobody in my neighborhood believed these disclaimers, at least not when my father was within hearing distance. Even as a re-tiree more than a decade later, my father would get red-faced angry re-calling it: "Beat a guy up just for disagreeing with you? What kind of union leader is that? If I'd've had my chance, I'd've popped *him* one." I remember him at the time, pacing the house in frustrated anger af-ter reading something in the paper or hearing it on the news—and I remember these moments, which occurred during my senior year in high school, much better than I remember anything about the strike the year before. On any other subject, my father could calmly and pa-tiently explain the most complicated kinds of things to me, but he couldn't talk about the beatings without that frustrated anger—which meant he couldn't *talk* about them at all. To someone with such an exalted sense of "the union," David J. McDonald was an insult and an injury.

Yet McDonald won reelection in 1961 without opposition. Only about one of five Steelworkers actually voted, and McDonald's total, 221,000, was less than the number Rarick had garnered in 1957. The 1962 contract was probably the worst in Steelworker history. Basically an extension of what already existed, with *no* increase in wages, it did make some improvements in SUB and in the possibility of early retirement, but these were more than offset by the discontinuance of COLA. Though McDonald would eventually come in for some fierce criticism for this contract, at the time most steelworkers accepted it as part of the continuing hard times they and the industry were experiencing. The 1962 convention was also pretty tame. The Protesters didn't need to be repressed, and the generally somber mood was lightened by real efforts on all sides for everybody to get along.[19] Hard times, like strikes, tended to pull everybody together.

But as work started to pick up in 1963 and 1964, so did union politics. Among the district directors and the staff, as well as among local leaders and the rank-and-file, there were both dissidents and loyal supporters. In 1965 the union's second-highest officer, I. W. Abel, pulled together a coalition of the dissidents to oppose McDonald. The election was conducted just like in a democracy—not without negative campaigning and lots of hurt feelings, bitterness, and division, but still focused on real issues concerning the way to conduct the union's affairs. When Abel won in a close vote, a door creaked open and a burst of fresh air blew away a lot of the earlier hatreds and divisions, along with McDonald.[20]

But democratic politics had become a way of life in the union. In 1969 Abel was opposed by an obscure staff lawyer, Emil Narick, whose main qualification seemed to be that his name rhymed with Rarick, and Abel beat him by less than two to one.[21] When Abel retired in 1977, his handpicked successor, Lloyd McBride, just barely beat Eddie Sadlowski, who had come up through the ranks with a little help from the Dues Protesters. And in 1983, when times were the hardest they had been in fifty years, three candidates (one with roots in the Dues Protesters) ran against one another in a free and fair election, with all the terrible issues facing the union being fiercely debated out in the open, and with the debaters still breathing fresh air from the door that had been pried open from 1956 to 1965. The Steelworkers, like other unions, have been roughed up pretty badly by employers in the past twenty years, but—unlike many other unions that didn't develop a democratic life in the good old days—they haven't been wanting for unity and discipline.

They have lost some memory, however. At the 1960 convention I. W. Abel, then the union's secretary-treasurer, was given the task of summing up the pros and cons of the 1959 strike. His account is basically in the same vein as the one in Chapter 2—"heroic workers and their families" won a decisive victory that consolidated union power against management's most formidable challenge in the postwar era.[22] In his 1965 campaign against McDonald, however, he remembered it differently; by that time, it had become a "costly and unnecessary" blunder by McDonald.[23] By 1965 McDonald had a different memory of it as well: He claimed on *Meet the Press* never to have called it. Rather than bragging about it as an accomplishment, the best McDonald could do was to claim that it wasn't his fault.[24] In his 1969 autobiography, however, McDonald remembers it as the great victory it was—minus the heroic workers and their families. But in retirement, Abel was still carping about how the 1960 contract undercut COLA, and he had convinced himself that the strike itself was McDonald's fault.[25]

That's the way it is in a democratic polity. The actors accumulate vested interests in remembering things in ways that suit their interpretations of themselves. Within the companies, there was a similar division; though local management complained for decades about how hopelessly powerful the union was after 1959, top management, particularly Blough and Cooper, whatever grousing they may have done in private, had the resources to control a public story that downplayed their miscalculations and defeat. Without outsiders like historians to correct or discipline the actors' memories, public events devolve into fragments of personal recollections with no public meaning. Most historians, unfortunately, are not interested in this kind of thing. They can scarcely remember that unions were even a part of the picture in those days.

I don't expect there to be a single meaning to the 1959 Steel Strike. But I would challenge anybody who thinks that it was a defeat or a stalemate, or that the union could have avoided it in any way other than by surrendering, to look at the rich public record of the time—particularly between June 10 and July 15. Even so, I don't expect that Joe Perriello and I will ever agree—except about the fact that, McDonald not-withstanding, workers and their families definitely were a part of it.

Disenchantment and Forgetfulness

Union politics and his position within it had a lot to do with why my fa-ther eventually, though only temporarily, forgot the debt we all owe the union. In most ways, so far as I know, he was never what most people would call a participant in those politics—he never went to meetings, circulated petitions, or took part in an organized group that called itself the Dues Protest Committee. All he did was "talk them up" to whoever would listen. But in our extended family, neighborhood, and church, and in his immediate work area, lots of people—probably more than a hun-dred, all told—*would* listen to him, and he influenced how they thought about these and other things. He didn't think of this as politics, which he associated with angling for some personal benefit, but it was. In fact, just arguing your view to friends, neighbors, and workmates is proba-bly the essence of a democratic politics. If you do *not* do it, you're un-dermining the very possibility of democracy.

Joe Perriello was undoubtedly "talking up Dave" to his circle of family, friends, and workmates as well. The group that participated in union politics in this broader sense went well beyond the union officers, grievers, and activists. Though I doubt they ever constituted much more than one of ten, we need to remember that the '50s and '60s were de-cades when civic participation exploded in American life. Voter partici-pation, for example, rarely reached more than a little above 50 percent in presidential elections and 40 percent in congressional elections in the '40s, '70s, '80s, and '90s, but it rose well above those marks in every elec-tion from 1950 through 1970.[26] For my father and thousands like him, there was a sense of connectedness between "chewing the fat" with fam-ily and friends and the kinds of outcomes you got and had to live with.

There is currently a rich debate about why his generation was so much better at being citizens than subsequent ones.[27] Only rarely is it noted that the glory days of civic participation are the same as the glory days of the American labor movement.[28] For my father, the connection between citizenship and unionism was clear. Before the union, chewing the fat about workplace and public issues was not permitted in company towns. After the union, it was required.

Johnny Metzgar was the kind of all-around pain-in-the-ass who can drive union leaders crazy—always raising objections at meetings, always expecting too much, and, completely without ambition, always very sure of his own rectitude. But a union—or any other institution—that doesn't take care of its true believers risks the culture it takes hundreds of thousands of living room and workplace conversations to cultivate and grow.

My father's disenchantment with the union, though it had roots in earlier years, undoubtedly began with the election of I. W. Abel in 1965. As long as David J. McDonald was president, "the union" was an absolute good, and whatever was wrong with it was merely the result of one bad leader. After Abel, that was no longer a credible view. What happened in the larger society in those years scrambled his earlier coherence and would have done so regardless of what happened in the union. But the union's capacity to give direction to him—and, through him, to others—weakened dramatically in the late '60s. It lost its weight as a moral force with him, and this loosed him from his fundamentalist Protestant version of social Keynesianism. For my father, the culture of unionism, only slightly eroded by more than a decade of David J. McDonald's moral insensibility, dissipated in the '60s and '70s, just as he needed it most.

In retirement, he endlessly repeated two stories from the second half of the '60s to explain why he'd quit being a griever in the late '60s. Other stories illustrated his frustrations, but none got repeated with the same intensity and emotion as these. The first story had to do with how long it took to get Uncle Stan his disability pension. By the mid-'60s, Stan had been a molder for more than thirty years. The kind of molding he did required him to be on his knees most of the time and to breathe silicon all of the time. By the time he was fifty, both his knees and his lungs were shot, and he was missing a lot of workdays—mostly because of his knees. According to Dad, he was entitled to a work-related disability pension, "no two ways about it." Dad and Stan had started together on the molding floor, but Dad had transferred to the lower shop just before the war; as a result, though he advised Stan and helped him with some of the paperwork, Dad couldn't use his formal status as a griever to shepherd the complicated process through which Stan would eventually get a disability pension. The company fought Stan's claim, and somehow "the union dropped the ball." Dad had to fight it through on the union side, making a nuisance of himself with the grievance chair, the local president, and the staff representative, so they would "push

Pittsburgh" until finally things were set right. The union's lack of concern bothered my father more than the company's: "It shouldn't have been that way. Stan was in the union right from the start. He never said much, but he was always there when we needed him. Thirty years of sticking with the union ought to mean something. And all they needed to do was their job. It hurt me. It hurts me still."

When I first started hearing this story, I didn't understand why this hurt him so much. Somebody in the union had screwed up, and he had set it right. What was the big deal? Nor could I understand why he'd get so upset when Aunt Ruth made a point to credit him and not the union with "getting Stan his disability." Why not just take the credit and be done with it?

Dad and his sister Ruth were two of a kind—bright, articulate, take-charge types, fully capable of dealing with the world's rough and tumble. They both married quiet, dependable people, Mom and Stan, who were not capable of fighting to get or keep their place in life, but who were models of Christian selflessness and humility. In family discussions, the best arguments were always between Dad and Ruth, and Ruth was the family's foremost skeptic about the union. Though others would pipe in with their views from time to time, Mom and Stan were uniformly silent, occasionally nodding in agreement with their spouses. About the union, Dad would sometimes appeal to Stan for confirmation of something he was saying. These were always tense moments, and almost everybody disapproved of Dad for doing it, because Stan didn't like to disagree with anybody, least of all Ruth. But when asked, he would speak his mind, and he was solid for the union. Because he spoke so seldom, Stan's words carried more weight than those of others, and on no other subject did he publicly disagree with his wife. This undercut Ruth's argument and advanced Dad's, but more importantly, it helped confirm Dad's exalted view of the union. Both Dad and Ruth saw Mom and Stan as model human beings and themselves as the flawed (though necessary) ones. Thus Stan's confirmation was worth far more to my father than a few debater's points.

Several years after Stan retired, so did Ruth—she had been a teacher, one who had resisted the union there, too, but with this balanced appraisal: "They did get us a pension, I'll give them that." For nearly a decade, Stan and Ruth took yearly trips "out West" through the national parks—trips that eventually turned into months-long journeys in a huge RV. We could not look at the pictures from these trips without Dad pointing out that the union had made them possible. Ruth would counter, "You're too modest, Johnny. We wouldn't have gotten anything from the union without your pull." In response, he'd snap, "Without the union, there'd have been nothing to get," but then he'd go silent, angry and humiliated. In the first place, the union was supposed to be about what was fair and right, who earned what by doing what, according to the rules that had been negotiated. It was not supposed to be about "pull"—about who you knew or who your brother-in-law was. Second, as he once explained to me, he didn't have any pull. His union brethren had told him he was meddling where he did not belong. He had gotten them to do the right thing with threats and maneuvering, not out of respect for his service to the union and its cause. He never told anybody that but me, and he was weeping when he did. Eventually, he stopped pointing out how Ruth and Stan's trips out West were made possible by the union.

For my father, the second story was "the final straw." It involved an industrial engineer who was timing Dad on a brand new machine, thus setting the base for the incentive rate for a new generation of machines, wherever they might eventually be placed in U.S. Steel. At the time there was only one other such machine at U.S. Steel—and an IE in Youngstown, Ohio, was also timing a union machinist on it. According to the IE who was timing Dad, the machinist in Youngstown was doing his jobs much faster than Dad could do them, and Dad knew this could easily be true because he was, of course, "not doing my best." He figured he needed to compare notes with the machinist in Youngstown, and there was evidently a procedure for doing this. Somebody from his local union called the union in Pittsburgh, and Pittsburgh was supposed to call Youngstown, get the information, and relay it back to Johnstown for Dad. Days went by and it didn't happen. Dad had exhausted his full bag of tricks, "arduously" inching up his performance, sometimes falling back a bit, day by day. But he knew the IE wasn't fooled: "The guy was not that dumb. He knew I was stalling him." Johnstown called Pittsburgh again, and they hadn't gotten to it yet. At this point, Dad took things into his own hands, calling the local union in Youngstown directly and eventually calling the machinist who was breaking in the new machine there. The two of them had a good time talking. They were doing the work at roughly similar rates, and the IE in Youngstown had been bragging about what a fantastic job the guy in Johnstown was doing! They fixed upon what they thought was a reasonable rate and agreed to hold to it.

It seemed like a happy ending, and he went to work the next day with considerable peace of mind. But near the end of his shift, he got a call to come to the local union's in-plant office. There the local president asked him if he'd called the Youngstown local, and when he said he had, he was told to call Pittsburgh, where an angry Steelworker official read him "the riot act," telling him that if he ever did that again, the union would bring him up on charges. Dad was stunned. He just listened—"I took my lumps," he'd say—and then he hung up. But as soon as he did, he started to boil, and he didn't stop boiling until the day he died.

"I waited three or four days for them to do it, and they couldn't find the time," he'd say. "But they sure had lots of time to talk to me once I did it on my own. I didn't have to wait at all then. You got to understand. I wasn't doing this for myself. I could have set that rate at whatever was comfortable for me and been done with it. I was looking out for the younger fellas, the guys who are going to have to work that machine year after year, and make a living off it." He'd point out that neither the two IEs nor the company were ever any the wiser, and a nice clean rate had been set on that machine: "I still don't understand the union's beef. Why shouldn't I talk to a guy in Youngstown? The industrial engineers were talking to each other, or at least they said they were. And who is he? He doesn't even know me, and he talks to me like a piece of dirt. I don't even get the courtesy of an explanation." Throughout his retirement, he'd ramble through something like this, getting more upset as he went along, wishing he had said this or that instead of having been intimidated into silence, and always ending with the lines, "I didn't do it for myself. I'm not one that just took from the union. I gave back. At least I should get an explanation."

Both stories involve a certain slackness among the union staff, but union staffers are often (even usually) overwhelmed with work. Both reveal a disrepect for a loyal member that does much more damage than could possibly have been intended. These were human errors—a guy in Baltimore, indeed a guy in his own plant, could have had a very different experience with a different staff guy on the other end. Anecdotes, as important as they were to my father, tell you nothing about how the instititution usually functioned. But the quick and angry response to his call to Youngstown tells you a lot about the Steelworkers union and, I suspect, all CIO unions. The leadership feared membership initiative— and punished it.

Some of this was politics. CIO unions didn't like local leaders in one plant talking with local leaders in another, because they knew that such relationships over time could nurture political opposition. A lot of work went into bringing local leaders into contact with one another only at carefully controlled national and regional meetings. After local leaders left these meetings, they were expected to run official business with other locals "through the International"—usually this meant through their staff representative. Staff representatives were full-time union officials, almost uniformly workers who had come up through the ranks of local leadership; in the Steelworkers, they were appointed by the International (not the DD) and could be fired by the International. Local leaders dealt with local staff reps, men who usually had deep roots and lots of contacts in their local communities, but who had to be 100 percent "loyal to Pittsburgh" (or extraordinarily savvy) to keep their jobs. There is an enormous difference between being a steelworker and being a staff rep—though the pay is only a little better, the working conditions (above all, the autonomy and control you have over what you do from day to day and hour to hour) are a lot better. Some observers, including Tom Geoghegan, think that the fear of being forced to return to "real work" after having a professional job with the union corrupts the institution and its leadership, opening up a gulf between leadership and membership and leading to panicky repression of even the slightest hint of political opposition.[29]

This is a part of the story, but only a part. Union staffers, then and now, include a high proportion of true believers—people who love their jobs because they get to "do good" almost every day, people invested in a cause who do the daily work of setting things right. Who wouldn't fight to keep such a job? Those who have gone from being a "shop rat" who gets paid to make U.S. Steel a profit to being a soldier in the cause of social justice have more to defend than the privileges and perogatives of a professional job. And they tend to perceive any interference with their work as challenging the cause upon which their identity—their sense of who they are and what they're doing—depends.

I. W. Abel, USWA president during these episodes my father recounted, was one of these former shop-rat true believers, as honest and decent a man as ever held power in postwar America. Having lived the union miracle, Abel understood how much of it depended on the centralization of authority at the top of the union. CIO unions had been founded on the idea that you couldn't organize just one company in an industry and expect to be able to make a difference; you had to control all or almost all the labor in an industry to change things. Though the Steelworkers were somewhat unique in bargaining with the industry as a whole (a method they had copied from the Mine Workers), unions that bargain company by company to establish a pattern contract have an equal need to have everybody coordinated around the same goals, with one leader able to speak for and give orders to every worker in the industry. This need for centralized authority fosters an exaggerated fear of unsupervised rank-and-file initiative. And by the '60s, USWA leaders had some well-tried practices and procedures for disciplining the ranks.[30]

When he took office in 1965, Abel did some things to democratize the union's governing processes,[31] but he also solidified staff unity in a way that led to more intolerance of initiative in the ranks. Precisely because he was an honest, decent true believer, Abel unified the staff and district leadership in a way that had never been characteristic under McDonald. Abel delegated some authority, but he did not disperse it, and like his predecessors, he still feared what Stan Weir once called "horizontal unionism"—organizational life based on direct contacts between local leaders to accomplish lower-level union business. McDonald's inattention to the daily work of the union had given the staff more autonomy, and his moral insensibility had motivated its true believers to form *sub voce* alliances with district and local leaders to protect "the union" from him. Under Abel there was much less need to engage in this kind of intramural organizational politics. Unlike with McDonald, staff could have confidence that top-down union discipline was being enforced for the good of the union. The union's "official family"—the full-time International leaders and staff and all the local leaders who identified wholeheartedly with them—became a tight-knit unit wedged between the recalcitrance of giant corporations and the inexhaustibly rising expectations of a restive membership. The history, the structure, and the very project of the Steelworkers union turned the whole bunch of them into "control freaks," a phrase coined sometime during the late 1960s, when every aspect of American life was getting looser and looser, less and less controlled. In that context, anybody going outside established channels, as Johnny Metzgar had when he made a phone call to Youngstown in 1968, seemed to threaten not just the union but the Great Chain of Being.

UNION culture dissipated in the late '60s not because of corrupt men or even bad leaders. Contrary to public perception, the gangsters were always few and far between and had almost no presence in the CIO unions. Upward mobility and the personal opportunism that often accompanies it were as much a part of the culture as a force that under-mined it, and opportunism was almost always mixed with genuine com-mitment to the union cause, to making things better (and better) for workers. The union's official family, like most staff cultures in well-run organizations, had developed such pride in its work that it began to see itself as "the union," and the members as unruly and ungrateful *clients* whose ignorance of the larger picture often threatened the enterprise and always made its work, the work of the union, more difficult.

The members, in turn, began to see things the same way. The staff was "the union," and they were not. The union became a mere practi-cal mechanism, a service for which you paid your dues and about which you complained if the service was not up to your standards. There had always been a strong element of this in the staff-member relationship, but between 1946 and 1959, when everyone in the union had to prepare for and conduct strikes regularly, the larger sense of the union as "all of us" (including families and entire communities) had to be enacted, lived, and suffered. The union's demands had to be publicly justified in terms of what was fair and right and what effect they would have on the economy as a whole. Union leaders in the '60s, both McDonald and Abel and all their minions, worked very hard to avoid strikes and to take labor negotiations off the front pages, where public posturing made practical negotiations more hot and difficult. There was good reason to do so; the vast majority of members had no romantic attachment to striking, and the contract was getting more and more complicated to explain to the members, let alone the general public. But this more pro-fessionalized, lower-key form of bargaining weakened the culture of social solidarity, the lived connection between self-interest and social justice that had so enchanted my father with the union.

As negotiations became more private, steelworkers no longer had to show a link between their contract provisions and the general public welfare, something my father had always been so good at. And then, in the '70s, the link disappeared. Until then, though steelworkers and other union workers had superior wages and conditions, they could le-gitimately argue that their improvements pulled up others—all others. But in the '70s, as real wages began to decline for everybody else, union workers with COLA clauses went on increasing their standard of liv-ing. Steelworkers, even before the union, had always earned a premium wage, but the premium had steadily decreased during the '60s. In the '70s it did an abrupt turnaround: By 1980 the individual steelworker's average wage was nearly 40 percent higher than the median income of all U.S. households.[32] When you add grievance protection and SUB, the specifics of the health and dental plan, vacations, holidays, and early retirement, by the early '80s steelworkers (like most other union workers) were living in a different world than the one in which most workers had to live. Worse, everybody knew this, and many resented it. And, still worse, steelworkers generally didn't seem to care. So when the wolf finally came in 1982, there was little sympathy for steelworkers among other workers and even a good bit of mean-spirited satisfaction that the steelworkers were "finally going to have to live like the rest of us."

During Christmas of 1982, my brother-in-law Albert Mikula was in his fifth or sixth month of what would be a three-year stretch of unemployment from the same mill where my father had worked. Albert was an outspoken opponent of the concessions the companies and the union leadership were asking for then (concessions they would eventually get). So was I, and we were stoking each other up as other family members listened. Albert's oldest son, David—a quiet young man, respectful of his elders in a way that was terribly old-fashioned by 1982—didn't argue with us. Albert, who had been making $13 an hour, declared, "I'll go hungry before I *ever* work for $8 an hour"—which was a rhetorical exaggeration, since the companies were only asking him to work for $11 at the time. At this point David exploded defiantly, "Well, I'll work for $8. And if I could get it, I'd take *your* job while you're making up your mind." Albert and I were speechless. While others thought David was being a little harsh, they joined in to make it clear that Albert and I were in a minority. Albert looked as if he'd just been kicked in the stomach. David was silent but defiant. Albert eventually went back to work for just a little more than $8 an hour, but my guess is that this moment in 1982 was more painful than that one was by the time he got to it.

This exchange took place in a union family in a union town—as union as America ever got. Yet while extreme, the incident was not untypical. By 1982 there was still plenty of unity and discipline within the union, but gone was that dense network of sympathies, power relationships, and personal bonds with the larger community that had been so important in 1959. It was nearly impossible even to remember it.

When Johnny Metzgar retired in 1969 at the age of fifty-six, he knew exactly how privileged he was and to what he owed his good fortune. Unlike so many others, he never forgot that. But the way he explained that to himself changed. In the early years of his retirement, he'd defend his privilege by claiming to be an "opening wedge" that would eventually win early retirement for everybody. Later, as that claim became less credible, he'd point to all the years he had spent in the mill to earn it—which was persuasive to middle-class professionals like me, but didn't go over too well with those for whom a job in the mill would have been like winning the lottery.

There is an enormous difference between these rationales for his privilege. Both make a claim to be just, but the latter looks to the past (he'd done something to deserve it) and claims a *personal* entitlement. "You tell me why I don't deserve it," he'd say, and nobody would. But they'd ask him, "Why do you deserve it and I don't?" To this, there was no answer. The opening-wedge argument, on the other hand, saw his retirement as acting on the future in the service of *social* justice. This is what had always enchanted him about the union. Anything he did for it or it did for him was "not just for myself," but was part of something much bigger that was "for everybody in the long run."

In retirement, he felt isolated from the union (there was no SOAR then that gave retirees a chance to be active), and he was disenchanted with it. With each year, it seemed to him to become more of a private service organization and less of a cause to which you could be loyal. As old men do, he'd hark back to the old days (which were my childhood) and regret what had been lost and what could have been, if only. Though he wouldn't bring it up, he'd agree with me (by the late '70s) when I'd say that the union was no longer the force for social justice it once had been, and he'd grant that that had been a part of its magic. Once disenchanted, he still valued the practical mechanism—and he could still eloquently defend it as such—but all the connections he had seen with the carpenter from Nazareth began to fall away. As they did, he became a smaller man with a shorter memory.

A Forgotten American

On February 1, 1960, just a few weeks after the Steelworkers had finished gloating over their victory, Ezell Blair Jr., Franklin McCain, Joe McNeil, and David Richmond insisted on being served a cup of coffee at a Woolworth's in Greensboro, North Carolina. Rarely do events so neatly divide decades. In January the steel industry finished off a piece of '50s business that had begun in the '30s. That done, four black college freshmen initiated "the '60s." Everything and everybody would be changed over the next decade—even those in an isolated mill town, a world away from the main battlefronts.

Soon enough, events on TV would have more significance than those happening around us—white mobs beating black protesters, assassinations, riots, body bags and death counts, protests and demonstrations; they would scramble our worldviews, rearrange our memories, and change our most intimate relationships. My father ended up on the wrong side of the generational and racial divides and, more importantly, he lost badly to a woman's liberation. And through it all was a class struggle: As I was becoming a middle-class professional, I not only had to separate myself from him, but I also denounced and ridiculed him as I did so.

The '60s was a particularly difficult time for parents. In 1960 Ezell Blair explained to his parents what he was about to do and asked for their support.[33] By the late '60s young people would not only not do anything like that, but we would choose to do things *because* we knew they would upset our parents and their world. When I think now of what my father had to go through in that decade, I regret many things I said and did to him. I had no idea then of how deeply adult (or semiadult) children can hurt their parents with even the smallest of slights, let alone full-scale assaults. But though, if I could, I would take back some words and change some details, the main line of what we did in the '60s had to be done, and there was no way he could have gotten through it without some permanent injury. In retrospect, I don't think either one of us handled it so badly—but that's easy for me to say, because as he became more narrow and self-protective, I was becoming larger.

Today it's hard to remember the huge and many-faceted impact the civil rights revolution had on white people in the industrial North in the early '60s. It's hard to remember the view Americans had of ourselves as a people who always did good and who represented the hope of humanity. Growing up in the glow of our victory over fascism, we found it easy to believe that there was something special about us; both good and strong, we really did stand for truth and justice. The early '60s civil rights struggles—the sit-ins of 1960, the freedom rides of 1961, Birmingham and the March on Washington in 1963—both appealed to those beliefs and challenged them in a way that required everybody, black and white, to either deepen their commitment to justice for all or to backpedal with reservations, qualifications, and provisos. Johnny Metzgar backpedalled, not because he was racist, but because he feared to upset the delicate balance that allowed him certain perogatives as a white man, husband, and father. My mother and I deepened our commitment to justice to undercut exactly those perogatives. In the early '60s, we both used the race issue as a part of our challenge to my father's patriarchal authority. That challenge had started before that and was never primarily about race, but Ezell Blair and his bunch lent us a hand by insisting on justice and inspiring us with examples of courage and persistence.

By the late '60s my mother and I were both independent human beings, completely free of my father's dominance ideologically, psychically, and financially. To get there we exaggerated his shortcomings, his hypocrisy—but so did he.

My mother was a college graduate, but nowhere near as smart as my father. He dominated our family (both the immediate and the extended ones) not only by his strength of will, but also by his intelligence. Overweight and unattractive, Mom had been a painfully shy girl who took refuge in religion and bookish learning at a very early age. She decided early that her fate was to be an old-maid schoolteacher, and she prepared herself accordingly. There was an extension of the University of Pittsburgh in Johnstown in the '30s (an old converted warehouse); she started there and finished at the main campus in Pittsburgh. How her parents —a milk truck driver and a cleaning lady—had afforded this, she wasn't sure, but she knew it had taken the kind of sacrifice she assumed was essential to the lives of Christians and parents.

She taught high school—French and German—for a while in the late '30s and then caught a piece of luck she had not anticipated. In his late twenties Johnny Metzgar, after a "born again" religious conversion, decided it was time to settle down and raise a family. He surveyed the young women in his church and chose Mom. She thanked God for the blessing. Teaching school had always been a second choice, well behind a first choice she'd never expected to have: that of being a dedicated wife and mother. And Dad was, according to her, "quite a catch"—a handsome young man, a good Christian with a good job in the mill, and best of all, a man "who knew his own mind," one who charted his course and stuck to it. She was thrilled with being his wife and our mother. In our childhood years, she was almost always smiling, with her eyes sparkling and with her lips pressing tightly closed, as if she were holding back bursts of joyous laughter. To say she loved her children is too pallid; she gloried in us. As painfully shy and reserved as she was, as slowly, tentatively, and cautiously as she moved about the house and neighborhood (particularly after the first heart attack), she was exuberant to be in our presence. Though she explained right from wrong to us and always faithfully enforced all Dad's rules and regulations, she never had to discipline us. My sister and I had the power to make her beam, to positively glow with joy, and we just naturally tried to do that whenever we could.

My mother had almost no self-esteem. She spoke so softly, when she spoke at all, that you had to strain to hear her. Her handwriting was so small, most people couldn't read it. She seemed always to fear that her mere presence, let alone any word or action, might disturb the really important things that everybody but her was engaged in. This changed as life progressed, but she never lost the belief that others' lives were more important and interesting than hers, and she somehow turned low self-esteem into a strength, and quite a formidable one. As a teenager my sister Marion was a beauty queen, and she had an interesting string of boyfriends—a few of whom kept coming back to our house to visit with Mom even after Marion was no longer interested in them. Mom was a gifted listener. She thought everybody else's life was fascinating, and she felt privileged to be included in it by listening to their problems and dreams. It was in her listening that her education and intelligence came out. Like all good listeners, she asked questions that required you to clarify details and thoughts and that initiated new lines of conversation. Her questions showed not only that she was listening intently to what you were saying (as few people do), but that she heard the things you meant to say but had not.

In the '40s and '50s Irene Metzgar was completely subservient to Johnny, subservient in a way that was extreme in our extended family and neighborhood. Our world was full of strong women—maybe not the kind of dominating forces that Aunt Ruth and Mom's mom, Lottie Lamison, were, but almost never the "superfeminine female" that Eldridge Cleaver saw in the professional, middle-class, white woman of the time.[34] Mom saw herself as weak, lacking in character and overly dependent on others. This weakness undoubtedly explained part of Dad's attraction to her. He knew that she would follow his lead and that he could run his family without interference from her and with lots of support, while at the same time he could take pride in and define himself by "taking care of her." What she called her weakness was attractive to everybody else as well. As they did Uncle Stan, everybody liked her, and everybody looked out for her.

My father ruled the roost in our family. Everything was done his way. He looked out for the rest of us, and he was more likely than any of us to know what was good for us, but he always did things to suit himself. As powerless and embattled as he often felt at work, he was in absolute control at home. And he abused his power—most of all, as almost everybody in the family bitterly remembers, he "abused Mom's good nature." There wasn't anything dramatic—no hitting, not even much shouting, just the kind of daily insensitivity and petty dominance for the joy of it that is both degrading and frightening if you have to live with it day after day. From as far back as I can remember, Marion and I both feared and resented the way he treated Mom—though Marion resented it much more than I did, and I'm not sure I would have resented it at all without her instruction.

Two kinds of petty incidents stick out in my memory, but these were repeated over and over again, amid thousands of other ways he abused Mom's good nature. When he was home, she served him—she brought him coffee, put the newspaper in his lap, helped him take off his shoes or put them away. Often when he was home in the evening, sitting in his chair and reading or watching television, Mom would come into the living room to finally "settle down" for the night. Just after she'd sit down and make herself comfortable, he'd think of something he needed her to do, and she would have to get up and do it. In earlier years, she never resisted or resented this, but there was hurt all over her face as she did what she was bidden to do. Though he hid his face in the newspaper or in his gaze at the TV, he sometimes (Marion thinks usually) seemed to be smiling. As Marion was coming into her teenage years, she'd tell Mom to sit still, and she'd do whatever Dad wanted done. Several times that I can remember, Marion asked with a special kind of acid in her voice, "Why don't *you* do it? Mom's tired. Why do you wait till she sits down? If you don't think of it before she sits down, *you* should have to do it, or do without." At that, Dad would be up in his chair, Mom on her feet in a flash; he'd give Marion a good talking to and then mete out her punishment (usually, having to stay home Saturday night, something that really hurt Marion at the time). Marion knew she would be punished when she spoke, but she did it anyway. Over time, this eventually got my mother to start sticking up for herself so that Marion wouldn't do it and get punished.

The other kind of incident occurred during Sunday drives, when Marion and I were little and we all spent Sundays together. We'd all be feeling good, enjoying the movement of the car and the good feeling of being a family and hurtling through space together—playing word games, counting cows, singing songs. Dad would be feeling good, effervescent, and this made the rest of us relax and feel good, too. At the height of his high spirits, he had a habit of reaching over and patting Mom just above her breasts. He did it out of exuberance and affection, but it always irritated her. At first she'd laugh and say, "Now, you stop that, Johnny Metzgar," and sometimes he would. But usually he'd keep on doing it in a teasing, playful way, and eventually she'd get mad, push his hand away, and turn to look out the window, sulking. Then he'd blow up. He hadn't meant anything by it. Why did it irritate her so? He had a tough life. Unlike her, he had to work in the mill. Why did she always spoil his good humor? Why didn't she understand him? Why didn't anybody appreciate him and the sacrifices he was making for his family? In the back seat Marion and I would clam up and look out our windows, frightened and ashamed, and disappointed at how quickly the good feeling had disappeared. This sequence of events happened so often that we usually clammed up and got tense right at the beginning of it; we knew what was coming. Once, when Marion was a very little girl, she lost it: She started slapping Dad on the shoulder, crying, "Don't do it, Daddy. Please don't do it!"—as if she were trying to stop an axe murder. He slammed on the brakes, almost throwing us into the front seat, and Marion got a spanking right by the side of the road as other cars whizzed by. Nobody was more ashamed than Mom.

Marion tried not to, but she rebelled early and often. Eventually, she would plead with Mom, "Why do you let him treat you like that?" But way before that, Mom started to change. She hardly ever stood up to him and never talked back, but she started to do things on her own. In the summer of '56 or '57, she crossed a Rubicon of some sort, and from that point on, slowly but methodically, she worked herself free of his dominance.

We were all in the living room, and Dad and Marion were wrestling on the floor, as he had always done with us kids when he was in good spirits. Marion was too old and well developed to be wrestled with at this point, but old habits die hard, and she didn't seem to mind at first. But when she wanted to stop, he kept on teasing, and she bit him on the arm—hard—to make him stop. He got up screaming, "Animal!" "Look at this," he yelled, showing Mom the teeth marks on his arm and the little droplets of blood. "You're an animal who's not fit to live with," he shouted at Marion, among other things. In addition to being angry, he seemed confused, humiliated, even frightened and ashamed. Marion looked right at him, saying nothing, definitely frightened but with a defiant expression, rock certain she had done nothing wrong.

A few days later, he left for one of his two-week fishing trips to Canada, and Marion's punishment was that she had to stay in the house the entire time he was gone. The day he left, Mom got us together to announce that she was not going to enforce Dad's punishment. We were amazed. At first we were exhilarated, particularly Marion, but then we got scared, frightened above all at what might happen to Mom. "What will you do if Dad finds out?" Marion asked, obviously thinking that this might not be such a good idea after all. Mom mumbled something we couldn't hear, and then looked up at us and said as loudly and as firmly as she had ever said anything in her life, "I don't care anymore. We'll cross that bridge if we come to it." The three of us sat in our living room, looking at each other in silence, for what seemed like a very long time, though not nearly long enough. I was the most frightened and Marion seemed the most grown-up person in the room, but there was a look on Mom's face we had never seen before; calm and determined, the look said that we'd be alright if we all stuck together. It was a luxurious silence that I can remember, that I can put myself into with all the feel and smell of it, any time I want to. About a decade later, as I was reading Trotsky's *The Russian Revolution*, the part where the soldiers in St. Petersburg waver and then decide not to fire on the people, this glorious moment of silence came back to me—and at the time, I had no idea why. But in that summer of '56 or '57, Marion broke the silence by getting up, walking over to Mom, and giving her a brief hug and kiss. Walking her sexiest teenage walk, the one Dad forbade her to use, she went to the door, threw it open with all the drama she could muster, and said without looking back, "I love you, Mom." Marion couldn't see it, but I'm sure she knew: Mom was glowing.

While Dad was gone, Mom finally did what she had been talking about doing for some time: She signed up to become a substitute teacher at my junior high school, not far from where we lived. That fall she started teaching a few days a month. Unlike other substitutes, she never had a problem with discipline. Everybody had always liked her and looked out for her, even children. Somehow it made her a wonderful teacher—the kind that middle-aged adults remember fondly. The more she taught, the more she wanted to teach. The only full-time job she could get when she was ready for it was a special education class at a junior high school across town—a class that had chased out the last few teachers but that Mom tamed with no trouble at all. It was a small but challenging class, consisting of fifteen or sixteen mostly overaged boys, black and white, who had been in various scrapes with the law and the school system most of their lives. She discovered that two-thirds of them were not "mentally retarded," and she made a fuss about it, eventually getting several of them into regular classes. One guy, who just couldn't stay out of trouble outside of her class, quit school before she could get the system to accept him in regular classes. Years later, after he'd turned himself into a solid, working-class citizen, he came to see her and told her what a big difference it had made to him to find out he wasn't "really a dummy." The students who *were* mentally disabled loved her even more; she was a gifted listener, and she actually knew quite a lot about making the most of your limitations.

Everything happened slowly, in measured steps, but from her first paycheck as a substitute teacher, she insisted on having a separate savings account. She negotiated the details with Dad: Part of her paycheck went to the household, but another part was for herself. From that part, she would buy things she wanted, which meant mostly stuff for Marion and me. But she also started to dress differently—like a schoolteacher instead of a housewife. She seldom bucked him directly, she just started living a separate life. He gradually learned to do things for himself and, with her own bank account, so did she. After I graduated from high school, she bought them a house with her own money. He loved the house as much as she did—it had an upstairs, and a shower in the basement—but he always called it "Mom's house," as if he were a guest in it. He was. Through the '60s they learned to live separate lives under the same roof, and though she was occasionally set back with another heart attack, she continued to distance herself from him until the summer before she died (in 1968), when she was getting ready to leave him entirely. This would have been a momentous step, since there had never been a divorce in our family, and because she died, there still hasn't.

My mother's liberation would have happened in some measure without the civil rights revolution, but it would not have gone as far. Ezell Blair and my sister, Marion, started college at the same time, in the fall of 1959, in the middle of the strike. Her leaving was a relief because she had battled Dad day in and day out since her early teens, and Mom and I had to support her without going against him directly. It was a relief to be without that tension in the house. But with Marion gone, Mom and I were on our own. Neither of us were strong enough then to directly oppose his control of our lives, but we were well practiced in indirectly supporting rebels with a good cause. Ezell Blair and his kind came onto our television screens just in time to take Marion's place. I was getting better and better at making arguments premised on what Jesus would have done. Mom just listened to Dad and me engage in these political-religious arguments and then did things nobody expected.

If you have the cartoon cut-out version of the white, working-class male in your head, you won't be able to grasp the complex dialectic of race, class, gender, and generation that went on in my family in the '60s. As Richard Hamilton and other sociologists who look at survey data and voting results have shown time and again, there is no evidence — and there never has been — for "the assumptions that liberal virtue [and racial enlightenment] resides in the middle class and that intolerance is disproportionately found in the working class."[35] But as Hamilton showed at the time, this set of class assumptions was essential to the liberal-middle-class worldview: "In the world view of liberal intellectuals, those persons who share decent and humane values form a tiny minority standing on the edge of an abyss. They are always standing there, the problem being that there are so few people who share those values and so many potentially powerful and, if aroused, dangerous groups in the society."[36]

Johnny Metzgar was no racist, even though by the late '60s he was full of complicated resentments and even though I would eventually call him one, both to his face and in characterizing him to others. As I was preparing myself for college, so was my mother, and with the help of the Civil Rights movement as seen through the eyes of the liberal media, we adopted the college-educated, liberal-middle-class view of ourselves as part of a tiny, virtuous minority. Martin Luther King Jr. was preaching exactly the opposite message then: that most people had decent and humane values they would act on if you forced the issue. But that message did not serve our purposes, did not provide us with a powerful legitimating identity like liberal self-righteousness did. To us Johnny Metzgar *was* powerful and dangerous, and the liberal-middle-class characterization of him helped us free ourselves from his domination. But it wouldn't have worked at all if he hadn't still had a firm commitment to social justice that we could use against him.

My father's reaction to the Civil Rights movement was not what I had expected. We had been sternly instructed as children about racial and ethnic prejudice—forbidden to use the hurtful words and told, "No-body's any better than you, and you're no better than anybody else." When I was a child, he had put forth Jackie Robinson as both a model baseball player ("He's not that fast," he explained about Jackie's ability to steal bases, including home, "he's just smarter than the rest of them") and a model human being ("Branch Rickey hired a man with a temper and asked him to hold it. Even the racists couldn't help but respect that"). And he positively gloried in explaining the Montgomery Bus Boycott to me when I was twelve: "You'd be surprised what can happen when everybody sticks together." But the intensity of Southern white racism in Little Rock in 1957 frightened him, as best I can remember, and as things began to develop in the early '60s, he became more frightened and confused. Though his sympathies were unswervingly with blacks, he tended to blame them for provoking the violence. For him everything was about tactics and the importance of patience, because, as he explained it, you can't change everything at once—which was not the kind of impatient "what's right is right" he preached in defending the union. The principles of Christian social justice that he could so powerfully articulate required some qualifications on this subject. Martin Luther King's broad appeals to brotherly love and equality in the eyes of the Lord didn't stir him the way they did my mother and me. Instead, he worried that they might somehow unravel the negotiated settlement upon which the postwar world "since the union" was based.

His union reacted pretty much the same way. Always supportive in the abstract and even the not-so-abstract areas of national and state legislation, the Steelworkers dragged their feet and actively resisted real changes in workplace relations and union governance. Some of this involved classic affirmative-action dilemmas, bids for special treatment for blacks to reverse the effects of previous and ongoing discrimination—things like appointing blacks to leadership roles to which they were unlikely to be elected or making some exceptions to the union's seniority system in order to break up departmental segregation within the mills.[37] Reasonable men, and they were all men in those days, could arrive at different conclusions on this without necessarily being racist. But the spirit of Steelworker stalling—in the ranks as much as in the leadership—hurt the union's culture more than a few accommodations ever could have.

Worse, racism in the mills violated the most fundamental principles of CIO unionism—that the workforce would not be divided by race, religion, or ethnicity; that who got what job would depend on blind rules (color-blind no less than blind to whose nephew or brother-in-law you were); that there would be no arbitrary authority, only rules and procedures negotiated in the contract. In fact, it didn't always work this way. Even within the system of company-caused departmental segregation, the union didn't always play by the rules for black men. All it took was a griever who failed to file a grievance, or filed it late, or didn't push it very strong, and black steelworkers were denied upward mobility in the job classification system—a system where the difference between a Job Class 6 and a Job Class 10 could be a couple of dimes an hour, which became over time the difference between owning a home or sending one of your kids to college or not. Moving up the job ladder within the mill was a fundamental part of the union miracle, and it wasn't always or even usually denied to black steelworkers. But it was denied a lot— not only in the notoriously racist mills in Alabama and Baltimore, but everywhere—and every time it was, it tore at the heart of CIO unionism, even before black steelworkers started to resist it, but especially once they had. This wasn't something reasonable men could disagree about. It was wrong—in fact, it was evil, both practically and metaphysically—according to the fundamental precepts of CIO unionism.

My father opposed the affirmative action measures based on his reading of these precepts, but I'm reasonably certain he was never one of those grievers who didn't enforce the contract 100 percent regardless of skin color. He once introduced me to Teddy, one of a handful of black men in his department, for the explicit purpose of my hearing Teddy's testimony that "your father is no racist." Teddy illustrated his assertion with a story that showed what a color-blind "good union man" my father was in comparison to others, which didn't impress me much at the time because I expected that to be the case, and it would shock me even now to find out otherwise. But Johnny Metzgar didn't buck those "others" who didn't pass on the grievances of black workers. Whoever they were, he feared them and disclaimed responsibility for them, which was rare for him. He also didn't talk up the black steelworkers' case when they started to make it.

This was surprising, because he had always been the one our family had to worry might do something unwise or impractical just because it was right. I started out genuinely puzzled, thinking there must be something I didn't understand, but it wasn't long before I started challenging him more sharply, throwing back phrases and precepts that I had heard him use hundreds of times. I was genuinely disappointed in his responses, and genuinely proud of (and a little uneasy with) my own superior virtue as it emerged, but I also instinctively knew that these arguments were a road to independence. I got bolder and bolder in challenging his religious convictions and sense of justice as the civil rights struggle heated up on our TV and in the mills. He started to dread my questions and then, occasionally, to tire of arguing with me. This gave me a little more space to think my own thoughts and live my own life. My mother encouraged me in this direction, but she was also genuinely moved by my arguments. Sometime in 1961, during my senior year in high school, she joined the local chapter of the National Association for the Advancement of Colored People (NAACP), which at the time was a breathtakingly radical thing for her to do. It wasn't clear in our neighborhood that the NAACP wasn't a bunch of Communists, and everybody—Dad, her two sisters, Aunt Ruth—tried to talk her out of it. They were afraid of what might happen to her; she could lose her job as a teacher, for example. She listened carefully, as always, but until her next heart attack, she was a (quiet but persistent) civil rights activist. This upped the ante for me.

My father had always encouraged me to argue with him . He saw it as a part of developing my mind, and I knew he would never punish me for anything I said. As long as I didn't challenge his authority to set rules and regulations for my behavior, I was free and clear to speak my mind. And I did. Though our arguments mush together in my memory, I'm pretty sure that the more bitter and hateful things I said to him (that he was "nothing but a racist," that Jesus would be ashamed of him, that he didn't have the courage of his convictions, that he was just looking out for himself, and that he was the reason I no longer believed in God) came out later in the '60s. But the main breaks, the most startling defiances, came in '60 and '61, when I was still in high school.

When I left for college in the fall of 1961, he warned me that some of those professors were "godless Communists" who could turn me against my own family and friends. I made a few stops and starts before those professors started getting to me, but by the late '60s it was clear that he had been right. Mentally, Mom came right along with me and so, in every way, did my wife, Judie; we all "got radicalized" by the times. By 1966 I had begun to define myself as a Marxist revolutionary, and I accused Dad of being a traitor to his class because he was a griever in the union. He thought things were getting pretty nutty by then: "I can't even talk to you any more. You college guys think you know everything.

Actually, every year you get dumber and dumber." In 1968, shortly after I finally got my bachelor's degree and shortly before she died, my
mother actually listened (intelligently asking questions, as always) as I
debated whether I could best serve humanity by running guns to guer-
rillas in Guatemala (which friends of mine were planning to do at the
time) or by mastering Hegel's *Phenomenology of Spirit*. She didn't try to
persuade me one way or the other but urged me to "open my heart to
Jesus," while noting that Hegel had been "a good Christian." Dad was
no good to talk with about things like this. He thought I was "off on another planet," and he was worn out with talking to me about anything.

To me the '60s was a great time to come of age, a blessing I'll never
forget or regret, but I wouldn't have wanted to be *my* father then. Some
things did get pretty nutty, but at the core of that tumultuous decade
was a serious purpose—a great leap forward for human freedom. I take
seriously the argument that the leap may have gone too far, that we lost
our sense of limits, that we glorified individual rights at the expense of
the larger community, that we overdid our assault on authority.[38] But it
has to be remembered that authority consistently overreacted and often defended its narrowest perogatives against its own publicly stated
principles. The '60s was a dialectic of overreaction, but we got through
it to a better world, because there was indeed more than a tiny minority of virtuous people.

What I regret about how the '60s were played out in my family is that
the way we blamed him caused him to become more worthy of our
blame. There was something malignant in the kind of control he exer-
cised in our home—a difference between his legitimate authority and
his petty domination just for the momentary satisfaction of it. But he
was always genuinely trying to sort things out, to do right by us and
everybody else, and at several crucial junctures he adjusted his needs
and views to align them with what he saw as fair and right. The problems came between the crucial junctures.

The strength of my father was that he saw himself and lived his life as
a necessary contradiction. As a man, a steelworker, a shop steward, he
had to be tough and cunning; he had to make himself "as hard as steel"
—which is not just hard (and brittle) like iron, but shrewdly tensile. As
a Christian, however, he was supposed to be soft, open, and vulnerable,
with charity for all and malice toward none, actively pursuing justice in
this life in order to earn a better one to come. He was a lot better at the
former, and he knew that, but even as he tired of achieving a synthesis

of those two existential ecologies, he never denied the legitimacy of the goal. Likewise, he hated the smugness and ambition of the college educated and loved the warm egalitarianism and sloppy diversity of working-class life, but he forced (and shrewdly manipulated) me out of the one class and into the other with an iron-like consistency that he must have known would eventually break his heart.

Mom used his internal contradictions to carve out a place for herself free of his domination and bad manners. But I blamed him in a careless and undisciplined way that was characteristic of the class I was joining through my long march in the university. Our orientation toward achievement, our competitive angling for esteem, seems to need somebody to be better than. In the '60s, I needed to feel I was a part of a virtuous minority—a lonely witness against a world that was not good enough for me. Every step the mainstream made toward my direction, I moved a little farther toward the margin in order to preserve my identity—in order to believe that I was better. And, incredibly, I wasn't the least bit suspicious that, as I shouted "racist" and "sexist," "imperialist" and "pig," I was systematically making a better life for myself as a middle-class professional. I wasn't suspicious that the burden of achieving racial justice was disproportionately put on him and people like him. I didn't appeal to his sense of justice, to his complicated sense of religion or the color-blind inclusiveness of his CIO unionism. I used these against him, to denounce him as a hypocrite—not to reach out and bring him toward me, but to distance myself from an exaggerated evil that I wanted to be pure of.

This is still not the part I most regret. Shit happens. Father and son stuff ain't no tea party, and he was the adult, not me. Besides, he needed to be opposed. He was no racist, imperialist, or pig, but he wasn't about to make the kinds of adjustments that were needed without some pressure. What I regret is that my denunciations—which made me feel so good, so "validated," in the jargon of my class—made him retreat into an angry defensiveness, one that he resorted to *only* when he recognized some truth in the charges, but one where he nursed his resentment at my inability to put him in a context that suited. That is, I backed him into a place where he handled everything worse than he otherwise would have. In 1961, when I graduated from high school, my father was a man who hated George Wallace and everything he stood for. He was a man you could never have imagined would vote for Ronald Reagan nineteen years later. I helped George Wallace get a hearing with that man, and then I helped Ronald Reagan get his vote. I helped make him part of the problem when he should have been part of the solution. I'm not taking all the blame, but that's the part I most regret.

In the '50s, he achieved for a while a powerful synthesis of CIO-bred social Keynesianism and trade union contractualism, and he made it fit within his evangelical version of the Social Gospel. You cannot look at the 1959 Steel Strike now without being impressed by the degree and kind of class unity that was achieved in the '50s. All that came apart in the '60s. The class war had resulted in a highly favorable "negotiated settlement," and that accomplishment made new liberations possible. There's no way this could have been done without unravelling previous syntheses and unities. But in the fading years of the twentieth century, I'm not convinced that the divisions and contentions among us had to strengthen the oligarchy of wealth the way they have.

Here's the mistake I think I made. Social justice needs to be related to rational self-interest, not posed and pursued as an abstract ideal. But I had thought that justice was one thing and self-interest another—that they didn't need to be, because they couldn't be, reconciled. I made some sacrifices, but in the main line of what I did, my pursuit of justice got reconciled with my self-interest behind my back. Justice and self-interest are sometimes, even often, opposed, but when you renounce the need to reconcile them, you cannot help but engage in bad faith. Self-righteousness almost always has a hidden agenda. Mine did.

My father's mistake was that he retired, retreated into a separate peace. He spent most of the '60s astonished and confused, and as his worldview unravelled, he gradually withdrew into a defensive protection of his self-interest, with less and less attempt to reconcile that with the broader public interest or the kind of metaphysical social justice that had always carried such weight with him. He had always defined himself as "just a little man," but coming into the '60s that phrase made an assertive claim for a sweeping social justice; the little man was the one who counted most, things should be arranged to accommodate him, and if a lot of little men stuck together, that could be achieved. Yet by 1969, when he retired, he used the phrase to indicate that he could neither do anything about nor be held responsible for what happened outside his own narrow precinct. Johnny Metzgar started to simply look out for himself—something he had always preached against, something he had always claimed would work against you in the long run. That's why he temporarily forgot the debt we all owe the union.

But he didn't permanently forget. His memory reached back to the '20s and '30s, and he saw the connections between things, the causes and effects within his life. Even when he felt most alone, he knew that none of us can ever be truly alone, that every human act leaves a residue, something for you to work with.

When Mom died in the fall of 1968, Dad fell apart. Not in a way the outside world could see very well—he didn't have a nervous breakdown, he kept going to work every day and church every Sunday. But he cried a lot, developed a host of physical ailments he had never had before, and he whined and complained to whoever would listen. Judie and I were back in Johnstown that year, saving money for graduate school (or maybe for running guns to Guatemala!), and I got to hear more of this than anybody else, with the possible exception of Aunt Ruth. I wasn't as sympathetic as I should have been. I wasn't feeling too good myself, and I was a lot better at dealing with him as a dominating son-of-a-bitch than as a whimpering, lost soul. He reached out to me in a way he never had, and though I did not make a conscious decision not to be there for him, I wasn't.

Yock, the Evil Foreman in the proletarian fairy tales my father told me as a child, could see that even six months after Mom had died, Dad was still reeling. The shop-floor wars between Yock and Dad had always been the kind of savagely personal vendettas that cannot be good for productivity. Some of Dad's greatest moments, according to him, were when he had "showed up" or humiliated Yock. By March of 1969, Dad's doctor had him on such a complicated mess of drugs (mood elevators and tranquilizers) that things were getting worse, not better. Smelling a final solution, Yock somehow found work that could only be done on "the Hot Rod"—an old machine that only a handful of guys were qualified to run. About the Hot Rod, my father explained, "If it had been just a piece of junk, it wouldn't have been so bad. But it was a precision machine, it could do beautiful work, but you had to run it fast and it was wildly unreliable. In the middle of a perfect cut, it would just go haywire. You had to hold onto the controls and pay attention every second." Everybody hated the Hot Rod. The union had filed grievances to get extra breaks for anybody running it, and numerous attempts had been made to fix it, "but it was like the Devil himself. It would run perfectly for weeks at a time, and then just go off on a tangent, and if you weren't right on top of it, it would ruin a job worth thousands of dollars. When they came to fix it, it would run perfectly again." And management, with Yock in the forefront, had always claimed that there was nothing wrong with the Hot Rod, that the machinists were just covering up for their own mistakes.

In March and April of 1969, Dad tried everything "to get off the Hot Rod." He got his doctor to file a temporary disability claim. Rejected. He filed grievances, but they would take months, maybe years, to settle. He appealed to the department superintendent for mercy and was told, "Whatever you can work out with Yock is fine with me, but I'm not going to go over his head." Finally, he did it. "My nerves were shot," he explained. "I couldn't sleep at night without dreaming the Hot Rod." He went to Yock, man to man, and appealed for mercy: "I'll train a younger guy on the machine. I don't care how long it takes me, at least I'll have an end in sight." Two other guys with more seniority, he told Yock, had agreed to rotate with him on the Hot Rod—two weeks on for Dad, one week on for each of them. How about that? Yock didn't say a word. He just let Dad ramble on, appealing for mercy. Dad didn't conclude, he just stopped rambling and waited for Yock's reaction. Yock, he said, "just laughed in my face." By the rules of the union contract, Dad had to work this machine; only Yock's discretion could save him from it. "I wish I could help you, Johnny," Yock said, meaning the opposite, "but I need you to work that machine, and I've got a year's worth of work for it."

Dad and I speculated on Yock's motives. I thought maybe he wanted Dad to retire, to be out of his hair. Dad said, "No, he knows I can't afford it yet. He wants to break me. He wants to either drive me crazy or for me to accumulate enough 'errors' on that machine that he can fire me with a reduced pension. And the way I'm going, he's going to get the one or the other. He's already got a lot of what he wants. I'm a mess. I just can't take it much longer." In the late '60s, shortly after the union had won "thirty and out," not many guys in their fifties actually used it—it wasn't rich enough yet. But my dad figured and refigured how he might live on it until his Social Security kicked in. Unlike others, he had some savings—he had sold Mom's house and moved to an apartment, and most of the money he'd put aside for his kids' college educations had not been used (Marion hadn't finished and, after my first year, I had paid for my own). He figured and refigured, and finally he worked it out. He shared all the details with me; it was a complicated contraption that I didn't understand too well, except to marvel at his ingenuity. He pulled some strings in the union, "called in some favors," and through some kind of technicality, got an immediate six-month disability that led right into retirement.

It all came together in a couple of days, and Dad was out the door by the end of the week. Yock was shocked and beaten. "I was right," Dad gloated. "He hadn't expected me to retire." What's more, Dad showed the two older guys who could run the Hot Rod how to retire if they wanted to—and they wanted to. By the end of the summer, Yock had a year's worth of work for the Hot Rod and nobody who could run it. Coming from way back in the bottom of the ninth, my father had won his last shop-floor war.

The victory reinvigorated him, and he started rebuilding his life— one that didn't include Marion and me, though we were welcome to visit. I was glad to be rid of him at the time, though later it hurt me that he didn't take more interest in his grandchildren. There was little left of his broader sense of unionism when I finally started trying to appeal to it in the late '70s. But with a little prodding, he could still be eloquent within his narrow, trade-union contractualism: "You can say what you want about the union, but Stan and me and lots of others would have been thrown on the scrap heap without it. I saw them do it to the old guys in the '30s. In the end, Yock couldn't do just whatever he wanted. The union couldn't do everything we wanted either, but it gave you something to work with, something to keep you from being on your knees begging for mercy. It might seem like a little thing to you, but to me it was everything."

At the very end of his life, he temporarily forgot the debt we all owe the union. But given all he had been through, that was understandable. On a comparative basis, he had remembered longer and truer than most. Besides, it had only been temporary, and I was there to remind him.

6

The Contest for
Official Memory

Calling the myth of classlessness larcenous is . . . no empty
figure of speech. . . . Because of its oversimplifying power,
pieces of the truth are constantly being mistaken for the
whole, connections between each part and every other part
are neglected, and immodesty and self-righteousness take
command.

—Benjamin DeMott, *The Imperial Middle*

To imagine . . . that America's middle-class prosperity in the
second half of the twentieth century sprang from wonderful
inventions and the bounty distributed by modern manufacturing requires one to forget. . . . In the sanitized version of
American history, the labor movement did not happen.

—William Greider, *One World, Ready or Not*

In the early 1980s, as the steel industry crashed, an outfit
called Mainstream Access tried to help displaced steelworkers get new jobs. This was difficult work because the
demise of steel was pulling down a lot of related activities,
and national unemployment was in the double digits for the
first time since the Depression. As Mainstream Access taught
steelworkers how to prepare resumes, it became the butt of
a lot of working-class jokes. Some of the jokes were self-

deprecating. Under "Accomplishments," someone would claim to have put, "I got up every day and went to work—well, almost every day." Others had a bitter tinge. Under "Objective" someone put, "A job like yours, so long as I don't have to wear a tie and act like you do." Another, knowing he'd likely never see his previous pay rate again, simply wrote "$13 an hour."

Resumes embody a certain way of looking at life, and most steel-workers resisted looking at it that way, even though they had to try. The professional middle class is, as is often noted, achievement oriented. We tend to measure ourselves by what we *do*, by our accomplishments, and we tend to be competitive with others. That's what resumes are about. We list our accomplishments, and this helps someone else evaluate us against our competitors. There's an art to writing a good resume: You have to present yourself in as positive a way as possible, covering up your negatives without telling outright lies. Lots of gaming and bad faith can go into developing resumes, but the act of defining yourself and re-counting your life in terms of what you have done is not superficial. At existential moments we put our resumes aside and ask, "What have I ac-complished? What difference have I made?" These questions ask about our lives as friends and lovers and parents, as whole human beings. But even so, if we have accomplished little in our work lives, we tend to feel worthless.

Listing accomplishments is not just recording the past. Past achieve-ments suggest our potential, and we look to them to gauge what we might yet be capable of doing. One of our best qualities as middle-class professionals is that we never think of ourselves as completed, as fixed entities with no further potential. We know that life has stages—that we are always developing, changing, becoming something we are not yet. We are more ready than other classes to believe that we can and should transform ourselves.

Mainstream Access's counselors were trying to get displaced workers to look at their past accomplishments in order to envision what they might yet become. But working-class culture emphasizes being and be-longing, not achieving and becoming. The kinds of work that working-class people do and the contexts in which they do them do not lend themselves to the listing of discrete, individual accomplishments. If working people consider themselves to have accomplishments, they lo-cate them in their private lives. But even so, defining yourself by your accomplishments seems superficial to them. What counts is the kind of person you are, day in and day out. They look to their personal qualities on the job and off, not to specific things they have done, to define themselves. And these qualities always come in human packages that include unchangeable deficiencies, immutable weaknesses.

Mainstream Access was trying to get steelworkers to look at themselves in a different way. Resume writing changed as a result. (It had already begun to change when "displaced homemakers" needed to redefine themselves for the work world in the '70s.) People were encouraged to look not for specific accomplishments, but for generalizable skills and abilities, even personal qualities, that they had gained and proved through experience. Like homemakers before them, displaced workers liked this idea, but they knew this was not the way the mainstream played the game, and they knew the mainstream knew that. But that was not the hard part. The hard part was the idea that you could and should transform yourself. Most steelworkers did not want to transform themselves, even if they thought they could. Even worse, it seemed like a bad strategy, unnatural, to try to eliminate weaknesses rather than to fit into a situation where your weaknesses were simply accepted because they could be offset by others' strengths, just as your strengths helped offset others' weaknesses. Even if you could eliminate your deficiencies, you would have to define yourself as self-sufficient, a fundamental error that inevitably leads to both loneliness and an inability to be honest with yourself. If others did not accept your weaknesses and compensate for them, you would have to be constantly adjusting to their view of what you should be, either covering up the weaknesses you couldn't change or making a show of trying to change them. This way of life seemed fraught with tension. You would always be striving to perfect yourself and to "get ahead" of others as you did so. Others would become part of the problem, not the solution.

The working-class sense of immutable personal insufficiency—and the need for others that results—is both the principal strength and the primary weakness of that culture. Mainstream Access's employment counselors in the 1980s were doing work similar to what I do as a general education teacher at an urban commuter university: coaxing adults to believe they can become something they are not without fundamentally changing who they are. Most of them know better. Most of them know that we're trying to make them over in our own image, that we're introducing them to middle-class ways and values that are not, in some respects at least, as good as their own. Even those who go along—and many are forced to go along in order to survive—know that there is a big loss as well as a gain in becoming middle class.

As a part of a steelworker family and community in the 1950s, you didn't need to become middle class. You could be yourself and still make progress in life. I grew up in a place where the workers lived in a valley and our betters lived on a hill, and though we resented them for "looking down on us," we didn't envy them. And for the most part, we didn't need them. We could be ourselves, among ourselves, and with our own way of doing things, we could make our lives better and better. We knew we were not a part of the mainstream, as defined by television, the movies, national newspapers and magazines. But we didn't want to be, and there was nothing forcing us to gain access to it.

My father was one of the few of his generation who realized that this could not last. There was no future in the mill, he'd say, and Marion and I had better get college educations if we hoped for a better life. Yet his illusion, like mine and those of most others I knew on the college track in high school, was that we could go to college and win middle-class jobs without becoming middle-class people. When I first began to prepare for college, during the 1959 strike, I was one of a tiny minority. Most of my male contemporaries thought they could progress by being auto mechanics, machinists, or printers—many of them did, for a while at least. Most felt sorry for me for being on the college track and were grateful they didn't have a misguided, tyrannical father like mine. Though many eventually would, hardly anybody *wanted* to "leave the valley" then. I didn't.

According to the standard conception of American history, none of this happened or could have happened. My father and I never existed, or if we did, we were not fundamentally different from Ozzie and David, Mr. Cleaver and Beaver, and Bob Anderson and his son, Bud. By 1959, it is said in the history books, we were "middle class"—or if we weren't, we aspired to be and shortly would be. There wasn't a culture and a way of life that was substantially different from the middle class one, and therefore, there were not unions that protected this way of life for a while. There didn't need to be strikes, because postwar prosperity was an impersonal tide lifting everybody into the middle class. Or if there were strikes, they were about narrow matters like wages and benefits, not grand ones like cultures and ways of life.

The organized working class and its unions get "disappeared" from postwar American history because they don't fit. To recognize and re-member a working class with distinct interests and values would require the professional middle class to recognize our values and interests as related to our class rather than as *the* social norm to which everyone should aspire. In the years after World War II, middle-class profes-sionals carved out a huge place in American life—large in numbers, larger still in power and prestige. The telling of history, the decisions about what to remember and forget, is generally the responsibility of middle-class professionals, and it usually gets told from our perspective. History is about doing and becoming, not being and belonging, and therefore we just naturally tend toward "great man" history, emphasiz-ing individual accomplishments—the first woman this, the first black that—not the collective action, the organization, and the constella-tions of belief and behavior among regular guys and ordinary people that actually drive real history, if you think about it. In short, Ameri-cans have forgotten the debt we all owe the union because to remember it would require us middle-class professionals to become class conscious.

Postwar Prosperity: The Official Story and What's Wrong with It

Imagine a history of the 1950s that began something like this: The 1950s were a great time for the American people—poverty decreased by a third, everybody's standard of living increased steadily and sub-stantially, and a powerful sense of equal rights took hold that would shape the rest of the century. But these improvements didn't just hap-pen. The 1950s were full of strikes and protests, organized collective ac-tion that pushed the limits of what a democratic capitalism would allow.

Such a paragraph could not fit in any of the eighteen major histories of postwar America (see Appendix A), not even the ones with titles such as *The Proud Decades*, *American High*, and *When the Going Was Good*, and certainly not the one titled *The Dark Ages*. Some see the '50s as a great time for the American people, and most mention the improvements in the standard of living (though often in negative terms, as part of dis-cussions of "consumerism" and "empty materialism"). Surprisingly few mention the substantial decrease in poverty—from a little less than one of three people in 1950 to a little more than one of five by 1960.[1] The acknowledgment of the emergence of a powerful sense of equal rights is restricted to African Americans, and great men such as Martin Luther

King get most of the attention, not organized collective action. But issues of emphasis and interpretation aside, the previous paragraph could not be in any existing account of the 1950s because of the phrase "full of strikes."

The 1950s *were* full of strikes. As Donald Barlett and James Steele point out in a book about the 1990s titled *America: Who Stole the Dream?*, the '50s was a strike decade: "During the 1950s, unions averaged 352 [major] work stoppages a year. That dropped to 283 in the 1960s, then held steady at 289 in the 1970s. It plummetted to 83 in the 1980s, and to 38 thus far in the 1990s. The number of workers involved in strikes has fallen from an average of 1.6 million a year in the 1950s to 273,000 in the 1990s."[2] The long-term picture of strikes this presents is somewhat deceptive, because the strike wave of the late 1960s and early 1970s gets averaged out of existence. But these figures and others indicate that the number and extent of strikes that occurred may be among the distinctive characteristics of what is usually seen as a placid decade. In fact, no decade in American history—not the 1890s, not the teens, and not the 1930s or 1940s—saw as many strikes as the 1950s did.[3]

Yet only one of the eighteen major surveys of the postwar period (Patterson) even looks at work stoppages in the 1950s, whether as a measure of working-class militancy or as anything else. Only three (Jezer, Patterson, and Perrett) pay any substantial attention to the existence and condition of the labor movement during that decade. In the others, unions are covered in three to six paragraphs (if at all) in highly stereotypical ways that would not be permitted if they were covering, say, "Italian-Americans" (which none do). Only seven of the eighteen mention that *any* strikes occurred during the 1950s. Diggins and Leuchtenberg mention the 1952 Steel Strike, during which President Truman took over the steel industry and the Supreme Court made him give it back; Manchester and Oakley note the 1959 Steel Strike in passing. Only Jezer, Patterson, and Perrett, who also note the 1959 strike, mention any other strikes.

By and large, labor and the working class are absent from the standard picture of America in the 1950s. Many of these books are focused on presidents and other celebrities who seem to symbolize their time. And most of the authors are consciously writing for a professional, middle-class audience, with an eye to elite university students preparing for leadership positions in our society. I suspect that most of these authors have had virtually no exposure to working people and their ways, and that few know anything of the labor movement beyond a few celebrity leaders. Except for Jezer, Patterson, and Perrett, none exhibits any evidence of such exposure or any substantial interest in the subject. That there should be a middle-class bias in how the postwar American story is told is neither surprising nor objectionable in itself. There's a middle-class bias to all aspects of our national culture. But the way unions are treated in these texts seriously distorts some of the guts of the American story.

Diggins may be taken as typical. He handles labor in brief summaries of the mid-1950s and then the late 1950s—a total of six paragraphs.[4] Characteristically, there is no effort to assess labor's *accomplishments.* Labor is assessed for its institutional strength (which is seen as weak and declining) and for its status as a political "special interest." One of the six paragraphs is devoted to "labor-union racketeering," with mention made of "murder, arson, blackmail, kidnappings, and beatings and torture." No mention is made of weekends, pensions, or health insurance, nor of labor's role in greatly expanding all aspects of the Social Security Act and the Fair Labor Standards Act under both Truman and Eisenhower. Meanwhile, and typically, postwar prosperity is discussed elsewhere as being the result of impersonal social-economic forces such as savings rates and demographics. Also typical is that racketeering is placed within the context of the disillusionment of liberal/Left intellectuals with their 1930s idealism. One gets the impression that the working class had had potential once, but had failed to live up to it. It could have been a contender but got lost in a morass of corruption, like Marlon Brando in *On the Waterfront.* Finally, Diggins repeats the conventional wisdom of the 1950s: "By 1956 white-collar workers outnumbered blue-collar workers. . . . Most [white-collar workers] regarded themselves as upwardly mobile professionals. The remaining unionized industrial workers shared their aspirations, if not their achievements."[5]

Diggins is the only one who includes "murder, kidnappings and torture" in his account of the labor movement, and most other authors give at least one sentence to the fact that unions improved wages and benefits for their members. But otherwise Diggins is typical. The more extensive treatments in Jezer, Patterson, and Perrett do not present a substantially different picture, though some emphases differ. Jezer, a '60s-style leftist, describes "Workers on the Defensive" and "Labor Defeated" during a postwar period he characterizes as *The Dark Ages.*[6]

Perrett calls the period from 1947 to 1957 "a decade of torpor" for the labor movement.[7] And Patterson sees "the stagnation of organized labor by 1950."[8]

This history-book picture is so out of kilter with the one I've presented, so at odds with my own memory and experience (not to mention my father's "before-the-union-and-since" version of American history), but it took me quite a while to convince myself that it was wrong. Most of the important gains that transformed the lives and prospects of everybody in my family and neighborhood—wages, pensions, health insurance, work rules, increased leisure time, and the possibility of early retirement—occurred after 1947 and after 1950, not before. The '50s were when the union really started to produce, steadily, relentlessly, consistently, like a slow, lumbering machine that could not be stopped, no matter how powerfully U.S. Steel, the president, or the Supreme Court opposed it.

Steelworkers did better than most union workers in the '50s, but they were atypical only in degree. Furthermore, unions represented one of three nonagricultural workers then, and that was enough to affect—management said "infect"—almost every urban workplace in America. Though they didn't accomplish it all in any one decade, unions played an essential part in changing the rules of the game in all aspects of American life. The dramatic improvements in working conditions and living standards that we still take for granted today would not be there for us to defend or to lose if the unions of the '50s had been as weak, corrupt, and inconsequential as they appear in the official memory of postwar America.

Reasonable people can—indeed, must—disagree about how they add up the pluses and minuses of American unions in the postwar period. But it is not reasonable to assume that unions were not there, that they played no role in creating or defending postwar prosperity, or that they had no accomplishments that need to be weighed against all the palpable deficiencies of a labor movement that remains dizzying in its complexity. No union in the '50s was more corrupt than the International Brotherhood of Teamsters, for example, but it delivered essentially the same package of life transformations for most of its members and families as the Steelworkers did. That doesn't justify the "murder, kidnappings and torture" that are about as uncharacteristic of American unionism as stealing home is of baseball, but that package is part of the picture, so big a part that its consistent absence from official memory requires an explanation.

How Did Labor Get Forgotten?

The Imperial Middle and the Fight for Professional Autonomy

The root cause of labor's virtual disappearance from the 1950s has to do with the middle-class imperialism that established itself during that decade and that still affects the way we conceptualize our society and our own lives within it. But in order to understand this, you have first to imagine how gloriously amazing, how disorientingly awesome, the initial experience of postwar prosperity was.

The "affluence" of the '50s was paltry compared to what most of us enjoy today, even after substantial erosions.[9] But it was new then— like a first kiss. It was unexpected, and it transformed what could be expected. Historians of the decade like to list the increases in auto and TV sales, the decreases in polio and tuberculosis victims, the wild expansion of higher education, the improvements in household technologies, and the explosions of paperback books, records, and teenage income. Such lists go on and on. Besides, as James Patterson points out, it was something new in human history for most people in a nation to have "the luxury of fairly secure food and shelter."[10] And though, as in my family, we worried about the progress of our souls amid this cornocupia of material progress, it was possible for a while to imagine that we were all middle class or that we soon would be. It seemed reasonable to define America as a "middle-class society." Doing so was as much of a mistake then as it is now, but back then it expressed the expansive spirit of the times. Now it's just an illusion.

Imagine this: When Michael Harrington published his classic exposure of poverty in America in 1962, the very existence of poor people was a surprise to many. That's how strong the concept of America as a middle-class society was by then. Reliable poverty statistics based on current definitions begin in 1959, because nobody had thought to count poor people until then. About 22 percent of Americans were poor that year. Throughout the '50s they had been, in Harrington's words, "socially invisible."[11] Somehow, the "poor" have been with us ever since, but the "working class" has not.

Look at a recent recollection of the nifty decade, Brett Harvey's *The Fifties: A Women's Oral History*. Harvey interviewed ninety-two women who had been "in their late teens to midtwenties during the fifties—a time of intense and critical decision-making about college, marriage, children and work." Her book, Harvey explains, "moves more or less chronologically through the *phases of a woman's life*. The first six chapters are about the progression from *college* to marriage to motherhood" (emphases added).[12] Harvey thinks that in the 1950s, going to college in your late teens and early twenties was a typical phase of a woman's life. It wasn't. Despite the enormous expansion of higher education in that decade, by the end of it only about 22 percent of eighteen to twenty-four year olds were enrolled in colleges and universities—about the same percentage as were poor at the time.[13]

Going to college is probably the single best identifier of middle-class status, then and now. College is where you're taught how to be middle class and given a ticket for admission to professional and managerial jobs. In 1960 only 41 percent of adults over twenty-five had graduated from high school, only 7 percent from college.[14] Still today, fewer than one of four Americans over twenty-five is a college graduate; among younger people, about 27 percent now graduate from college "at normal age."[15] The tremendous expansion of higher education is one of the great achievements of postwar America, but it's an achievement that is still not shared by a majority of the population. Yet Harvey is not alone in casually assuming that college is a normal developmental stage of everybody's life. This is middle-class imperialism—mistaking your part for the whole. When we do it, we make the other parts socially invisible.[16]

In the '50s (and still today), many of "the poor" were also working class. But if we set the poor to one side and the college educated to the other, what's in between is the working class, and it was then and still is larger than either the poor or the middle class. As I explained at the beginning of this book, the standard conception of class in America includes three classes—rich, poor, and middle—and this scheme hides the working class from view. We've had that vernacular conception since Michael Harrington's *The Other America* required us to include the poor in our vision of a middle-class society. In my view this three-class schema is both grossly inaccurate and disabling. The mistake began in the '50s, fueled not only by the disorienting effect of postwar prosperity, but also by the professional middle class's fight for autonomy within the giant organizations that seemed fated to rule everybody's life then. Defining America as a middle-class society then was not just an illusion; it was a mission.

The two most influential books of the 1950s (and into the 1960s) were works of what Paul Carter calls "imaginative sociology," a genre that flowered in that decade—David Riesman's *The Lonely Crowd* (1950) and William H. Whyte's *The Organization Man* (1956).[17] With their complex critiques of the "other-directed" individual and "the social ethic," they defined the '50s as a decade of "conformism" and gently urged readers to assert their individuality against it. Though both books generated a lot of interest and discussion among intellectuals, their main impact occurred through their widespread use in college classrooms, where these books required students to confront the culture, values, and way of life they were preparing to take on. Riesman and Whyte thought they were merely describing the inevitable character of "modern life" as shaped by large, hierarchical, and rigidly structured organizations, but neither hesitated to inflect a little nostalgia for an earlier time, when the "inner-directed," entrepreneurial individual had more social space and internal resources to exercise his or her creativity in shaping a life. In fact, they were sounding a *cri de coeur* for middle-class professionals to carve out a space for themselves within large organizations, to assert their professional autonomy to act in the best interests of the organization, without day-to-day supervision and semi-independent of the rules and guidelines.

Those of us in the '50s and '60s who were preparing to become college professors (though often we didn't know this was what we were doing) would be more influenced by other imaginative sociologists, such as C. Wright Mills, Paul Goodman, and Herbert Marcuse. We would eventually reject our society, root and branch, and would try to stand outside it and protest. But the much larger group in the '50s and later who were consciously preparing for careers in business or government were forced to read Riesman and Whyte in college, and they took these analyses to heart, even as they entered the huge organizations and highly scripted suburbs Riesman and Whyte had warned against. Though often in bitter opposition to one another, the managerial-technical professionals and the cultural-communications ones worked together to ensure that both the organizational and personal lives of middle-class professionals were more loose, more individualistic and less totalitarian than Riesman and Whyte had feared.

Today American national politics and culture are pretty much defined by the unities and oppositions within the professional middle class. Liberalism and conservatism, the key terms of American politics, are a unity of opposites within our class, for example. Usually the managerial-technical wing is more conservative, the cultural-communications wing more liberal, but not always, and each is constantly informing the other. It's a rich and complex dialectic that is constrained, but not controlled, by the power of the market and of Big Money. We are, after all, hired hands, wage labor, and at the margins we are not free to act and think as we want. But we're usually not at the margins, and our society has given us, or we have won, a great deal of power to shape both the terms of debate and the final action. But a lot of our power as a class, and certainly our cultural hegemony, is based in the fact that to become middle class you have first to pass through the university, where despite all the rich oppositions among us, professionals are given a way of seeing and being and a prejudice toward doing and becoming that make us more homogenous than all those—a majority—who have not passed through our ivied walls. The working class is now and has always been wildly more diverse, more defined by ethnicity and religion, by locality and region, by the immediacy of family, friends and neighborhood, by the specificity of occupation, and by the presence or absence of money, of decent wages, pensions and benefits. Despite the middle-class commitment to individualism and personal autonomy—indeed, because of it—we are much more uniform as a class, and it is one source of our power.

The working class, lacking the homogenizing effect of a college education, pays much less attention to the national culture and is therefore less constrained and less influenced by it—that is, by us. Its members are also more likely to break apart into ethnic, racial, religious, and local subcultures, and to have fierce, nonnegotiable personal and familial loyalties that constrain their ability and willingness to reach out beyond those spheres. But they are also much more used to dealing with diversity, to getting along with people unlike themselves. Despite their best efforts, they can't avoid it, at least not the way most middle-class professionals can.

As members of a class that takes itself as the norm, we tend to see everybody else as essentially like us, just closer or farther from fulfilling the norm. Many of us (the liberals, usually) have a charming faith that everybody, no matter how deviant, can be brought up to the norm. Mainstream Access's outplacement counselors had this faith, for example, and displaced steelworkers I talked with appreciated it. But the college-educated counselors couldn't help but patronize the steelworkers whom they were trying to help make progress toward the norm; it could never have occurred to them that they were dealing with a culture unlike their own. The steelworkers, on the other hand, knew they were dealing with folks of a different social class; they dealt with them, and then they made jokes about it.

By defining everybody else as either like us or aspiring to be like us, we don't have to deal with the diversity all around us. This kind of middle-class imperialism was a lot less possible in the 1950s. The college educated were a much smaller group then, as were professional and managerial workers, and the working class was a much more organized, powerful, and visible presence in American life. But to establish yourself as the social norm, you've got to be both precipitous and bold—and a little sloppy with your definitions. That's why so much attention got paid to a 1956 Census Bureau report showing that for the first time in history, white-collar workers outnumbered blue-collar workers. This was taken then as evidence of the amazing progress that was being made toward becoming a middle-class society—and historians repeat it today for the same reason.

From 1950 to 1960, "manual workers" declined as a percentage of the work force, from 41 to 38 percent, while "white-collar workers" increased from 36 to 43 percent. But this hardly indicated the disappearance of the working class. Though "professional, technical workers" increased dramatically during that period, so did the larger group of "clerical workers," who were included in the "white collar" category, as were "sales workers," most of whom should, like clerical workers, be counted among the working class. If you include farm laborers and "service workers" like maids and janitors in the working class, then about 70 percent of the gainfully employed were in working-class occupations in 1960.[18]

For a society that has defined itself by its middle-classness for more than four decades, you'd think we'd have a fairly clear definition of middle class by now. But the confusion over occupational categories is among the more precise (and correctable) confusions. Ordinarily, the usage of "middle class" is not based on a single definition and is highly flexible in adjusting to a variety of contexts. Often "middle class" is used to refer only to income, with no reference to occupation, culture, or other life circumstances. But even this usage is highly indefinite, as the income scale it defines varies wildly, often moving up to the income level of the professional class. In using "middle class" to refer to income level, then, most users ignore altogether the need for a middle class to be in the middle. I often ask students and others how they would define a middle-class income, and they almost always start well above the median family income. This is because "middle class" has the strong connotation of "comfortable," or at least of "having enough for a decent existence." Indeed, the economist Juliet Schor explicitly defines the middle class as the top 40 percent of the income distribution by showing that the 1990s median "is no longer a sufficient income to put a family into the middle class."[19] In Schor's three-class schema, this would make the bottom 60 percent "poor," but she avoids that conclusion because we already have a clear definition of "the poor," and they're about 15 percent. This leaves about 45 percent of families without a class to be a part of. If there were that class between middle and poor, it would be the largest in a four-class schema.

These discussions get tedious pretty quick. If you just say that almost everybody is middle class often enough and long enough, most people may begin to define themselves that way. As Todd Gitlin has pointed out, "middle class" has become "a catch-all label . . . beloved by pollsters and politicians. . . . To identify oneself as part of that great blur [is merely] an affirmation of normality."[20] Indeed, pollsters often find that the vast majority of Americans identify themselves as middle class; President Clinton's pollster, for example, claimed that today "90 percent of Americans think of themselves as middle class." But that's because the pollsters do not usually offer their respondents the opportunity to identify themselves as working class. When offered that option, about an equal number of Americans (45 percent) identify themselves as working class and middle class.[21]

More than four decades of middle-class imperialism have succeeded in removing the working class from *our* minds, but not from theirs. It's pretty extraordinary, if you think about. They know that both we and they exist and that they're different from us. Usually, we don't.

Europeans often remark on this strange illusion. "In the period after 1945, the use of class as a social determinant was considered almost un-American, as if to breathe the phrase 'working class' was to deny America's accomplishments," notes the British journalist Michael Elliott. "In fact, there may be no modern society where elites have so lost touch with the lifestyles and aspirations of the working class."[22] In the first flush of postwar prosperity, in the midst of a battle for professional autonomy against the forces of Bigness, believing we were all middle class (or could be) had a progressive quality it no longer has. One paradox in the way postwar prosperity is now remembered is that shadows of a working class show up more often in intellectual histories of the time than in social or general histories. Listen, for example, to Richard Pells in a book subtitled *American Intellectuals in the 1940s and 1950s:*

> One of the major consequences of America's postwar prosperity was that writers turned their attention to the social predicaments of the middle class. . . . Where social critics had once insisted on the need for collective action, they now urged the individual to resist the pressures of conformity. . . . The primary danger was no longer social inequality but standardization and uniformity, not economic exploitation but the moral consequences of abundance. . . . What the writers of the 1930s had called 'community,' the postwar intelligentsia labeled 'conformity.' Cooperation now became 'other-direction'; social consciousness had turned into 'groupism'; solidarity with others implied an invasion of privacy; 'collectivism' ushered in a 'mass society'. . . .[23]

The postwar ideology of individualism this describes, indiscriminately watered by the traditions of the American Revolution and the Hollywood western, was a necessary part of the fight for professional autonomy in a world ostensibly controlled by Big Business, Big Government, and yes, Big Labor. The remembrance of the 1950s as repressive is based on the reality of rigidly authoritarian institutions— from International Business Machines to Jim Crow, from the House Un-American Activities Committee to the military-industrial complex, from *Good Housekeeping* to the International Brotherhood of Electrical Workers—all dedicated to preserving a rigid set of social norms that allowed little room for personal deviance or initiative. In the period of our class formation, the liberal part of the middle class eventually sided with the poor and the black, the young and the female—or at least enough of us did—to create a series of individual rights, both formal and informal, which few of us would choose to give up today.

But the fight against hierarchy and control was also a reaction to the power of the organized working class and a part of a larger middle-class need to assert our own interests and authority as a class. Look at what Riesman and Whyte and the others were railing against: being and belonging, the virtues of solidarity and organization that were (and still are) essential to working-class prospects. The strikes of the '50s were mostly civilized affairs, with workers going out together and back together as if by habit. Few heads got busted; almost nobody got shot in the back. But that's not because the organized working class was complacent and lacking in the kind of militance it had shown in what Geoffrey Perrett nostalgically calls "the tear gas days of the late 1930s."[24] Rather, in steel, auto, rubber, electric utilities, construction, telecommunications, and dozens of other industries, the culture of "groupism" and "conformity," of solidarity and collective action, was so strong that tear gas and bullets were no longer options. As a result, the business class had to hand over a lot more of its power and money, its work rules and fringe benefits, than it had a mind to. That's why there were so many strikes in the '50s—because Big Business was not prepared to share postwar prosperity without a fight.

To remember the strikes of the '50s, then, would require us to look at the causes of postwar prosperity, not just at its effects. It would challenge the concept of America as a middle-class society, then and now. And it might require us to remember the virtues of being and belonging, of unity and social discipline that middle-class professionals often think we can live without.

Ruling-Class Propaganda and the Disenchantment of the Left

There are additional causes for the disappearance of the organized working class from postwar memory. Big Business, as I showed earlier, made a concerted and sophisticated effort that had both short- and longer-term effects. In addition, the American Left, suppressed by the postwar Red Scare, sustained a disproportionately influential tradition of evaluating unions by what they had not accomplished, rather than by what they had. Both of these efforts, executed for the most part by middle-class professionals, gelled nicely with the mission of an emergent middle class to establish its hegemony within an expanding national culture. Finally, the working class, increasingly out of sight and out of mind in the national culture, eventually settled for a separate peace that allowed it to advance by degrees but that narrowed its larger social vision and facilitated its social invisibility.

I probably underestimate the role of ruling-class propaganda in this process, but I do so in hopes of retaining a sense of how difficult and complicated it was for a ruling class to rule from the 1940s into the

1980s. Coming out of World War II, a genuinely democratic spirit refreshed and deepened the values of liberty, equality, and fraternity among the people. The rise of the black, the young, the female, and the poor asserting *their* rights—all of which took root in the '50s—was fed and watered by the popular ethos of the immediate postwar period. So was unionism. That life should and could be good for all people—these ideas were not widespread in hearts and minds prior to World War II, but they were common coin after—not only in America, but throughout the world.[25] Tear gas and bullets, expulsions and blacklists, fire hoses and attack dogs could not extinguish that spirit; in fact, they often stimulated and deepened it.

The distinctive thing about the sophisticated public relations strategy devised in the late 1940s by groups such as the Advertising Council and the National Association of Manufacturers (NAM) was that it did *not* attack unions directly. Despite initial funding by some of the most ferociously anti-union companies of the time, after 1948 it left attacks on Social Security, unions and the New Deal to the ideologically more primitive (like Senators McClellan and Goldwater and editorial writers Lawrence and Krock). Rather, it focused on determining who got credit for postwar prosperity.[26] New Dealers wanted to give Big Government some of the credit. Unionists thought they deserved some. The Advertising Council–NAM strategy was to ignore rather than deny these claims, and to claim credit for something it called "people's capitalism."

The Advertising Council's promotion of people's capitalism was no simple bumper-sticker slogan without substance. As spelled out in full-page ads, pamphlets, and high school educational materials, the new and improved version of capitalism had eight essential characteristics that mixed things like "opportunity for each individual to develop to his highest potential" with things like "high volume at prices within reach of all." "High wages" and "high purchasing power" were included as well, but as a natural part of the system, not as a result of unions and strikes. From the very beginning, the effort was tightly focused on enhancing the image of business and businessmen, not on attacking their adversaries. Whatever frustration with government and unions businessmen might vent in private or at industry association meetings, the public story had to stick with the positive. It had to acknowledge the claims of the people to more rights and better lives without acknowledging the necessity for any non-market institutions to nurture and advance those claims.[27]

The sheer magnitude of the business effort is impressive—the Advertising Council's thirteen million lines of newspaper advertising and eight thousand billboards, the NAM's eight million pamphlets in 1950 and its TV program, *Industry on Parade*, after that[28]—but equally impressive is its extent and subtlety. The American Iron and Steel Institute, for example, committed more than $2 million to restoring a colonial ironworks in Saugus, Massachusetts, one of dozens of museums, historical sites, and tours that "showcased companies, explained how products were made, and demonstrated what industry gave to individuals, communities, and the nation."[29] As historian Mike Wallace explains, these efforts generally followed the example of Henry Ford's Greenfield Village, shifting historical attention away from politics and wars and toward the artifacts of everyday life and the ways that inventors and other men of genius fueled progress. Industry-sponsored museums and historical sites did not rail against Big Government and Big Labor; they just left them out of the picture.[30]

Throughout the 1950s, organized labor combatted the business effort as best it could. There were about eight hundred labor newspapers then, with a circulation of more than twenty million, not counting local union newspapers and shop newsletters. Unions funded their own radio stations and TV shows, agitated and educated for labor education programs at state universities, and developed systematic community service efforts to put their members and staff on the boards of public schools, social service agencies, and sanitation and transportation authorities.[31] As we've seen in the 1959 Steel Strike, some of this was not without effect—people still hesitated to root for U.S. Steel. But in the long run, labor could not match either the money or the reach of the business effort. What happened in Akron, Ohio, the center of rubber tire production in the United States in those days and a union stronghold, is typical: "[U]nionists unsuccessfully fought the introduction into the schools of a history text that was written and published by the Chamber of Commerce. This text ignored unions and devoted fifty-four pages to the rubber companies and a whole chapter to the Quaker Oats Company."[32]

Ignoring and crowding out unions with genuinely educational and seemingly neutral material about technology and economics was a highly effective long-run strategy. James Loewen's 1995 study, for example, found that high school history textbooks made "unions appear anachronistic" by displaying some tragic events of the distant past, such as the Pullman Strike and the Triangle Shirtwaist Fire, while making no mention of labor in the past fifty years.[33] The controversial *National*

Standards for United States History, reputed by conservatives to be leftist and multicultural, nevertheless displays the same absence of unions in its "Era 9: Postwar U.S. (1945 to early 1970s)."[34]

Mike Wallace speculates that the absence of unions from popular presentations of American history is "rooted in the ongoing challenge labor represents to the capitalist system,"[35] but today that strikes me as fanciful. Rather, labor has been so thoroughly excluded from the story for so long that to include it now seems highly ideological and politically intrusive. Besides, what would the *National Standards* include about labor in the last fifty years? The social historians, including most labor historians, have not done much better than general historians or museum curators in remembering the unions. Though a flourishing academic discipline, labor history has ignored the postwar period, for the most part.[36] Writers of textbooks and general histories cannot include a balanced assessment of the role of unions in postwar America if the specialists upon whom they rely pay no attention to it. And though there are more mundane reasons, the main reason the specialists have been silent is that labor history as an academic discipline is a franchise of the American Left, and for the Left, the 1950s are McCarthyism and little else—that is, the story of its own suppression.[37]

The revolutionary Left, communist and noncommunist, was a powerful presence within the labor movement in the 1930s and 1940s, and this made it a powerful presence in American life coming out of World War II. By 1950 its adherents had been rooted out of the labor movement and were on the run in their other stronghold, the culture industry. This was a shameful episode of American life, and it distorted many parts of that life, none more than the labor movement.[38] If after 1948 businessmen and mainstream Republicans had to declare acceptance of the changes the New Deal wrought, the American labor movement had to show even greater ardor in declaring its acceptance of the capitalist system. This *was* the postwar consensus, and it involved a lot of suppression of deviant views. To members of the Left it appeared that only they were being suppressed, but the consensus also marginalized the anti-New Deal Right, allowing a considerable social and economic space for unions to transform American life, one workplace at a time. If there was an executive committee of the ruling class then, by 1948 it knew it could not eliminate that space without ruining the opportunities for profit the postwar period was providing; instead, it would try to *contain* working-class power, to keep it limited to what already existed. In the '50s and into the '60s, the extent and degree of that containment—or, conversely, of what could be made of the space government-regulated collective bargaining provided—were open questions. But to the Left the fight was over once they had been cast out and suppressed. Compared to the workers' commonwealth they had envisioned, the contracts and strikes of the '50s were meaningless, the rise of real wages was "consumerism" in a "mass society," health insurance and pensions were "fringe benefits" for a "labor aristocracy," and the grievance system, a "counterfeit liberty."

The nonrevolutionary Left—liberals and social democrats, anticommunists all—celebrated the achievements of the labor movement for a while, but as collective bargaining became more complicated and difficult to follow, and as labor's power seemed thoroughly entrenched, it gradually lost interest. The postwar generation of labor historians dedicated themselves to showing how bad things were in the past and how free collective bargaining and the New Deal had permanently changed that. These historians tended to have a "celebrationist" quality reflective of the liberal consensus of the time, a view that couldn't help but glorify the present in comparison to the past, and a view only somewhat broader than my father's before-the-union-and-since version of twentieth century America. The New Left generation of labor and social historians reacted against this celebration and dedicated itself to pointing out those denied their fair share of postwar prosperity—blacks, the poor both in the United States and in suppressed countries like South Vietnam, and, eventually, women. But they also sought to downgrade the achievements of the unions—not only for their disappointing records on race and their acceptance of the Cold War consensus, but for their focus on bread-and-butter material benefits, their ambivalence toward rank-and-file militance, and their abandonment of revolutionary aspirations in favor of the genteel politics of the Democratic Party.[39]

The Left in all its variants, powerless in American politics since the mid-1970s, still has a certain weight within universities and the broader professional, middle-class culture that universities help shape. There, the Left, within which I include myself, is deferred to on matters of labor and the working class. We get to draw the picture, and others will repeat it—or parts of it, at least. Given our aspirations and tradition, we can't help but measure any existent working class or labor movement against the hopes and dreams of Karl Marx and Friedrich Engels, and though revolutionary romanticism waxes and wanes, we always tend to emphasize what yet needs to be done rather than what has thus been accomplished. Therefore we tend to be suspicious of celebrations of achievements, to such an extent that we often seem to deny the achievements themselves.

The New Left generation of labor historians knew the achievements of the American labor movement, but they chose not to emphasize them. The picture of unions they purveyed emphasized the things labor had not achieved—influence over corporate policies like pricing and investment, national health insurance and a broader social safety net like the ones Western Europeans have, greater class consciousness and political activism, and a shop steward system like the one the British are thought to have had.[40] When unions were strong, this attitude had a critically progressive quality. But in a professional, middle-class culture that measures life itself in terms of doing and becoming, this lack of attention to accomplishments left an image of labor in the 1950s as defeated and contained, as no longer becoming and therefore decaying, its accomplishments confined to the tear gas days of the 1930s.

There's some truth to the Left critique of postwar unionism, and we all owe leftists a debt for leading the charge out of the postwar American celebration. But the Left view of labor in the '50s as "defeated," "on the defensive," and "in decline" confuses the labor movement with itself and supports the mainstream view of labor as "complacent" and "corrupt"—and therefore not worth much attention. The result has been that the period of labor unions' greatest power, a veritable golden age of unionism from the late 1940s into the 1970s, has been virtually unexplored by labor historians. Social scientists and journalists sometimes look at this history in order to understand how organized labor has arrived at its pitiful state today, but this simply reinforces the story of defeat and decline.[41] Thus, there is no history of what unions accomplished when they were powerful, of the impact they had on workers' lives, or of how, in Joshua Freeman's incautious words, unions achieved "a basic transformation in the social status of American workers. . . [and thereby] a redefinition of the very notion of what America was."[42]

Above all, the Left view misses the gee-whiz sense of liberation and rising expectations that were such a prominent part of the experience of union families like mine. It grossly overestimates the narrow-mindedness and selfishness of unionists, and underestimates the contribution they made to the emerging sense that life should and could be good for everybody. It also undervalues the solidarity and faithfulness of working hard and playing by the rules that were endemic in the working class then and that had so many wonderful payoffs for a while.

The '50s with a Working Class in It

As a part of my research, I went to Washington, D.C.'s National Museum of American History, where I established that it too includes nothing about labor or the working class in postwar America. While in Washington, my wife and I stayed at a moderately fancy hotel in the DuPont Circle area; walked for miles up, down, and around the Connecticut Avenue corridor; and used the Red Line of the Metro to explore some of the northwest quadrant of the city. This was in May 1997, when unemployment was at 5 percent, inflation was practically nonexistent, the stock market was a wonder to behold, and most of our leaders thought we were once again the envy of the world. It sure looked good where we were—clean, green, civilized. Friendly, generous people, many of them vigorously young, were crowding into bookstores, coffee shops, and restaurants of every ethnicity in the world, obviously enjoying spending their money. We knew there were poor people in destitute neighborhoods nearby; friends had given us some basic directions for how to avoid them. But we were amazed at how far we could go without bumping into them, at how large a piece of the city was so wealthy, prosperous, and vibrant.

You can do that in almost any city in America. In fact, unless you're a country bumpkin or a sociological explorer, you're quite likely to have a similar experience as a middle-class professional, whether you're a tourist or a business traveller. American cities are carefully organized today to take middle-class professionals where we'll feel comfortable and safe, and we have internal maps that help us read the cues of where and where not to go. Our everyday lives are not dissimilar. Professionals who live in D.C.'s Connecticut Avenue corridor and work downtown are not unusual in being able to traverse the main points of their lives without bumping into people of other social classes. We know there's a ruling class—the rich and the powerful—and we sometimes have contact with it, but for most of us, most of the time, they, like the poor, are a felt but invisible presence. Some, like me, have to traverse an ugly urban ghetto to get to work downtown from our comfortable, inner-ring, suburban homes. Others live and work in a suburban world that sure looks and feels classless, even when it isn't.

For all practical purposes, then, middle-class professionals in America don't need to have a very sophisticated grasp of the class structure of our society. We know we're "in the middle," between rich and poor, and we don't need to know much more than that. A lot of our moral and political culture has to do with how we relate to these other two classes. Some of us admire the rich and powerful and work hard to be among them, but many of us don't. A lot of us have sympathy for the poor and worry about them, but many of us fear and avoid them. As a practical matter, I'm not sure how important it is to realize that there's a working class in the middle with us, a class that is separate and distinct, with different values and interests, prospects and possibilities, and strategies for achieving them. But if you're making a conscientious effort to understand our society and its history, being unaware of the working class seriously distorts your picture of yourself and the world you live in.

When visiting cities, you have to search for the working class or you won't know it's there. It's almost always located in neighborhoods and suburbs we are unlikely to traverse. But if you know where to look, you can find mile after mile of folks who are visibly, palpably, neither poor nor middle class. If you stop and talk with some of them, even superficially, you'll see that they are different from middle-class professionals and disorientingly various among themselves.

I've described some cultural differences between the working and the middle classes earlier, and more need to be explored, but the most important difference between them and us today has to do with standards of living. The greatest distortion caused by including them in a vast middle class is that it causes us to think that they are moving in the same direction as we are—up. That was true in the '50s and '60s, but it hasn't been so for quite some time.

The Average Real Weekly Wages graph here charts wages for production and nonsupervisory workers, who constitute about 80 percent of all wage and salary employment in the private sector. Because it is adjusted for inflation, it offers the single best line for charting the standard of living of the vast majority of the American people. 1947, when this Bureau of Labor Statistics series begins, was the year after the great postwar strike wave, the year that Geoffrey Perrett thinks started a "decade of torpor," just before James Patterson's "stagnation" and Marty

Figure 1. Average Real Weekly Wages
Production & Non-Supervisory Workers
(Bureau of Labor Statistics, Series EEU00500051)

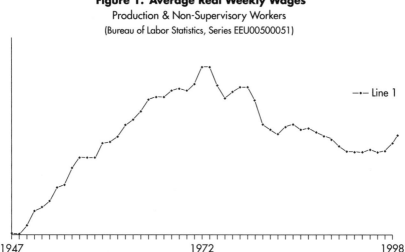

—·— Line 1

1947   1972   1998

Jezer's "Dark Ages." From 1947 to 1972, that line charts a 62 percent improvement in the standard of living. Then it weakens in the 1970s before turning decisively downward in 1978. Today, production and nonsupervisory workers have about the same real wages as they had in 1959, which is more than 15 percent below where they were in 1972. This is an average, so it hides a lot of variation within that bottom 80 percent and can seriously distort what actually happened to individuals whose incomes increased over a lifetime, but this line shows that for most people, the American standard of living has been declining for the last quarter of the twentieth century.

That's not so for us. Though there is no comparable data series for managers and professionals, stitching together what there is shows that our class shared roughly the same trajectory until the early 1980s. The increases in our salaries in the 1950s and 1960s were higher than those for production and nonsupervisory workers (about 23 percent higher in the 1950s and 37 percent higher in the 1960s), but we were all going in the same direction—up. In the 1970s we shared roughly the same fate; nominal wages for male managerial and professional workers, for example, increased at exactly the same rate as they did for production and nonsupervisory workers, meaning that we too suffered a decline in our standard of living. But from 1983 to 1994, we increased our nominal salaries 48 percent more than they increased their wages. Today, as we continue to improve, they are barely holding steady at where they were in 1959.[43] As is often noted, the marginal value of a college education has never been higher than it is right now. We benefit from that disproportionately.

In absolute numbers, our median salary is nearly double their average wage, but the direction is even more important than any specific amount. Most middle-class professionals do not realize that, as we're improving the material conditions of our lives, adding to our personal autonomy in a hundred little and a few big ways, most everybody else is moving in the opposite direction. When we mix the working class into the middle class and use what Benjamin DeMott has called "the imperial 'we,'" we cannot help but think that their experience is like ours, varying only in degree. Likewise, those of us who complain about "the disappearing middle" often think we're a part of that. We're not. When everybody was advancing together, it was perhaps not so important that the professional middle class forgot the working class and defined ours as a middle-class society, but now this error leads to a cascade of illusions that distorts our politics, our culture, and our self-understanding.

There is now some recognition—among the liberal part of our class, for example—that people without college educations are falling behind. Clinton's first secretary of labor, Robert Reich, made a habit of pointing this out, even when it was inconvenient for the administration.[44] But Reich defined this group—which is at least two-thirds of everybody working—as "the anxious class" and prescribed education as the remedy, even though his own Labor Department consistently produced employment projections that showed seven of the ten occupations with the largest job growth don't require anything like a college education.[45] As an adult educator, my life's work involves helping people get out of the working class one by one, but no matter how hard I and others like me work, there's not enough room in the professional middle class for everybody—in fact, there's not enough room for the majority. If Reich's "anxious class" were called by its historical name, we might be more likely to view it as a group with a history, a history we might look at to see what has worked and not worked in improving its condition. If the working class could be called by its name, it might be clear that circuitous individual routes like going to college cannot begin to compete with things like solidarity, organization, collective action, and unions.

Being for or against the 1950s is an important part of our national culture wars and political debate. Conservatives hark back to that time as a touchstone of family values, moral rectitude, and respect for authority. Liberals detest the decade for its suppression of women, blacks, and nonconformists. The '50s remembered in these debates are a time when there could not have been a 1959 Steel Strike. There was no working class then, so there were no unions or strikes. If, on the other hand, you remember a working class with unions and strikes and you keep your eye on real wages, you will need to reconstruct postwar American history.

The immediate postwar decade was characterized by a dialectic of liberation and repression. People came roaring out of our victory over Fascism with a sense that they would never allow things to be as they had been. The 1945–46 strike wave was the primary institutional expression of this spirit, but it was everywhere. Blacks expected and were determined to fight for a systematic, if slow, rollback of segregation and discrimination. Women were less focused on a single goal, but their expectations for themselves were no longer as confined as they had been. This spirit called forth its opposite: The forces of repression mobilized to suppress and contain, and they were particularly fierce because the spirit of liberation was so strong. The Ku Klux Klan was revitalized and the White Citizens Councils were initiated because they were now more necessary than before. The rigid sexual and family norms of the '50s were set in stone in the national culture because the traditional trajectory of women's lives was now in doubt. The radical Left was tarred and feathered because it had become a legitimate voice for radical social change. By 1955 it was possible to think that all those hopes and possibilities, all that determination, had been utterly and permanently suppressed.

But look at that real wages line. Something was making it go up, year after year, as never before. Unions, though tamed by Taft-Hartley and suppressed in the South, were *not* defeated. They were the one force for liberation that had a clear path for advancing despite the repression, and keeping that path open stimulated others. Contract by contract, strike by strike, grievance by grievance, they were building up a realm of freedom for about one-third of the workforce, affecting lots of others. This realm of freedom was nothing to brag about by professional, middle-class standards today, but it was going in the right direction, and it maintained and opened up possibilities for others.

Organizationally, unions were a strong and consistent voice for "the common man," and though the common person as then envisioned was both male and pale, publicly beating or just routinely standing up to the likes of U.S. Steel, General Motors, or General Electric increased every common person's sense of possibility. And the steady rise of real wages had its own impact, without anybody being aware of the statistics. When the average goes up like that, it means that each year daily life gets a little easier to handle; each year there is an incremental increase in personal discretion. This has an impact on morality for those of average means, because it slowly increases hope and makes doing the right thing, working hard, and playing by the rules more rational and feasible behavior. On the other hand, it means that each year a little less self-repression is necessary to live a life, and then all the external repressions begin to seem more intolerable and less justified.

Most historians of the 1950s emphasize the existence of an optimism that now looks naive and that many think led to an overconfidence, a hubris, that resulted in our leaders mistakenly thinking we could simultaneously fight national liberation in Asia and poverty at home. It may be true that the ruling and middle classes became overconfident, but on the evidence of my personal observation and experience, this was not true of the working class. Because life improved incrementally and because there was always so much rollback rhetoric, like R. Conrad Cooper's vow to "reverse the mistakes of the last eighteen years," working-class optimism was more like a patient hope, better geared for holding one's ground than for going on the offensive, but shrewdly aware of the incremental possibilities and stubbornly pushing to achieve them.

The way things played out in my family was unique, but it can help us understand postwar America better than we do now. Most families didn't have a CIO-bred shop steward in the house to articulate a common man's ideology of spending power and social justice, but they breathed some of that air nonetheless. To my father, making the world more right and fair was a daily, practical struggle, and our lives depended on it. He didn't get that from his religion or from his father's knee. His family, as he often pointed out, were "Somerset County Germans," known among steelmasters for their blind obedience and their capacity to carry heavy loads without complaining. No, his sense of social justice and a route for achieving it arrived one day in the form of a union card that he had had to risk his livelihood to sign.

Once the rest of us saw that his actions could play a role in making U.S. Steel howl with anguish over a few pennies per hour, we began to hope. Once we understood not only why it was right to oppose Evil Foremen like Yock but that it could be effectively done, it was inevitable that others would find the heart to challenge other limitations and re-pressions. Some would passively refuse to ride segregated buses. Some would defiantly "shake that thing" to the sounds of a forbidden mu-sic. Some would challenge a war machine that seemed both benign and impregnable at the time. And some, like my mother, would simply go about living a life of their own as if they were entitled to it. The libera-tions of the '50s and '60s inevitably competed with each other, but they also fed and watered each other—at least so long as real wages were rising.[46]

Now that the American labor movement is small and weak, it has be-gun to dawn on some of us within the liberal wing of the professional middle class how important labor was when it was large and strong. But the telling of history hasn't caught up with that perception yet. Because it hasn't, we still defend the '60s against the '50s. I have no problem de-fending what we did in "the '60s," but it is a mistake to oppose it to "the '50s," to give over that wonderful, liberatory decade to the forces of repression. There would have been no '60s without the rising expecta-tions the labor movement seeded so deeply among the American people in the postwar period.

Family historian Stephanie Coontz, a liberal feminist who knows we're not all middle class, notes without dismay that today the largest group of Americans choose the 1950s as their favorite decade:

> [D]espite the research I've done on the underside of 1950s families, I don't think it's crazy for people to feel nostalgic about the period. For one thing, it's easy to see why people might look back fondly to a decade when real wages grew more in any single year than in the entire ten years of the 1980s combined. . . .
>
> What most people really feel nostalgic about has little to do with the internal structure of 1950s families. It is the belief that the 1950s provided a more family-friendly economic and social environment, an easier climate in which to keep kids on the straight and narrow, and above all, a greater feeling of hope for a family's long-term future, especially for its young. The contrast between the perceived hopefulness of the fifties and our own mis-givings about the future is key to contemporary nostalgia for the period. Greater optimism *did* exist then, even among many individuals and groups who were in terrible circumstances. But if we are to take people's sense of loss seriously, . . . we need to develop a historical perspective on where that hope came from.[47]

I think I know where the hope came from, and it's not coming back un-til we have a bigger and stronger labor movement than the one we have now. I took it for granted once, but now I remember.

Appendix A

Histories of Postwar America

Carter, Paul A. *Another Part of the Fifties*. Columbia University Press, 1983.

Chafe, William. *The Unfinished Journey: America since World War II*. Oxford University Press, 1986.

Diggins, John Patrick. *The Proud Decades: America in War and Peace, 1941–1960*. W. W. Norton, 1988.

Goldman, Eric F. *The Crucial Decade—and after: America, 1945–1960*. Vintage, 1960.

Halberstam, David. *The Fifties*. Villard Books, 1993.

Hart, Jeffrey. *When the Going Was Good! American Life in the Fifties*. Crown, 1982.

Hodgson, Godfrey. *America in Our Time: From World War II to Nixon, What Happened and Why*. Vintage Books, 1976.

Jezer, Marty. *The Dark Ages: Life in the United States, 1945–1960*. South End Press, 1982.

Leuchtenberg, William E. *A Troubled Feast: American Society since 1945*. Little, Brown, 1983.

Manchester, William. *The Glory and the Dream: A Narrative History of America, 1932–1972*. Little, Brown, 1973.

Miller, Douglas T., and Marion Nowak. *The Fifties: The Way We Really Were*. Doubleday, 1975.

Oakley, J. Ronald. *God's Country: America in the Fifties*. Dembner Books, 1986.

O'Neill, William L. *American High: The Years of Confidence, 1945–1960*. Free Press, 1986.

Patterson, James T. *Grand Expectations: The United States, 1945–1974*. Oxford University Press, 1996.

Perrett, Geoffrey. *A Dream of Greatness: The American People, 1945–1963*. Coward, McCann and Geoghegan, 1979.

Siegel, Frederick F. *Troubled Journey: From Pearl Harbor to Ronald Reagan*. Hill and Wang, 1984.

Solberg, Carl. *Riding High: America in the Cold War*. Mason and Lipscomb, 1973.

Zinn, Howard. *Postwar America: 1945–1971*. Bobbs-Merrill, 1973.

Appendix B

Interviews

Balanoff, Betty. Professor of history emeritus, Roosevelt University, Chicago, and wife of Jim Balanoff (see below). Interview by author. July 13, 1995.

Balanoff, Jim. Machinist, Inland Steel, East Chicago, Indiana; a member of Local 1010 in 1959 and subsequently president and USWA District 31 director. Interview by author. July 13, 1995.

Baxter, Russ. Bricklayer, Youngstown Sheet and Tube, Youngstown, Ohio; a member of Local 2163 in 1959 and subsequently president. Interview by author. July 12, 1995.

Borbely, Steve. Turned sixteen years old in 1959. Son of Joseph, who was labor relations manager at Inland Steel, East Chicago, Indiana. Interview by author. February 29, 1996.

Bowser, Charles. Turned sixteen years old in 1959. Son of William, who was a roll turner at Bethlehem Steel, Johnstown, Pennsylvania, and griever for USWA Local 2632. Charles was subsequently an inspector at Bethlehem and a member of Local 2632. Interview by author. January 3, 1999.

Bracken, Dean. Inspector, U.S. Steel, Johnstown, Pennsylvania; a member of Local 1288 in 1959 and subsequently president. Interview by author. October 7, 1994.

Carlini, Joseph. Welder, Republic Steel, Youngstown, Ohio; vice president of Local 1331 in 1959 and subsequently president. Interview by author. July 11, 1995.

Coon, Jim. Motor inspector, Fairless Works, U.S. Steel, Morrisville, Pennsylvania; a member of Local 4889 in 1959 and subsequently vice president. Interview by author. July 13, 1995.

Corcoran, Eugene. Bricklayer, Republic Steel, Buffalo, New York; a griever in Local 1743 in 1959 and subsequently president. Interview by author. July 11, 1995.

Dishong, Albert. Stock handler, Bethlehem Steel, Johnstown, Pennsylvania; a member of Local 2644 in 1959. Interview by author. July 1983.

Dishong, Dennis. Turned sixteen years old during the strike. Son of Albert (see above). Interview by author. July 1983 and numerous subsequent conversations.

Dishong, Mary Lou. Wife of Albert (see above). Interview by author. July 1983.

Filotei, Chris. Electrician, U.S. Steel, McKeesport, Pennsylvania; a griever in Local 1408 in 1959. Interview by author. July 10, 1995.

Fiore, James. Instrument repairman, U.S. Steel, Clairton, Pennsylvania; a griever in Local 1557 in 1959 and subsequently president. Interview by author. July 13, 1995.

Foutz, John. Inspector, Bethlehem Steel, Lackawanna, New York; a member of Local 2604 in 1959 and subsequently president. Interview by author. July 11, 1995.

Frombach, Wilfred. Electrician, U.S. Steel, Johnstown, Pennsylvania; a member of Local 1288 in 1959 and subsequently grievance chair. Interview by author. October 7, 1994.

Gavini, Joseph. Rolling mill scarfer, Ohio Works of U.S. Steel, Youngstown, Ohio; assistant griever in Local 1330 in 1959 and subsequently grievance chair. Interview by author. July 12, 1995.

Grace, Dick. Crane repairman, U.S. Steel, McKeesport, Pennsylvania; a member of Local 1408 in 1959 and subsequently president. Interview by author. July 11, 1995.

Gyurko, Joseph. Motor inspector, Inland Steel, East Chicago, Indiana; a griever in Local 1010 in 1959 and subsequently grievance chair. Interview by author. July 13, 1995.

Harmon, Bonnie. Clerical worker, U.S. Steel, Gary, Indiana. Member of Local 2695 in 1959 and subsequently steward. Interview by author. October 7, 1992.

Hodos, Joseph. Rolling mill turner, Jones and Laughlin, Pittsburgh; a member of Local 1843. Interview by author. July 12, 1995.

Ingersoll, John. Rigger, U.S. Steel, McKeesport, Pennsylvania; a griever in Local 1408 in 1959. Interview by author. July 10, 1995.

Kuczkowski, Joe. Bricklayer, Republic Steel, Buffalo, New York; a member of Local 1743. Interview by author. July 11, 1995.

Martinez, Frank. Millwright, Bethlehem Steel, Bethlehem, Pennsylvania; a member of Local 2600. Interview by author. July 11, 1995.

Matson, James. Electrician, Wheeling-Pittsburgh Steel, Allenport, Pennsylvania; a griever in Local 1187 in 1959 and subsequently recording secretary. Interview by author. July 11, 1995.

Metzgar, Johnny. Machinist, U.S. Steel, Johnstown, Pennsylvania; an assistant griever in Local 1288 in 1959. Interview by author. July 8, 1980.

Meyers, Harry. Loader helper, Republic Steel, Youngstown, Ohio; a member of Local 1331. Interview by author. July 12, 1995.

Mihailidis, Irene. Wife of Nick (see below). Interview by author. December 24, 1994.

Mihailidis, Nick. Rolling mill operator, Inland Steel, East Chicago; a member of Local 1010. Interview by author. December 24, 1994.

Mikula, Albert. Was eighteen years old in 1959. Son of Joseph, a rolling mill heater at Bethlehem Steel, Johnstown, Pennsylvania. Albert was subsequently a machinist at U.S. Steel, Johnstown, and a member and an officer of Local 1288. Interview by author. August 24, 1998.

Moore, Willie. Snag grinder, Republic Steel, Canton, Ohio; a shop steward in Local 1200 in 1959 and subsequently vice president. Interview by author. July 13, 1995.

Nophsker, Marion. Daughter of Johnny Metzgar. Interview by author. March 4, 1993.

Park, Howard R. Millwright, Fairless Works, U.S. Steel, Morrisville, Pennsylvania; an assistant griever in Local 4889 in 1959. Interview by author. July 13, 1995.

Pasnick, Ray W. Former aluminum worker in New Kensington, Pennsylvania; in 1959 was Midwest editor of *Steelabor* and Midwest director of education, USWA; subsequently was editor of *Steelabor.* Interview by author. October 24, 1994.

Perriello, Joe. Machinist, Jones and Laughlin Steel, Aliquippa, Pennsylvania; a member of Local 1211. Interview by author. July 12, 1995.

Peulen, Matt J. Millwright, Colorado Fuel and Iron, Pueblo, Colorado; a member of Local 2102 in 1959 and subsequently grievance chair. Interview by author. July 12, 1995.

Prajsner, Marion. Roll grinder, Jones and Laughlin, Aliquippa; a member of Local 1211. Interview by author. July 13, 1995.

Reed, Bettie. Wife of Bill (see below). Interview by author. July 3, 1992.

Reed, Bill. Inspector, Bethlehem Steel, Johnstown; a member of Local 2632. Interview by author. July 3, 1992.

Reis, Harry. Cutter, Wheeling-Pittsburgh Steel, Allenport; a griever in Local 1187 in 1959 and subsequently president. Interview by author. July 11, 1995.

Saylor, Ruth. Wife of Stan, who was a molder at U.S. Steel, Johnstown, Pennsylvania. Interview by author. June 30, 1992.

Schenck, Bud. Freight car repairman, Republic Steel, Buffalo, New York; a member of Local 1743. Interview by author. July 10, 1995.

Sheehan, Elizabeth. Wife of Nelson (see below). Interview by author. July 10, 1995.

Sheehan, Nelson. Overhead crane operator, Republic Steel, Buffalo, New York; a member of Local 1743. Interview by author. July 10, 1995.

Swindle, James F. Finisher in hot strip mill, U.S. Steel, Fairfield, Alabama; grievance chair of Local 2122 for twenty-eight years, including 1959. Interview by author. July 18, 1995.

Thomas, Don. Son of John, who worked at U.S. Steel in Braddock, Pennsylvania. Interview by author. July 14, 1995.

Toth, Albert. Mobile equipment mechanic, U.S. Steel, Irwin, Pennsylvania; a member of Local 2227. Interview by author. July 10, 1995.

Uehlein, Joe. Seven years old in 1959. Son of Julius (see below) and subsequently secretary-treasurer of the Industrial Union Department, AFL-CIO. Interview by author. May 24, 1996.

Uehlein, Julius. USWA staff representative in Lorain, Ohio, in 1959, and subsequently president of Pennsylvania AFL-CIO in 1980s. Interview by author. November 7, 1998.

Vukelich, Theodore. Pickling furnace operator, Crucible Steel, Midland, Pennsylvania; a member of Local 1212. Interview by author. July 12, 1995.

Wadolny, John. Machinist, Bethlehem Steel, Bethlehem, Pennsylvania; president of Local 2599 in 1959 and subsequently an international staff representative for USWA. Interview by author. July 11, 1995.

Werkheiser, William. Electrical repairman, Bethlehem Steel, Bethlehem, Pennsylvania; a trustee in Local 2600 in 1959 and subsequently recording secretary. Interview by author. July 10, 1995.

Zetz, George. Rolling mill grinder, Crucible Steel, Midland, Pennsylvania; a member of Local 1212. Interview by author. July 12, 1995.

Notes

Key:

HCLA-PSU—Historical Collections and Labor Archives, Pennsylvania State University

IEB—Minutes of meetings of the Steelworkers International Executive Board, at HCLA-PSU

NYT—New York Times

WSJ—Wall Street Journal

Introduction

1. Richard Feldman and Michael Betzold, eds., *End of the Line: Autoworkers and the American Dream, an Oral History* (University of Illinois Press, 1988).

2. See Erik Olin Wright, *Class Counts: Comparative Studies in Class Analysis* (Cambridge University Press, 1997). Wright finds twelve classes based on an occupation's relation to scarce skills, authority, and the means of production and then reduces these to six classes of employees, among whom "the extended working class" constitutes at least 70 percent. Though much more nuanced and complex, Wright's basic categories are compatible with a simplified four-class model; see his discussion of "The problem of the 'middle class' among employees," 19–26. For a rich set of reflections on the cultures of class, see C. L. Barney Dews and Carolyn Leste Law, eds., *This Fine Place So Far from Home: Voices of Academics from the Working Class* (Temple University Press, 1995).

Part One: Prologue

1. Thomas Geoghegan, *Which Side Are You On? Trying to Be for Labor When It's Flat on Its Back* (Farrar, Straus and Giroux, 1991), 67.

2. John Strohmeyer, *Crisis in Bethlehem: Big Steel's Struggle to Survive* (Adler and Adler, 1986), 70–73.

3. Alessandro Portelli, *The Death of Luigi Trastulli and Other Stories: Form and Meaning in Oral History* (State University of New York Press, 1991), 2 and 26.

Chapter One: Getting to 1959

Epigraphs: The Molony quote is from John Herling, *Right to Challenge: People and Power in the Steelworkers Union* (Harper and Row, 1972), 238. The Ditka quote is from my memory of his televised news conference at the time; the rhetorical question "What have I got to complain about?" was a standard one where I grew up, not far from Ditka.

1. The eighteen deaths in steel in 1937—ten of them at the Memorial Day Massacre in Chicago and three at the Massillon (Ohio) Massacre—brought to 550 the men, women, and children killed in labor disputes since the mid-1870s. Robert Zieger, *The CIO, 1935–1955* (University of North Carolina Press, 1995), 62. In addition to Zieger, my brief account of the CIO story is based primarily on Irving Bernstein, *Turbulent Years: A History of the American Worker, 1933–1941* (Houghton Mifflin, 1969); Art Preis, *Labor's Giant Step: Twenty Years of the CIO* (Pathfinder Press, 1972); and Nelson Lichtenstein, *Labor's War at Home: The CIO in World War II* (Cambridge University Press, 1982).

2. Bernstein, 229–98.

3. Preis, 72, and Zieger, 91–94.

4. Michael Goldfield, *The Decline of Organized Labor in the United States* (University of Chicago Press, 1987), 10.

5. Joshua Freeman, "Delivering the Goods: Industrial Unionism during World War II," *Labor History* 19 (fall 1978), reprinted in Daniel J. Leab, ed., *The Labor History Reader* (University of Illinois Press, 1985), 402.

6. See Freeman, "Delivering," and Lichtenstein, *Labor's War.*

7. Goldfield, 10.

8. Preis, 260–63.

9. Ibid., 267–76.

10. Ibid., 276.

11. Zieger, 227–52, and Irving Richter, *Labor's Struggles, 1945–1950: A Participant's View* (Cambridge University Press, 1994).

12. Lichtenstein, *Labor's War,* 227, and Nelson Lichtenstein, *The Most Dangerous Man in Detroit: Walter Reuther and the Fate of American Labor* (Basic Books, 1995), 233.

13. William Z. Foster, *The Great Steel Strike and Its Lessons,* 1920 (reprinted, Da Capo Press, 1971), 42–49 and 187–91. Johnstown, which Foster called "an industrial jail of a city," played a central role in the 1919 strike and in Foster's account of it.

14. Bernstein, 490–97; Curtis Miner, *Forging A New Deal: Johnstown and the Great Depression, 1929–1941* (Johnstown Area Heritage Association, 1993), 53–77; and Keith Sward, "The Johnstown Strike of 1937: A Case Study of Large-Scale Conflict," in George Hartmann and Theodore Newcomb, eds., *Industrial Conflict: A Psychological Interpretation* (Cordon, 1939), 74–102.

15. Steven Fraser, *Labor Will Rule: Sidney Hillman and the Rise of American Labor* (Free Press, 1991), 506–14.

16. See George Lipsitz, *Class and Culture in Cold War America: "A Rainbow at*

Midnight" (Bergin and Garvey, 1982) and Marty Jezer, *The Dark Ages: Life in the United States, 1945–1960* (South End Press, 1982).

17. Some of the details in this section, particularly those from the 1930s, are based on a tape-recorded interview I did with my father on July 8, 1980.

18. "Workplace Contractualism: A Historical/Comparative Analysis," in David Brody, *In Labor's Cause: Main Themes on the History of the American Worker* (Oxford University Press, 1993).

19. The average hourly wage in steel in 1936 was sixty-six cents, according to Vincent D. Sweeney, *The United Steelworkers of America: Twenty Years Later, 1936–1956* (USWA, n.d.), 66–67. Other wage figures are calculated from the American Iron and Steel Institute (AISI), *The Competitive Challenge to Steel*, AISI, 1963. My account of the bargaining history of the Steelworkers in the 1940s and 1950s is based on Jack Stieber, "Steel" in Gerald G. Somers, ed., *Collective Bargaining: Contemporary American Experience* (Industrial Relations Research Association, 1980), 151–208; "The Steel Industry" in Benjamin M. Selekman, Sylvia K. Selekman and Stephen H. Fuller, *Problems in Labor Relations* (McGraw-Hill, 1958), 466–520; E. Robert Livernash, *Collective Bargaining in the Basic Steel Industry: A Study of the Public Interest and the Role of Government* (U.S. Department of Labor, January 1961); Richard Betheil, "The ENA in Perspective: The Transformation of Collective Bargaining in the Basic Steel Industry," *Review of Radical Political Economics* 10, 2 (summer 1978); Richard Kalwa, "Collective Bargaining in Basic Steel, 1946–83," Ph.D. dissertation, Cornell University, 1985; and Garth L. Mangum and R. Scott McNabb, *The Rise, Fall and Replacement of Industrywide Bargaining in the Basic Steel Industry* (M. E. Sharpe, 1997).

20. Livernash, 267.

21. Mark McColloch, "Modest but Adequate: Standard of Living for Mon Valley Steelworkers in the Union Era," paper delivered July 7, 1992, at three-day conference, "Homestead 1892 Strike Centennial," Homestead, Pennsylvania, 5–6.

22. For a history of the weekend, see Witold Rybczynski, *Waiting for the Weekend* (Viking, 1991). For the worrying, see Daniel Bell, *The End of Ideology: On the Exhaustion of Political Ideas in the Fifties* (Free Press, 1962), 257–59.

23. Bell, 258.

24. William Greider, *Who Will Tell the People: The Betrayal of American Democracy* (Simon and Schuster, 1992), 182–201.

25. Bell, 259.

26. C. Wright Mills, *The New Men of Power: America's Labor Leaders* (Harcourt Brace, 1948), 35.

27. David Riesman, with Nathan Glazer and Reuel Denney, *The Lonely Crowd: A Study of the Changing American Character* (Yale University Press, 1950), 174.

28. On the sophisticated public relations of the CIO during its organizing days, see Sward, 82–83, 98, and 100–102. For the labor movement's efforts at the public education of its members in the 1950s, see Elizabeth A. Fones-Wolf, *Selling Free Enterprise: The Business Assault on Labor and Liberalism, 1945–60* (University of Illinois Press, 1994), 108–28.

29. Nelson Lichtenstein and Howell John Harris, eds., *Industrial Democracy in*

America: The Ambiguous Promise (Cambridge University Press, 1993), 16. Also in this volume, see the debate between Lichtenstein, "Great Expectations: The Promise of Industrial Jurisprudence and Its Demise, 1930–1960," and David Brody, "Workplace Contractualism in Comparative Perspective."

30. Duane Beeler, *How to Be a More Effective Union Representative* (Roosevelt University Press, 1966), 5–8.

31. See Fones-Wolf, particularly 1–57.

32. Thomas R. Brooks, *Toil and Trouble: A History of American Labor*, 2d ed. (Delta, 1971), 216–22.

33. Ronald L. Filippelli, "The Historical Context of Postwar Industrial Relations," in Bruce Nissen, ed., *U.S. Labor Relations, 1945–1989: Accommodation and Conflict* (Garland, 1990), 138.

34. Richard Edwards, *Rights at Work: Employment Relations in the Post-Union Era* (Brookings Institution, 1993).

35. Mills, 40.

36. Melvyn Dubofsky, *The State and Labor in Modern America* (University of North Carolina Press, 1994), 207.

37. David L. Stebenne, *Arthur J. Goldberg: New Deal Liberal* (Oxford University Press, 1996), 154–56. On the U.S. economy in the late 1950s, see chapter 3 of Sam Rosenberg, *Growth, Decline and Rejuvenation: The American Economy since 1940* (Macmillan, forthcoming).

38. Mike Davis, *Prisoners of the American Dream: Politics and Economy in the History of the U.S. Working Class* (Verso, 1986), 123 for the direct quote and 121–27 for Davis's account of the management offensive. The most thorough account of the management offensive is in Stebenne's two chapters on "The Postwar Order Under Stress," 154–232 of *Arthur J. Goldberg*. Among contemporaneous sources, see the inaugural issue of *Industrial Relations* 1, 1 (October 1961), the centerpiece of which was a symposium of labor relations scholars called "The Employer Challenge and the Union Response."

39. Davis, 123–24. For the situation in auto, see Kevin Boyle, *The UAW and the Heyday of American Liberalism, 1945–1968* (Cornell University Press, 1995), 135–36, and Lichtenstein, *The Most Dangerous Man*, 294–98. On the 1960 GE strike, see James J. Matles and James Higgins, *Them and Us: Struggles of a Rank-and-File Union* (Beacon Press, 1974), 254–56, and Ronald W. Schatz, *The Electrical Workers: A History of Labor at General Electric and Westinghouse, 1923–60* (University of Illinois Press, 1983), 226–29.

40. Leon Fink and Brian Greenberg, *Upheaval in the Quiet Zone: A History of Hospital Workers' Union Local 1199* (University of Illinois Press, 1989), 63–90.

41. Brooks, 300–323, and Robert Zieger, *American Workers, American Unions, 1920–1985* (John Hopkins University Press, 1986), 163–67. For the rise of AFSCME see Richard N. Billings and John Greenya, *Power to the Public Worker* (Robert B. Luce, 1974) and Joseph C. Goulden, *Jerry Wurf: Labor's Last Angry Man* (Atheneum, 1982). On the 1970 postal strike, see Aaron Brenner, "Striking Against the State: The Postal Wildcat of 1970," *Labor's Heritage* 7, 4 (spring 1996), 4–27.

42. See Michael K. Honey, *Southern Labor and Black Civil Rights: Organizing Memphis Workers* (University of Illinois Press, 1993), particularly the last chapter,

"Legacies," 279–91; Sanford D. Horwitt, *Let Them Call Me Rebel: Saul Alinsky—His Life and Legacy* (Knopf, 1989), especially 303–48 on Alinsky's late-1950s organizing in both black and white neighborhoods in Chicago; and Peter B. Levy, *The New Left and Labor in the 1960s* (University of Illinois Press, 1994).

43. Livernash, 20–21.

44. Though it's not clear exactly when Cooper made it, this early remark was widely referred to after June 10, when a strike began to seem inevitable. See *Iron Age*, July 2, 1959, 40, and A. H. Raskin, "Labor: A New 'Era of Bad Feeling'?" *New York Times Magazine*, July 5, 1959, 18. *Steelabor* regularly referred to it, sometimes substituting "twenty-two years" in order to reference the union's epic beginnings in 1937; so did the union's most thorough television presentation of its case, titled "No Backward Steps," available at HCLA-PSU, "USWA Films," Box 10, Film 57, Item 7 (n.d., but probably aired in July 1959). McDonald claims in his autobiography to have quizzed Cooper about the remark at the time, eliciting a reaffirmation of Cooper's view that "everything done in collective bargaining in the steel industry since 1941 had been wrong." *Union Man* (Dutton, 1969), 266.

Chapter Two: No Backward Steps

1. Livernash, *Collective Bargaining in the Basic Steel Industry*, 23.

2. The following account of the strike is based primarily on tracking it day by day in four newspapers, which I did in the following order: *Johnstown Tribune-Democrat, Steelabor, WSJ*, and *NYT*. This was supplemented by the minutes of USWA Executive Board (IEB) meetings from January 1959 through August 1960 and other archival materials at HCLA-PSU. Of course the bargaining histories listed in note 19 for Chapter 1 include brief accounts of the strike, as does Stebenne, *Arthur J. Goldberg*, 197–215. The most extensive treatment of the 1959 strike is Anthony F. Libertella, "The Steel Strike of 1959: Labor, Management, and Government Relations," Ph.D. dissertation, Ohio State University, 1972.

3. For a thorough account of the public-education campaigns run by both general business and the steel industry from the mid-1950s through 1959, see Libertella, 78–105. According to Libertella, the steel companies' lengthy ads ran in "some 430 newspapers at two-week intervals starting in January [1959] and concluding before contract negotiations in May" (89).

4. The National Council of Churches, for example, commissioned a widely publicized report after the strike that vigorously complained about the companies, the union, the press, and the government all "misleading" the public with their different presentations of the facts. See *NYT*, November 26, 1960, 1.

5. See McDonald, *Union Man*, 264–80, and Dwight D. Eisenhower, *Waging Peace, 1956–1961* (Doubleday, 1965), 453–65.

6. 1956 was actually the first year the companies *formally* coordinated their bargaining, but this was simply a matter of formally recognizing their informal practice since World War II. For the view that basic steel negotiations prior to 1956 were more like classic "pattern bargaining," see Mangum and McNabb, *The Rise, Fall and Replacement of Industrywide Bargaining*, 8–11.

7. In 1959 McDonald faced a well-organized opposition of local union leaders,

"the Dues Protesters," who had done embarassingly well in contesting his election as union president in 1957 and who were in the process of laying the foundation for his eventual unseating in 1965. A fuller account of these developments is given in Chapter 5, where it helps explain how union politics affected steelworkers' memory of the strike. Though Cooper was undoubtedly hoping that the union's internal political strife would undermine steelworker solidarity, that strife disappeared during the strike period. At the beginning of negotiations in May, the Dues Protesters called a news conference to announce that they were "100 per cent behind the McDonald leadership in the wage talks" (*NYT*, May 5, 1959, 66), and they never deviated from that stance until the strike was over. Thus, though the upsurge of union democracy in the USWA is important background information, it played virtually no part in the events of 1959—an extraordinary disappearance of union politics, which is discussed more fully in Chapter 5 as part of the culture of unionism of that time.

8. IEB, June 25, 1959, 1–7.

9. See June 25 IEB minutes, particularly 35–36 and 42–43, versus McDonald's later account in *Union Man*, 267.

10. *Monthly Review* (February 1960), 353, and American Iron and Steel Institute, *Steel at the Crossroads: The American Steel Industry in the 1980s* (AISI, January 1980), 89.

11. *WSJ*, April 30, 1959, 28.

12. *NYT*, July 15, 1959, 1.

13. Loretto R. Nolan, "A Review of Work Stoppages During 1959," *Monthly Labor Review* (June 1960), and Harold J. Ruttenberg, *How to Save and Create Jobs in the Pittsburgh Area: An Analysis of Chronic Unemployment* (Humanation Associates, 1964), 54–55.

14. *Iron Age*, July 2, 1959, 40.

15. David Brody, *Labor in Crisis: The Steel Strike of 1919*, 1965 (reprinted, University of Illinois Press, 1987), 147.

16. See Dishong, Albert, in Appendix B, Interviews.

17. *WSJ*, May 4, 1959, 1.

18. Lloyd Ulman, *The Government of the Steel Workers' Union* (John Wiley and Sons, 1962), 47–50, lists the international union's net worth in June 1959 at $32 million, some of which was in real estate. There was, however, an additional $30 million in local union treasuries then, much of which was drawn down during the strike. The CIO International distributed $11 million in direct strike relief and another $6 million in loans to local unions.

19. HCLA-PSU, IEB Miscellaneous Files—Record Group A1: Box 37, File 11, "Correspondence Sent from International (1954–1959)."

20. *WSJ*, June 15, 1959, 17.

21. Ibid.

22. Ibid.

23. See George Soule, "Civil Rights in Western Pennsylvania," in *Public Opinion and the Steel Strike*, 1921 (reprinted, Da Capo Press, 1970), 163–223.

24. Irving Bernstein, *Turbulent Years*, 490–97.

25. *WSJ*, June 19, 1959, 8. Also see Ulman, 48, for the USWA's program of

building "community centers" (228 of them by 1960) as a way "to improve their position in the wider community." These centers "housed Boy Scouts, wedding parties, local politicians, high school debates, dances, art shows, cultural and recreational activities for the elderly, Alcoholics Anonymous, YMCAs, and school boards."

26. Pennsylvania's two senators, Democrat Joseph Clark and Republican Hugh Scott, were among the complainers. *Johnstown Tribune-Democrat*, August 7, 1959.

27. *WSJ*, June 19, 1959, 8.

28. IEB, August 25–26, 1959, 50.

29. *WSJ*, June 15, 1959, 1.

30. Ibid.

31. *WSJ*, May 4, 1959, 1.

32. *WSJ*, August 4, 1959, 1.

33. *WSJ*, September 10, 1959, 1, and October 22, 1959, 1.

34. *WSJ*, September 29, 1959, 1.

35. *WSJ*, May 4, 1959, 1.

36. *WSJ*, June 15, 1959, 1.

37. *WSJ*, September 29, 1959, 1.

38. IEB, October 4, 1959, 28–29.

39. IEB, October 19, 1959, 2–3.

40. IEB, June 25, 1959, 25.

41. IEB, August 25–26, 1959, 2–3.

42. Eisenhower, 455.

43. Eisenhower, 455. For a more thorough analysis of the economic and defense impacts of the steel shortage by October, see Libertella, 181–89.

44. Eisenhower, 456.

45. IEB, November 12, 1959, 26.

46. *NYT*, November 10, 1959, 53.

47. IEB, November 12, 1959, 14–22 and 26–31.

48. Ibid., 20–22.

49. Stebenne, 207–10, and McDonald, 275.

50. *Steelabor* (December 1959), 10–11.

51. Ibid.

52. IEB, November 12, 1959, 23–25.

53. Ibid., 23.

54. *WSJ*, December 1, 1959, 32.

55. IEB, November 12, 1959, 18–30.

56. *WSJ*, November 18, 1959, 1.

57. *NYT*, December 24, 1959, 1. HCLA-PSU has results of the Steelworkers' postcard poll by district and company, "Membership Ballots 1959 Strike," Microfilm Roll 7022.

58. The companies also surveyed steelworker opinion in late December, using the scientific apparatus of the giant p.r. firm Hill and Knowlton; it recorded a rejection rate of 80 to 95 percent. *Year Book of the American Iron and Steel Institute 1960*, 246–47. Also see Libertella, 223–25.

59. McDonald, 269–70, and Libertella, 105. For the Auto Workers, see *NYT*,

September 18, 1959, 12, and for the German metal workers, *NYT,* October 28, 1959, 9.

60. McDonald, 277–79.

61. Eisenhower, 458.

62. *NYT,* January 5, 1960, 1, and Livernash, 307.

63. For Cooper's post-strike analysis, see his remarks at the trade association's afternoon session, May 26, 1960, *Year Book of American Iron and Steel Institute 1960,* 220–21. Libertella, 142, thinks McDonald would have settled in May for fifteen to twenty cents.

64. *NYT,* January 5, 1960, 19, and January 6, 1960, 1.

65. *NYT,* January 9, 1960, 25, and January 16, 1960, 8.

66. *WSJ,* January 8, 1960, 5, and McDonald, 280.

67. *NYT,* January 14, 1960, 1 and 14.

Part Two: Prologue

1. See Richard Betheil, "The ENA in Perspective," 5; William T. Hogan, S.J., *Economic History of the Iron and Steel Industry in the United States,* Volume 4, Part 6 (Lexington Books, 1971), 1637–41, and Libertella, "The Steel Strike of 1959," 229–38. On the other hand, the most recent look at the strike, Stebenne, *Arthur J. Goldberg,* 213, has it right: "[S]teel managers finally caved in. . . . Blough and his brethren had emerged the losers, and they knew it."

2. A. H. Raskin, "Deep Shadow Over Our Factories," *New York Times Magazine,* November 29, 1959, 28. The article's subhead, written in the first month of the Taft-Hartley cooling-off period, warned of "the threat of a new 'class war' in basic industries."

3. A. H. Raskin, "The Rout of Big Steel," *NYT,* January 6, 1960, 43.

4. See Herbert R. Northrup, "Management's 'New Look' in Labor Relations"; Jack Barbash, "Union Response to the 'Hard Line'"; and Arthur Ross, "The Prospects for Industrial Conflict"; all in *Industrial Relations* 1,1 (October 1961). Also Libertella, 251–53.

5. James T. Patterson, *Grand Expectations: The United States, 1945–1974* (Oxford University Press, 1996), Chapters 7 to 14, is the most recent and, to my mind, the most accurate and revealing account of the '50s; see 311–12 for his characterization of the mid-'50s. The periodization of the '50s into "The Age of Fear" (1948–53) and "The Time of National Reassessment" (1958–1960) is from Douglas T. Miller and Marion Nowak, *The Fifties: The Way We Really Were* (Doubleday, 1975).

6. Stebenne, 95, describes Eisenhower as "the candidate of sophisticated business realists such as Thomas J. Watson Sr. of IBM." But my debt to Stebenne is broader than that, as he carefully tracks a dialectic of divisions within the business community throughout his book, beginning with the immediate postwar years, 55–57 and 63–64, through what he calls the "revolt against the postwar New Deal" in 174–232, 253–304, and 318–42.

7. In addition to Stebenne, see Patterson, 272–73, and the justly famous essay by Robert Griffith, "Dwight D. Eisenhower and the Corporate Commonwealth," *American Historical Review* 87 (February 1982).

8. Fones-Wolf, *Selling Free Enterprise*, 8. Also see Libertella, 78–105.

9. Roger M. Blough, "Has the Power of Big Unions 'Gotten Out of Hand'?" *U.S. News and World Report*, November 2, 1959, 82–84.

10. *NYT*, January 7, 1960, 28, and *WSJ*, January 5, 1960, 10, and January 6, 1960, 10.

11. Stebenne, 156–97.

12. Cf. Stebenne and Nelson Lichtenstein, *The Most Dangerous Man in Detroit*, 294–98.

13. Mike Davis' Eastern Front analogy is in *Prisoners of the American Dream*, 123. The right-wing political offensive stimulated a renewed political mobilization of the labor movement, beginning in 1958 and ending in organized labor's best showing in American history in 1964, when 83 percent of union households decisively rejected Barry Goldwater in favor of Lyndon Johnson's Great Society. See James L. Sundquist, *Politics and Policy: The Eisenhower, Kennedy and Johnson Years* (Brookings Institution, 1968).

14. Given what has happened to employee health insurance in the 1980s and 1990s, the 1960 agreement on health insurance sure looks like a "new principle" from today's perspective. Before 1960 steelworkers paid one-half of their insurance premiums, whereas the 1960 contract obligated the companies to pay 100 percent. But this was not viewed as a breakthrough in principle at the time, because it was seen as just one way among many to raise workers' take-home pay. Because of tax consequences, eliminating employee contributions to health insurance actually resulted in more take-home pay than an equivalent direct wage increase would have; it had, therefore, been given top priority by the union since early in the negotiations. The added increase in take-home pay, not the principle of noncontribution, was what was most important then. See Arthur Goldberg's explanation of the 1960 contract in *Proceedings of International Wage Policy Committee, USWA, January 5, 1960*, 23–44, HCLA-PSU.

15. See Jack Stieber, "Steel," in Somers, ed., *Collective Bargaining*, 151–208.

16. In addition to Strohmeyer, *Crisis in Bethlehem*, 64–77, others who see the 1959 strike as a turning point for the industry are Donald F. Barnett and Robert W. Crandall, *Up from the Ashes: The Rise of the Steel Minimill in the United States* (Brookings Institution, 1986), 36; Mangum and McNabb, *The Rise, Fall, and Replacement of Industrywide Bargaining*, 47 and 188–89; and Paul A. Tiffany, *The Decline of American Steel: How Management, Labor, and Government Went Wrong* (Oxford University Press, 1988), vii and 160–68.

Chapter Three: 2-B or Not 2-B

1. Irwin L. Herrnstadt and Benson Soffer, "Recent Labor Disputes over 'Restrictive' Practices and 'Inflationary' Wage Increases," *Journal of Business* 34 (October 1961), 453–70.

2. Christopher L. Tomlins, *The State and the Unions: Labor Relations, Law, and the Organized Labor Movement in America, 1880–1960* (Cambridge University Press, 1985), 327. Also see Katherine Van Wezel Stone, "The Post-War Paradigm in American Labor Law," *Yale Law Journal* 90, 7 (June 1981).

3. "What Work Rules?" *Fortune*, December 1959, 215–18.

4. Strohmeyer, *Crisis in Bethlehem*, 68.

5. "What Work Rules?" 215. Also see Libertella, "The Steel Strike of 1959," 189–207.

6. *Time*, January 18, 1960, 15.

7. "What Work Rules?" 215–16.

8. Marvin Miller, oral history interview, November 17, 1970, New York City, at HCLA-PSU, 9–11. Also see Miller's interim progress report on the 2-B study at IEB, August 8–9, 1960, 140–50.

9. Strohmeyer, 68–69.

10. Libertella, 197–99, gives an excellent brief explanation of the "2-B problem" based on the hearings of the Board of Inquiry appointed under the Taft-Hartley process. For the view of George W. Taylor, chair of the Board of Inquiry, see "Remarks Upon Conclusion of Steel Board Testimony," *Monthly Labor Review*, December 1959, 1330–32. The most comprehensive treatment of 2-B's history is James D. Rose, "The Struggle over Management Rights at U.S. Steel, 1946–1960: A Reassessment of Section 2-B of the Collective Bargaining Contract," *Business History Review* 72 (autumn 1998), 446–77.

11. Art Preis, *Labor's Giant Step*, 449–51, and Duane Beeler, *Arbitration for the Local Union* (Union Representative, 1977), 41.

12. "What Work Rules?" 218. Though both the strike itself and post-strike activity eventually focused narrowly on the past-practice clause, the entire section *was* a long-standing issue for the companies, who had wanted to centralize negotiations completely and to eliminate this "domain reserved to local unions and their plant negotiating committees." See Ulman, *The Government of the Steel Workers' Union*, 77–82, for a brief history from 1947 through 1959 of management efforts to completely eliminate Section 2-B, as well as of local unions' fierce determination, beginning in 1944, to have these powers rather than to delegate them to the International.

13. Marvin Miller, oral history interview, HCLA-PSU.

14. Ibid.

15. "What Work Rules?" 216.

16. "Steel: 2B or not 2B," *Fortune*, August 1959, 174.

17. Bruce S. Feldacker, *Labor Guide to Labor Law*, 3d ed. (Prentice Hall, 1990), 274–80. For a very different view of the Steelworkers Trilogy, see Thomas Geoghegan, *Which Side Are You On?*, 163–66.

18. For the history of production and employment in the postwar U.S. steel industry, see Table A in Chapter 4.

19. American Iron and Steel Institute, *Steel at the Crossroads*, 89.

20. See Appendix B, Interviews.

21. Though theoretically easier to control than steelworkers, workers on assembly lines have a long record of creativity in avoiding, shirking, and resisting management control. See Ben Hamper, *Rivethead: Tales from the Assembly Line* (Warner Books, 1991).

22. Stieber, "Steel," in Somers, ed., *Collective Bargaining*, 192.

23. David A. Peach and E. Robert Livernash, *Grievance Initiation and Resolution:*

A Study in Basic Steel (Harvard University Press, 1974), 117 and 120, found that management generally wanted incentive rates limited to 135 percent.

24. David Montgomery has detailed such practices in a number of industries in the late nineteenth and early twentieth centuries. In the nineteenth-century iron industry, for example, craft unions established their own work practices and rules governing "the stint": "What is important to notice is that these rules were not negotiated with the employers, but were unilaterally adopted by the workers. . . . He who upheld them in his daily work was 'honorable' or 'manly.' He who exceeded the stints was a 'hog,' a 'rooter,' a 'chaser,' a 'blackleg.' . . . Unlimited output . . . led to irregular employment, slashed piece rates, drink, and debauchery. Rationally restricted output reflected 'unselfish brotherhood,' personal dignity, and 'cultivation of the mind.'" *The Fall of the House of Labor: The Workplace, the State, and American Labor Activism, 1865–1925* (Cambridge University Press, 1987), 17. My father would have been heir to these traditions from his years as a teenage molder under the tutelage of Runt Espey. CIO unionism, with its negotiated work rules, did not replace these earlier union traditions, but was laid atop them, often strengthening and protecting them, just as these older shop-floor norms gave life and weight to the formal grievance system.

Chapter Four: When the Wolf Finally Came

Epigraph: Odorcich's statement is from John Hoerr, *And the Wolf Finally Came: The Decline of the American Steel Industry* (University of Pittsburgh Press, 1988), 23. The Golden-Ruttenberg quote is "Principle of Union-Management Relations 32" in their book *The Dynamics of Industrial Democracy* (Harper, 1942), xxvi.

1. For a list of blamers, see note 16, Part Two, Prologue. Unless otherwise noted, all steel industry data in this chapter are from the American Iron and Steel Institute (AISI)'s Annual Statistical Report from various years.

2. On the role of the strong dollar, see Mangum and McNabb, *The Rise, Fall, and Replacement of Industrywide Bargaining*, 64: "At 1984 exchange rates, the United States was the world's highest-cost steel producer, whereas, had exchange rates of the late 1970s prevailed, only Japan would have had lower production costs and that not by a substantial margin."

3. The steel industry in the United States, unlike every other in the world, is expected to be profitable. Other countries, both advanced and developing, subsidize their steel industries in one way or another, and by keeping the price of steel low, they subsidize the entire metalworking sector of their economies. In the 1970s (from 1969 to 1977), the American industry posted annual profit rates averaging 6.7 percent (net income as a percentage of net fixed assets). This is an anemic profit rate compared to what American companies require, then and now, but it was double what the Japanese industry and triple what the German industry made in those years; the rest of the world was operating its steel industries at a loss. See AISI, *Steel at the Crossroads*, 8.

4. The measure "Annual Tons Shipped Per Wage Worker" is my own invention, using American Iron and Steel Institute (AISI) numbers that were uniformly reported over this period in AISI's *Annual Statistical Report*. There are several prob-

lems with using this measure—most importantly, that shipments are not always produced in the same year as they are shipped—and it cannot be relied on for precision. But it is the only comprehensive, long-term, industry-wide measure of *actual* productivity, as opposed to indexes and productivity *growth* rates. Professionals at the Bureau of Labor Statistics (BLS) have thoroughly explained to me why they measure only the productivity of specific steel mill products (not aggregates) and why they aggregate productivity only in indexes and in year-to-year percentage changes, never in absolute numbers. (See BLS, "Technical Note: Steel Industry— SIC 331," January 1981.) But though my measure lacks precision, it—or something like it—is absolutely essential for public understanding. And it results in an annual rate of productivity growth in the basic steel industry that is very similar to the BLS's highly reliable indexes, which unfortunately do not begin until 1947. (See BLS, "Steel SIC 331, Output Per Production Worker Hour.")

The key problem for me with the way productivity has been publicly discussed is that the *decline in productivity growth* (in steel, in manufacturing, and in the economy as a whole) in the 1970s and early 1980s is often seen (and sometimes reported in the press) as an *actual decline in productivity*. People think that workers were actually producing less per hour of work in 1982 than they were in 1972! Economists and even many journalists know better, but most people I've asked (including students in my classes and professorial colleagues, as well as friends, relatives, and people I've met at baseball games and bars) do not—and most of the worrying about our national "work ethic" in those years was rooted in this misunderstanding. In order to avoid this misunderstanding (which some folks are not at all interested in avoiding), you need absolute numbers, like those in Table A, that measure things like workers and tons of steel. Though it lacks methodological precision, Table A makes clear at a glance that there was a huge increase in steel productivity over the forty years of the union era. It also makes it hard to see how the Steelworkers could have "throttled productivity" or how "overmanning had begun at the end of World War II and was steadily worsening."

5. McKinsey Global Institute, *Service Sector Productivity* (McKinsey and Company, 1992), 4–8.

6. Donald F. Barnett and Louis Schorsch, *Steel: Upheaval in a Basic Industry* (Ballinger, 1983), 55–57.

7. For the "capital shortage" debate, see Office of Technological Assessment, U.S. Congress, *Technology and Steel Industry Competitiveness*, June 1980; U.S. General Accounting Office, *New Strategy Required for Aiding Distressed Steel Industry* (EMD-81-29), January 8, 1981; and Jack Metzgar, "Would Wage Concessions Help the Steel Industry?" *Labor Research Review* 2 (winter 1983) and "Public Policy and Steel," *Dissent* (summer 1982).

8. Barnett and Schorsch, 107–39.

9. Donald Barnett, research director, AISI, telephone conversation during the fall of 1982.

10. See David Brody, *Workers in Industrial America: Essays on the Twentieth Century Struggle* (Oxford University Press, 1980), 195–98.

11. John A. Orr, "The Rise and Fall of Steel's Human Relations Committee," *Labor History* 13, 1 (winter 1972).

12. For a thorough review of the effect of unions on productivity, see Dale Belman, "Unions, the Quality of Labor Relations, and Firm Performance," in Lawrence Mishel and Paula B. Voos, *Unions and Economic Competitiveness* (M. E. Sharpe, 1992), 41–107.

13. Adrienne E. Eaton and Paula B. Voos, "Unions and Contemporary Innovations in Work Organization, Compensation, and Employee Participation," in Mishel and Voos, 191.

14. Maryellen R. Kelley and Bennett Harrison, "Unions, Technology, and Labor-Management Cooperation," in Mishel and Voos, 255.

15. See Richard Freeman, "Is Declining Unionization of the U.S. Good, Bad, or Irrelevant?" in Mishel and Voos, 143–69.

16. Livernash, *Collective Bargaining in the Basic Steel Industry,* 117.

17. Health and safety conditions in the mills have stopped improving, if they have not worsened. See Michael Arndt, "Steel Belt Hardly a Safe Belt," *Chicago Tribune,* November 30, 1997, Sec. 5, 1: "[D]espite advances in automation and decades of federal safety regulation, the percentage of workers killed or grievously hurt in the steel industry is no better than it was 10 or 20 years ago, with fatality rates three times greater than in the overall economy. Every year, thousands of people are still injured in steel mills, and, on average, someone is killed at a U.S. steel mill almost every week."

18. William Serrin, *Homestead: The Glory and Tragedy of an American Steel Town* (Times Books, 1992), 303–5.

19. Strohmeyer, *Crisis in Bethlehem,* 77.

20. "Steel: 2B or Not 2B," *Fortune,* August 1959, 174.

21. See Strohmeyer, chapter 6, which is titled "The Years of Self-Destruction."

22. Serrin, 283 and 299.

23. Serrin, 281.

24. See, for example, AISI's 1963 special report, *The Competitive Challenge to Steel.* Also Libertella, "The Steel Strike of 1959," 23–28.

25. Serrin, 299 and 303–4. Though Serrin is not a reliable analyst of the steel industry, *Homestead* is a wonderfully evocative narrative of steeltown and working-class life across the twentieth century.

26. Mark McColloch, "Modest But Adequate."

27. The best brief explication of this view is Barnett and Crandall, *Up from the Ashes,* particularly chapter 3, "The Decline of the Integrated Sector."

28. For what the steel industry's future looked like in the early 1970s, see William T. Hogan, S. J., *The 1970s: Critical Years for Steel* (Lexington Books, 1972).

29. After the crisis hit in the 1980s, both the Steelworkers and progressive advocates argued for such an "industrial policy" approach. The most effective argument for such a policy, along with a poignant rendering of the decline of the mills in Chicago, is in David Bensman and Roberta Lynch, *Rusted Dreams: Hard Times in a Steel Community* (McGraw-Hill, 1987).

30. Hourly wages and benefits are from AISI. Inflation adjustments are calculated from Consumer Price Indexes in *The Statistical History of the United States* (Basic Books, 1976), 210, and in "U.S. City Average Consumer Price Index," Bureau of Labor Statistics, U.S. Department of Labor, March 30, 1994.

31. Barnett and Crandall, 42.

32. *Chicago Tribune*, August 8, 1993, Sec. 7, 1–2.

33. *Statistical History*, 75–76, and U.S. Bureau of the Census, *Statistical Abstract of the United States: 1993*, 118–19.

34. Infant mortality was 29.2 per 1,000 population in 1950, 20 in 1970, and 9.2 in 1990. *Statistical Abstract: 1995*, 73.

35. Eisenhower's Council of Economic Advisers, for example, heartily accepted the macroeconomic multiplier effect, claiming that "unemployment benefits were paid in high-powered dollars that turned over a dozen times each year, compared to ordinary dollars that turned over only six times." Edward D. Berkowitz, *America's Welfare State: From Roosevelt to Reagan* (John Hopkins University Press, 1991), 65. Also see Sundquist, *Politics and Policy*, 13–56.

36. For an excellent account of the intellectual and class background of New Deal policy, see Ronald W. Schatz, "From Commons to Dunlop: Rethinking the Field and Theory of Industrial Relations," in Lichtenstein and Harris, eds., *Industrial Democracy in America*.

37. Rybczynski, *Waiting for the Weekend*, 143–44.

38. Berkowitz, 55–65.

39. *Statistical History*, 345–46 for Social Security retirees and 354–56 for UC and AFDC recipients.

40. Barry Bluestone and Irving Bluestone, *Negotiating the Future: A Labor Perspective on American Business* (Basic Books, 1992), 35.

41. Eric Hobsbawm, *The Age of Extremes: A History of the World, 1914–1991* (Pantheon Books, 1994), 286.

42. Stephen J. Whitfield, *The Culture of the Cold War* (John Hopkins University Press, 1991), 69–70.

43. Hobsbawm, 261.

Part Three: Prologue

1. For Tomko's role in Steelworker history, see Herling, *Right to Challenge*, 55, 66, 69, and 114, and Hoerr, *And the Wolf Finally Came*, 330–32.

2. Joshua Freeman, *Working-Class New York* (New Press, forthcoming).

3. Robert J. Samuelson, *The Good Life and Its Discontents: The American Dream in the Age of Entitlement, 1945–1990* (Times Books, 1995), 5.

4. Samuelson, 111.

Chapter Five: Steel Family Memories and the Culture of Unionism

1. See Appendix B, Interviews, Reed, Bettie and Bill, and Saylor, Ruth.

2. Patterson, *Grand Expectations*, 321–26.

3. Herling, *Right to Challenge*, 5.

4. Fink and Greenberg, *Upheaval in the Quiet Zone*, 204.

5. Selekman, Selekman, and Fuller, *Problems in Labor Relations*, 517 for the quote and 507–19 for the 1956 negotiations and strike.

6. McDonald, *Union Man*, 253.

7. Herling, 47.

8. Herling, 48.

9. Herling, 48–50.

10. Herling, 50–54.

11. Herling, 56–68.

12. For the poststrike assessment of industry leaders, see Libertella, "The Steel Strike of 1959," 233–38.

13. *U.S. News and World Report*, January 18, 1960, 44.

14. *U.S. News and World Report*, May 30, 1960, 93.

15. See Table A in Chapter 4.

16. *U.S. News and World Report*, May 30, 1960, 92–96.

17. Herling, 69, and Ulman, *The Government of the Steel Workers' Union*, 147–48.

18. Herling, 69–71.

19. Herling, 72–76.

20. Herling, 131–273.

21. Herling, 379.

22. *Proceedings of the Tenth Constitutional Convention of the USWA, September 19–23, 1960*, 241–44, at HCLA-PSU.

23. Herling, 145–48.

24. Herling, 257.

25. I. W. Abel, oral history interview, June 12, 1979, at HCLA-PSU, Interview II, 10 and 51.

26. *Statistical Abstract: 1995*, 290.

27. See Robert D. Putnam, "The Strange Disappearance of Civic America," *American Prospect* 24 (winter 1996) and "Unresolved Mysteries: The Tocqueville Files," *American Prospect* 25 (March-April 1996). Putnam locates what he calls "the long civic generation" as those born between 1910 and 1940.

28. Richard M. Valelly argues the following in "Couch-Potato Democracy?" *American Prospect* 25 (March-April 1996), 26: "Civic disengagement has not caused trade union decline; trade union decline has caused civic disengagement."

29. Geoghegan, *Which Side Are You On?* 196–98. Geoghegan is talking about local union officers, but what he says is even more applicable to appointed staff reps.

30. See Jim and Betty Balanoff, "Democracy and Bureaucracy in the USWA," *Labor Research Review* 3 (summer 1983).

31. For Abel's reforms, see Herling, 301–29, and Kalwa, "Collective Bargaining in Basic Steel," 42–44.

32. Steel wages are from AISI. Household income is from *Statistical History*, 303, and *Statistical Abstract: 1993*, 457.

33. William H. Chafe, *The Unfinished Journey: America since World War II* (Oxford University Press, 1986), 168.

34. Eldridge Cleaver, *Soul on Ice* (Dell, 1968), 181–86.

35. Richard F. Hamilton, "Liberal Intelligentsia and White Backlash," in Irving Howe, ed., *The World of the Blue-Collar Worker* (Quadrangle Books, 1972), 229. Also see Godfrey Hodgson, *America in Our Time* (Vintage Books, 1976), 486: "Polls have consistently found Catholic voters more liberal than the population as a whole on racial issues, and the same has been broadly true of union members. Working-

class Americans are no more likely, and may be less likely, to have racist views than the professional and executive classes."

36. Hamilton, 227.

37. Black steelworkers had long been relegated to the hot end of the mills—coke ovens, blast furnaces, open hearths—where it was not only hotter, but also dirtier, more dangerous, and more unhealthy, and where many of the jobs paid less. Because the union contract vested seniority rights by department rather than plantwide, a steelworker who left one department for another (as my father had left molding in 1940) lost his seniority in the new department, meaning he started at the bottom in the bidding system for better jobs in that department. This forced black steelworkers to choose between remaining at the hot end or taking lower-paying jobs that were subject to more layoffs in the more desirable parts of the mill. This dilemma was rooted in the racist hiring policies of the companies, about which the union had no say, but the union could have opened up opportunities for its black members by negotiating a change in the contract from departmental to plantwide seniority; though involving no "racial preference," this would have been an "affirmative action," one the USWA refused to take until a federal court forced it to in 1974. See Dennis C. Dickerson, *Out of the Crucible: Black Steelworkers in Western Pennsylvania, 1895–1980* (State University of New York Press, 1986), 215–46; Ruth Needleman, "Black Caucuses in Steel," *New Labor Forum* 3 (fall/winter 1998); and, above all, Tony Buba and Ray Henderson's video *Struggles in Steel: The Fight for Equal Opportunity*, 58 minutes, 1996 (available from California Newsreel in San Francisco). For a sympathetic analysis of the way the union dealt with these issues, see Judith Stein, *Running Steel, Running America: Race, Economic Policy, and the Decline of Liberalism* (University of North Carolina Press, 1998), 37–195.

38. See Alan Ehrenhalt, *The Lost City: The Forgotten Virtues of Community in America* (Basic Books, 1995).

Chapter Six: The Contest for Official Memory

Epigraphs: Benjamin DeMott, *The Imperial Middle: Why Americans Can't Think Straight about Class* (Yale University Press, 1990), 192, and William Greider, *One World, Ready or Not: The Manic Logic of Global Capitalism* (Simon and Schuster, 1997), 41.

1. For poverty rates prior to 1959, which are often hard to find, see Derek Bok, *The State of the Nation: Government and the Quest for a Better Society* (Harvard University Press, 1996), 335; Reynolds Farley, *The New American Reality: Who We Are, How We Got Here, Where We Are Going* (Russell Sage Foundation), 1996, 65–66; and Frank Levy, *Dollars and Dreams: The Changing American Income Distribution* (Norton, 1988), 47, 56, and 66.

2. Donald L. Barlett and James B. Steele, *America: Who Stole the Dream?* (Andrew and McNeel, 1996), 19.

3. In total work stoppages (major and minor), the 1950s far surpasses the 1930s. Only one year in the 1930s (1937) saw more than 4,000 strikes, versus five of the ten years from 1950 to 1959. Nothing in the 1930s compares to 1952 in terms of the number of workers involved in strikes as a percentage of total employed—only

1945–46 and 1919 rival 1952 in that regard. 1959 is the record for "days idled per worker involved"; this number, of course, is bloated by the massiveness of the steel strike that year. But the 1959 Steel Strike was no anomaly; it was typical of its time, just bigger. See *Statistical History*, 179.

4. John Patrick Diggins, *The Proud Decades: America in War and Peace, 1941– 1960* (Norton, 1988), 133–34 and 321–22.

5. Diggins, 133.

6. Jezer, *The Dark Ages*, 203 and 208.

7. Geoffrey Perrett, *A Dream of Greatness: The American People, 1945–1963* (Coward, McCann and Geoghegan, 1979), 527.

8. Patterson, *Grand Expectations*, 55.

9. Bok, 359–89, and Farley, 64–107.

10. Patterson, 342.

11. Jezer, 201, and Patterson, 533–34.

12. Brett Harvey, *The Fifties: A Women's Oral History* (Harper-Collins, 1993), xviii.

13. Patterson, 313, and *Statistical History*, 383.

14. *Statistical History*, 380.

15. Bok, 61.

16. I have borrowed the concept of middle-class imperialism from Benjamin DeMott's *The Imperial Middle*, where an imperial attitude is described as not necessarily exploitative or physically oppressive. Rather, "imperialists" assume themselves to represent a norm in a way that erases the experience and values of others and grossly oversimplifies the social reality around them. Many authors have complained about the resulting working-class invisibility, none more revealingly than Lillian B. Rubin, *Families on the Fault Line: America's Working Class Speaks about the Family, the Economy, Race, and Ethnicity* (Harper Perennial, 1994), and Joshua Freeman, "Hardhats: Construction Workers, Manliness, and the 1970 Pro-War Demonstrations," *Journal of Social History* 26, 4 (summer 1993).

17. For the impact of Riesman's and Whyte's books, see Paul A. Carter, *Another Part of the Fifties* (Columbia University Press, 1983), 85–113, and Richard H. Pells, *The Liberal Mind in a Conservative Age: American Intellectuals in the 1940s and 1950s*, 2d edition (Wesleyan University Press, 1989), 232–48.

18. *Statistical History*, 139. The superficiality of collar color as an indication of occupational reality or class position has been repeatedly explained since 1956. Some of the best examples are in Andrew Levison, *The Working-Class Majority* (Coward, McCann and Geoghegan, 1974), 17–51; Harry Braverman, *Labor and Monopoly Capital: The Degradation of Work in the Twentieth Century* (Monthly Review Press, 1974), 377–401; and Erik Olin Wright, *Class Counts*, 45–113.

19. Juliet B. Schor, *The Overworked American: The Unexpected Decline of Leisure* (Basic Books, 1991), 113.

20. Todd Gitlin, *The Twilight of Common Dreams: Why America Is Wracked by Culture Wars* (Metropolitan Books, 1995), 63.

21. S. M. Miller and Karen Marie Ferroggiaro, "Class Dismissed?" *American Prospect* 21 (spring 1995), 100–104.

22. Michael Elliot, *The Day before Yesterday: Reconsidering America's Past, Redis-*

covering the Present (Simon and Schuster, 1996), 201–2. For similar perceptions from natives of Great Britain, see Godfrey Hodgson, *America in Our Time*, 81–90, and Patrick Renshaw, *American Labor and Consensus Capitalism, 1935–1990* (University Press of Mississippi, 1991), xx.

23. Pells, 183, 187, and 247.

24. Perrett, 531.

25. Hobsbawm, *The Age of Extremes*, 257–343.

26. Fones-Wolf, *Selling Free Enterprise*, 38.

27. Miller and Nowak, *The Fifties*, 110–11.

28. Fones-Wolf, 51–52.

29. Fones-Wolf, 52, and Mike Wallace, *Mickey Mouse History and Other Essays on American Memory* (Temple University Press, 1996), 17.

30. Wallace, 10–12.

31. Fones-Wolf, 108–28.

32. Fones-Wolf, 208.

33. James W. Loewen, *Lies My Teacher Told Me: Everything Your American History Textbook Got Wrong* (New Press, 1995), 195–207.

34. *National Standards for United States History: Exploring the American Experience*, Grades 5–12 Expanded Edition, National Center for History in the Schools, University of California, Los Angeles, undated. Also see Harvey J. Kaye, *"Why Do Ruling Classes Fear History?" and Other Questions* (St. Martin's Press, 1996), 146–47.

35. Wallace, 152.

36. See John Schacht, "Labor History in the Academy: A Layman's Guide to a Century of Scholarship," *Labor's Heritage* 5, 3 (winter 1994). This article was part of what originally inspired me to focus attention on the 1959 Steel Strike, and it includes a complex explanation of why the postwar period, the period of organized labor's greatest success, has been ignored by labor historians. Schacht defines "the new labor history" by its rejection of the old labor history's singular focus on the trade union, and divides it into two camps—those focused on the workplace (following David Montgomery) and those focused on community life (following Herbert Gutman). "What the two camps have had in common," Schacht writes, "is a Thompsonian concern for workers who fought valiant but mostly losing struggles against corporate industrial capitalism" (14). Another labor historian, Ronald W. Schatz, makes a similar complaint: "The late 1950s, like nearly all American labor history since 1950, need much more study." Schatz, "From Commons to Dunlop," in Lichtenstein and Harris, eds., *Industrial Democracy in America*. It is now clear that labor historians have begun to respond to those complaints. Lichtenstein's biography of Walter Reuther and Stebenne's biography of Arthur Goldberg, as well as other works I've cited in earlier chapters, are evidence of this. Two books on the textile industry in the South deserve special mention, I think, for emphasizing the accomplishments of unions in the 1950s within what is basically a tragic story: Timothy J. Minchin, *What Do We Need a Union for? The TWUA in the South, 1945–1955* (University of North Carolina Press, 1997) and Daniel J. Clark, *Like Night and Day: Unionization in a Southern Mill Town* (University of North Carolina Press, 1997). The spirit of Clark's book, with its frankly celebratory and poignant defense of the grievance system, is similar to my own, though he is a much more thorough

scholar than I am. Finally, Joshua Freeman's *Working-Class New York*, which I have been privileged to read in manuscript, will change everything once it appears; though focused on one city, New York's labor movement was particularly strong and creative, and Freeman covers the unions and working class there—in all their daunting complexity—across the entire second half of the twentieth century.

37. See tapes from a conference sponsored by *The Nation* in April 1996, *All Shook Up: Lessons and Legacies of the 1950s* (Nation Institute, 1996).

38. Steve Rosswurm, ed., *The CIO's Left-Led Unions* (Rutgers University Press, 1992).

39. The New Left generation of labor and social historians has been involved in a much grander project than I can recognize in this brief analysis. They have consciously sought to create a people's history as an alternative to "great man" and institutional history. This has involved shifting the focus of historical inquiry away from unions as institutions and onto workers as people—people whose lives and identities were more directly shaped by their race, gender, ethnicity, and occupation than by their membership (or nonmembership) in unions. The American Social History Project's extraordinary two-volume *Who Built America? Working People and the Nation's Economy, Politics, Culture and Society* (Pantheon, 1989–92), for example, has attempted a complete recasting of U.S. history from the perspectives and experiences of working people. My complaint against this large and varied group of historians is a narrow one having to do with their treatment of the postwar period. My debt to them, on the other hand, is large: Without them, I would never have recognized that most of the material in this book is worthy of historical attention.

40. Steven Tolliday and Jonathan Zeitlin have shown that there was little for American unionists to envy in the British system in the 1950s: "Until the mid-1960s. . . . those to be laid off were generally selected by the supervisors without consultation." Tolliday and Zeitlin, "Shop Floor Bargaining, Contract Unionism, and Job Control: An Anglo-American Comparison," in Nelson Lichtenstein and Stephen Meyer, *On the Line: Essays in the History of Auto Work* (University of Illinois Press, 1989), 226.

41. Kim Moody, *An Injury to All: The Decline of American Unionism* (Verso, 1988), and Goldfield, *The Decline of Organized Labor*.

42. Joshua B. Freeman, *In Transit: The Transport Workers Union in New York City, 1933–1966* (Oxford University Press, 1989), v.

43. *Statistical History*, 304, and *Statistical Abstract: 1995*, 433. For comparisons since 1973, see Lawrence Mishel, Jared Bernstein and John Schmitt, *The State of Working America, 1996–97* (M. E. Sharpe, 1997), 142.

44. E. J. Dionne Jr., *They Only Look Dead: Why Progressives Will Dominate the Next Political Era* (Touchstone, 1997), 67.

45. Barlett and Steele, 140, and *Monthly Labor Review*, November 1997, 58–83.

46. Cf. Nelson Lichtenstein's contention: "The modern civil rights movement arose out of the proletarianization and unionization of black America." *The Most Dangerous Man in Detroit*, 207.

47. Stephanie Coontz, *The Way We Really Are: Coming to Terms with America's Changing Families* (Basic Books, 1997), 33–35.

Acknowledgments

I started work on this book as a hobby and a refuge after a period of burnout, and I received such enthusiastic encouragement from family and friends that I just kept going. Many people aided me in a variety of practical ways, but above all else I appreciate the encouragement I received from all of them.

I was particularly fortunate to have five friends who read the manuscript chapter by chapter as I produced it—Joshua Freeman, Greg LeRoy, Arny Reichler, Bill Smoot, and Carol Williams. Bill and Carol were particularly helpful on style and grammar, Josh on facts, Greg on both words and numbers, and Arny on the politics of President Eisenhower, but all five helped me clarify both my narrative and my thinking. For each mistaken judgment or interpretation that remains, I can assure you that at least one of them tried to talk me out of it.

Near the end, after I had chiseled the manuscript into a perfectly crafted work of art but still needed to cut four thousand words, Roberta Lynch and Bill Smoot volunteered to potentially jeopardize our friendships by helping me find four thousand unnecessary words. They found the cuts, and the book is better for their work, but I am even more thankful for the offer of help and the effort from friends who have such busy lives and so many better things to do.

Other friends who read parts of the manuscript are David Bensman, Andy Banks, Lynn Feekin, Mickey Jarvis, and John Russo—all of whom, along with Greg LeRoy, helped shape my thinking, for good or ill, during our years together at the Midwest Center for Labor Research. For thorough readings and pointed criticisms of the manuscript, I am particularly grateful to Stephen Brier, series editor for Temple University Press, and Nelson Lichtenstein, the external reviewer for Temple University Press. My sister, Marion Nophsker, read the entire manuscript and was delightfully uncritical. Mike Locker and Ken Blum helped me with steel industry facts and figures, as did John Olson and Chris Kask of the Bureau of Labor Statistics. Denise Conklin at Pennsylvania State University's Historical Collections and Labor Archives went above and beyond the call of duty to make my visits to the Steelworkers Archive there both pleasant and productive. My colleagues at Roosevelt University granted me a one-semester research leave at a time when the project seemed particularly unwieldly and improbable.

Besides his very helpful readings of my manuscript, Josh Freeman helped in numerous ways, sharing his boundless knowledge on numerous topics, his good name in places where it mattered, and, above all, the manuscript of his masterwork on postwar labor, "Working-Class New York." Janet Francendese, editor-in-chief at Temple, has been a friend to the book, and to me, from beginning to end of the editorial process; her shrewd insights, sense of humor, and people skills made what should have been a trying experience both insightful and enjoyable. Her working-class background didn't hurt, either. Janet Benton edited the manuscript with a skill and a dexterity that improved almost every page, and she taught me more than I care to admit about clarity, syntax, and usage; I also appreciate her willingness to promise never to tell my students about all the errors she found and corrected.

I also want to express my gratitude to Emily Rosenberg, Bob Breving, and all the alumni of the Labor Leadership Certificate Program, now at DePaul University, for teaching me about the varieties of unionism and inspiring me to become a better teacher; to Illinois AFSCME for reminding me what a union can be and for allowing me to educate and be educated by its local leaders and staff; and to all the folks associated with the Center for Working-Class Studies at Youngstown State University for renewing my spirits just when I thought I was exhausted.

Finally, I want to thank Judd Metzgar for his early encouragement and late research help and Judie Blair for going steady with me since October 1959, just before the Taft-Hartley injunction.

Index